ELIZABETH FRY
Quaker Heroine

ELIZABETH FRY

QUAKER HEROINE

By JANET WHITNEY

WITH ILLUSTRATIONS

BOSTON

Published by LITTLE, AND COMPANY

1937

Copyright, 1936,
BY JANET PAYNE WHITNEY

All rights reserved

Published November, 1936
Reprinted November, 1936
Reprinted February, 1937

THE ATLANTIC MONTHLY PRESS BOOKS
ARE PUBLISHED BY
LITTLE, BROWN, AND COMPANY
IN ASSOCIATION WITH
THE ATLANTIC MONTHLY COMPANY

PRINTED IN THE UNITED STATES OF AMERICA

*To my husband
and
my father*

FOREWORD

ACKNOWLEDGMENTS are due and are hereby gratefully rendered to Pendle Hill, Wallingford, Pennsylvania, Quaker Graduate Centre, whose grant of a Research Fellowship suggested the work in the first place and afforded the peace and quiet in which to get on with it, in the second. To Francis R. Taylor of Philadelphia, for his generous loan of the manuscript of William Savery's journal. To Quintin Gurney of Norwich and to Miss A. Isabel Fry of Loughton, England, for making available the use of a number of hitherto unpublished letters, journals, and family pictures. To John Nickalls for the facilities of the Friends' Reference Library, London; to the authorities of the Library of the British Museum for similar courtesies; to the librarians of Haverford and Swarthmore Colleges for their coöperation in obtaining for me the loan of rare books; and to Edward Weeks of the Atlantic Monthly Press for many valuable suggestions.

Quotations whose origin is not otherwise given are from the unpublished manuscripts aforementioned.

More personal acknowledgments would be too numerous, but a single exception must be made of Miss Rosemary Gurney, great-granddaughter of Daniel Gurney, for her tales of family traditions, and for the conveyance, in her own person, of the Gurney quality.

JANET WHITNEY

CONTENTS

	FOREWORD	vii
I	THE FAMILY AT EARLHAM	3
II	BETSY	19
III	LONDON	46
IV	THE CHANGE	64
V	JOSEPH FRY	78
VI	THE YOUNG WIFE	98
VII	FAMILY MATTERS	122
VIII	THE LADY OF THE MANOR	157
IX	STEPHEN GRELLET	180
X	INTRODUCTION TO NEWGATE	190
XI	NEWGATE IN EARNEST	205
XII	REMEDIES FOR CRIME	226
XIII	PUBLIC LIFE	248
XIV	TROUBLED WATERS	266
XV	ROYAL PROGRESS	297
XVI	TIME AND THE HOUR	330

ILLUSTRATIONS

ELIZABETH FRY IN 1823 . . . *Frontispiece*	
ELIZABETH GURNEY, AGED ABOUT NINETEEN . .	80
THE QUAKER WEDDING	96
SAMUEL GURNEY	136
ELIZABETH FRY ENTERING NEWGATE PRISON . .	194
ELIZABETH FRY READING TO THE PRISONERS AT NEWGATE, 1823	250
JOSEPH FRY IN 1823	278
THE CHILDREN OF JOSEPH AND ELIZABETH FRY LIVING AT HOME, FEBRUARY 1830 . . .	298

THE FAMILY AT EARLHAM

	Born	Married	Died
John Gurney	Nov. 10, 1749	May 26, 1775	Oct. 28, 1809
Catherine Bell [1]			Nov. 17, 1792

Their Children

	Born	Married	Died
Catherine	March 28, 1776	——	June 26, 1850
John	Oct. 28, 1777	——	May 24, 1778
Rachel	Nov. 21, 1778	——	Sept. 17, 1827
Elizabeth	May 21, 1780	Joseph Fry (Aug. 19, 1800)	Oct. 12, 1845
John [2]	June 17, 1781	Elizabeth Gurney (Jan. 6, 1807)	Aug. 9, 1814
Richenda	Aug. 5, 1782	Rev. Francis Cunningham (Jan. 1816)	Aug. 12, 1855
Hannah	Sept. 15, 1783	Sir Thomas Fowell Buxton, Bart. (May 7, 1807)	March 20, 1872
Louisa	Sept. 26, 1784	Samuel Hoare, III (Dec. 24, 1806)	Aug. 1836
Priscilla	Nov. 27, 1785	——	March 25, 1821
Samuel	Oct. 26, 1786	Elizabeth Sheppard (April 7, 1808)	June 5, 1856
Joseph John	Aug. 2, 1788	1. Jane Birkbeck (Sept. 10, 1817) 2. Mary Fowler (July 18, 1827) 2. Eliza Paul Kirkbride (Oct. 21, 1841)	Jan. 4, 1847
Daniel	March 9, 1791	Lady Harriet Jemima Hay (Dec. 12, 1822)	June 16, 1880

[1] Catherine Bell was a great-granddaughter of Robert Barclay, author of Barclay's *Apology*.
[2] Second of the name.

CHILDREN OF JOSEPH AND ELIZABETH FRY

	Born	Married
Katherine	1801 (d.1886)	
Rachel	1803	Francis Cresswell (1821)
John Gurney	1804	Rachel Reynolds (1825)
William Storrs	1806	Juliana Pelly (1832)
Richenda	1808	Foster Reynolds (1828)
Joseph	1809	Alice Partridge (1834)
Elizabeth	1811 (d.1815)	
Hannah	1812	Wm. Champion Streatfield (1832)
Louisa	1814	Raymond Pelly (1835)
(Samuel) Gurney	1816	Sophia Pinkerton (1838)
(Daniel) Henry	1822	Lucy Sheppard (1845)

HOMES

Earlham Hall	1780–1800
Mildred's Court	1800–1809
Plashet	1809–1829
Upton Lane	1829–1845

ELIZABETH FRY
1780–1845

I

THE FAMILY AT EARLHAM

1

Spring in the eighteenth century in England. The Norwich coach toils at a heavy trot up the sloping road towards Lynn. The passengers do not observe the passing landscape very closely. The sight of a ploughman in a round-frock driving a team consisting of a horse yoked with an ox is too commonplace to excite remark. Those inside feel somnolent and stuffy, as in a greenhouse, with the sun shining on the small glass windows. Those outside hug their overcoats around them against the brisk March wind. But suddenly an exclamation from the young gentleman next the coachman rouses everyone.

"My faith, what's that? That red thing — like a ribbon across the road?"

"Summat red summun's dropped, likely."

"'T ain't on the ground," said the Inside, a clergyman, looking out. "It's strung across the road, like a red rope. No, it flacks in the wind! Someone's strung a long red flag across on a rope!"

"Flag er rope er ribbon, 't won't be there long!" growled the coachman behind his collar. "Soon see *it* busted when my leaders breasts it!"

But he was wrong. They were all wrong, as most of them soon saw. It was — by Jiminy, yes it was! — a row of frisking girls! There they stood across the road, arms linked firmly, red cloaks flying in the wind, skirts awhisk. One, two, three — seven of them, by Jove, or I'll eat my hat. The three tallest stood in the middle, with the four younger ones arranged two on either flank. The centre three were steady, and as grave as goddesses, but the younger four were giggling and excited, and skipped with their feet now and then, to keep warm or to express their excessive delight in this spring madness. Their ages perhaps might range altogether from ten to twenty. Their bright hair, auburn, golden, or flaxen, flew out from their scarlet hoods. And now it was possible to see the bright shine of their seven pairs of eyes.

What, then, was it a joke, then? The outraged coachman perceived that it *was*. With audacity unprecedented in his experience, these flibbertigibbets were out with a wicked intention, a preconceived plot — to make him look an ass and stop the London mail! Never. He flourished his whip, and lashed the horses to a gallop.

"Out o' the way, ye hussies! I'll show ye! I'll run ye down! Out o' the way there!"

The guard sounded the horn, chokily, gasping with laughter. The young man on the box was shouting through his cupped hands, "Two to one on the girls!" The Inside, leaning out, shook angry fists.

"Break up! Break up! You bad young ladies! I know you. You're the Gurneys of Earlham. Your father's my banker! Make way, or I'll tell yer father — I'll tell yer Uncle Joseph! Stop the coach, would you! Out of the way! Get you into your home!"

But the wind blew back all their words into their teeth. It could not be told whether the saucy Miss Gurneys had heard or not. One thing only was certain — they would not budge. They tightened their linked arms, braced themselves together, set their little feet firm. And with a sudden impulse of bravado running along their line, they threw up their heads in the face of danger, with a flash of white teeth. Yes, they were laughing! And one big saucy girl, of the younger Four, put out her tongue with a quick impish gesture.

All of them horsewomen, they knew that the four great horses, snorting and smoking, would not run them down if they maintained an unbroken front. But not many girls could have done it!

The coach stopped.

Then the scarlet line broke into units, dancing in momentary triumph round the conquered, captured coach. Two of them produced apples for the horses, the smallest one threw a placating kiss to the coachman — promptly returned, with éclat, by the lively young man on the box. And then they all swooped like birds into a side avenue of budding limes, through which could be seen the mellow red brick front of a stately house. The coach proceeded, smiling in spite of itself.

" 'T was the prettiest adventure I ever encountered!" said the young man. "For all the world like an unbelievably natural, spontaneous *corps de ballet!*"

Oh, shocking, shocking! As the Inside, who banked with their father, could have told him. For these young maids were Quakers.

Their father, John Gurney, was a wealthy wool stapler and banker, a member of a notable Norwich Quaker family, a widower, hard put to it to train up his madcap girls. Catherine, Rachel, and Elizabeth, the three elder; Richenda, Louisa, Hannah, and Priscilla, the four younger; and four sons to boot, John, Samuel, Joseph John, and Daniel. A houseful, certainly, for any man.

Earlham Hall, beyond the lime avenue, contained them

all, their weal and woe, their pranks and tasks, their loves and fears and hopes. And fortunately for posterity they belonged to a journal-keeping age.

2

It is possible to look back at the 1790's as a very sunlit period. One form of civilization had reached its peak, and, unaware that, like a ripe fruit, it was about to fall, it looked cheerfully forward to further steady progress along its own familiar path. The experience of daily life was so interesting and so delightful that men and women and boys and girls everywhere found it natural, found it almost irresistible, to keep a record of it in diaries.

With some, like Parson Woodforde (who held the living of Weston near Norwich, and banked at Gurneys' Bank), this habit seemed merely to intensify the charm of the present by delaying and prolonging it. Stay, stay, pleasant meal, comfortable friend, kind talk, sunshine on the apricots, trout twinkling in the brook; and even stay, for contrast, the less agreeable but interesting incidents of disaster, accident, and disease. There they are, embalmed in the easy amber of daily remembrance; and for us too they become the present and not the past. Us too they deliver by their simple magic from fleeting time.

But with others again, the intense interest of self-contemplation eclipsed the passing scene. The diarist gave expression to the fascinating pursuit of self-betterment. Moral perfection, nothing less, spurred on the lofty aspiring heart, day by day noting its faults and their remedy.

There were some notable exceptions to the itch for personal recording. Jane Austen did not keep a journal, unfortunately; nor Dr. Johnson; nor Charles Lamb. But the universality of the custom is all the more manifest by the few exceptions. And most of those made up for it by voluminous letters.

Of the eleven Gurneys of Earlham, all kept journals but one. John, the eldest son, was immune. Parents and teachers regarded it as a valuable instrument of education. "When we arrive in England," wrote Mrs. Hare, mother of Augustus, in 1797, to an eleven-year-old son, "I shall hope to find a long and interesting journal of all you do and all you think; it will improve you in the facility of writing English, and it will continue you in the habit of treating your parents with that confidence which their indulgence and affection have a right to claim. I expect to hear all your faults candidly told, that my advice may assist you in mending and correcting them; if you tell me you are always good, I shall not believe it, for it is neither for your age nor for human frailty."[1]

So Catherine Gurney, in encouraging it in her brothers and sisters and practising it herself, was merely following conscientiously the accepted best pedagogy of the period.

It took up time. What countless hours all over Europe were spent in this manner! But there was plenty of time. Never in the history of the world has there been more time. To the savage, time hardly exists. But in the eighteenth and early nineteenth centuries the finest development of the human mind, keen in senses, subtle in thought, cheerful and hopeful, found ample leisure in which to operate. Even Charles Wesley, a byword for energy, who declared that leisure and he had taken leave of one another, had eight or ten hours a day, most days, alone in a carriage as he pursued his constant journeys. And the habit of reading and writing in the slow-moving chaise was as usual then as it is now in the trains which destroy leisure by taking passengers too rapidly from place to place. It was a criticism of Madame de Staël

[1] Augustus J. C. Hare, *Memorials of a Quiet Life*, I, 124.

that she would pass through the most striking scenery without seeing it, absorbed in her book of writing. And long letters poured forth, filled with the cherished detail of the daily scene and kept more often than not by their recipients. Volumes and volumes of journals were piled up in cupboards for the attention of mice and spiders, seldom meant for publication or for any eye but the writer's; and with what pleasure their owners sometimes took them down and dusted them off and pored here and there over the neat yellowed page of a day of their lives long past; smelt again the honeysuckle of a youthful spring, or savored the fine venison of a sturdy middle age; heard again the simple, hearty voice of a friend long dead; and forgot the present gout, the empty house, the rain on the roof, and the nearing approach of the great forgetfulness.

So the young journal of Betsy Gurney, seventeen years old, third daughter and fifth child of John Gurney of Norwich (one infant son deceased), transports us instantly to the year 1797, and into the heart of the family at Earlham Hall. But most remarkably into the actual immediate youth of Elizabeth Gurney herself.

3

"I must not mump when my sisters are liked and I am not," wrote Betsy in her secret little book. There were seven sisters in the Gurney family, and seven sisters means a lot of competition. Betsy was not commanding, like Catherine, or beautiful, like Rachel. And then, those two were hand in glove. Betsy belonged to their group, one of the older ones, but there were times when her sensitive heart perceived, or suspected, that two were company, three were none.

Below her was a brother, away at school, and after him the Four, led by Louisa, who was so tall and handsome that at twelve years old she received at a party an intentional kiss from the young man who was to be her future husband. "Young Sam Hoare was most disgusting; we were on most good terms the first part of the evening, but at last he went so far as to give me a kiss; it was most disgusting. Still I was very agreeable last night; I felt so both in mind and body; how seldom can I say this of myself!"

Thus Louisa's little secret book. And it was far from seldom that she could say that of herself.

Sometimes Betsy felt rather out of it. She was the delicate one, she was the "stupid" one, of the lively, handsome, energetic brood of children who called John Gurney their father and Earlham Hall their home.

She did not know that even the triumphant, full-blooded Louisa had her jealousies, which made her not mump, but rage. "I was very angry with Rachel for treating Chenda differently, just because she is a little older than me; there is nothing on earth I detest so much as this. I think children ought to be treated according to their merit, not their age. I love democracy, whenever and in whatever form it appears."

And with still more candor: "For years past I have had a jealousy about Chenda, which circumstances now and then bring forth. She is far the most pleasing character of us four and all those by whom I should most wish to be admired prefer her."

But Louisa, unlike Betsy, had an easy disposition. She recovered quickly her essential mood of hearty self-content. "I have been in a good mind all day. The others have been truly disagreeable and idle. I was much inclined to catch the contagion, but I *would* not. I gave my mind entirely to my lessons. How far better it is to give our minds to the things we are about; it is the only way to do them well."

And another day: "I got up early and made a pincushion for nurse's sister. I think it is quite right to pay these sort of attentions to servants, and if we do it out of kindness it is more virtue to give a present to a person who has been rather ungrateful to you."

But dark moments would recur, and, though incapable of profound unhappiness or subtle self-analysis like Betsy, Louisa was an honest girl and tried to look her faults in the face. "I felt extremely cross in the morning, so many little things came to cross me. I have been quite struck lately with my own disagreeableness. We four did something in the afternoon which Kitty had forbidden us, and my conscience pinched me the whole time. I have also been rather selfish to-day."

But up she comes again. "A great many Friends came to tea. I did all I could to please them. How charming it is to feel one is giving pleasure! though I never can say how stupid they were to me."

How surprised Betsy's book would have been to interview Louisa's. Betsy's pen could never write such airy, confident words. Her sensitive desire to please was never fully satisfied. She wanted to please — oh, deeply, deeply. Her sisters all found it so easy; even her two little brothers, Joseph and Sam, promised to be charming men. And yet Betsy felt the superficial pleasing, the charming of people at a tea or at a dance, was really worthless. It was only exciting. It made no links between the soul and reality, it gave one no real love. When she achieved it, she was exalted, yet afterward, in her little book, the mirror of her soul, she despised it. "My mind feels very flat after this storm of pleasure."

Somehow it had happened that Betsy, in a healthy-minded family, was temperamental. Her spirits were more delicately poised, her feelings more sensitive. When she was down, she was so very far down.

Was there not in the world an awful thing called Death?

Louisa writes in her little book, "Betsy is so ill, I look forward with the most gloomy thoughts concerning her."

And another day: "To Betsy I feel a particular sort of attachment; her ill-health and sweetness draw my heart to her entirely."

But then: "Dearest Betsy! she seems to have no one for her *friend,* for none of us are intimate with her."

Betsy was older, and more out in the world, and when she was well no one could be gayer than she. Louisa notes with a little touch of chagrin: "Betsy went to the assembly last night and danced a great deal. How most droll! quite a new excursion!"

And when it was one of Betsy's flowering days, not Rachel's beauty or Richenda's color or Louisa's abundant vitality could put her in the shade.

"The Prince has been here again, and we have had a gay, pleasant, bustling time. I really don't know which of the days he was here was the pleasantest. Betsy had an *offer* from one of the officers; I never knew anything so droll as the whole thing was."

So the gay, pleasant, bustling life of Earlham Hall went on, and John Gurney's eleven motherless children brought themselves up, under the guidance of Catherine, the eldest, with a governess and tutors, and good Uncle Joseph Gurney not far off.

Catherine had a difficult path to tread.

"She now and then takes us up and does not allow us to have any opinion. These things would not be observed in anyone else, but she is usually so kind, so good and so charming that even a cool word seems odd in her. And her present plan of treating us as children rather hurts me," complains the candid Louisa, "being of a rather forward disposition."

But Kitty was a person of rare character indeed. Mrs. Gurney, exhausted mother of seven daughters and five sons, had written in her journal before she died the praiseworthy but fatigued resolution "to endeavour to enjoy each one individually"; but Kitty, unexhausted by maternity, did not need to make any such resolve. Their individual characters were all clear-cut and well-known to her, and she did her young best by them all.

"Here then we were left," she writes, "I not seventeen, at the head, wholly ignorant of common life, from the retirement in which we had been educated, quite unprepared for filling an important station and unaccustomed to act on independent principle. Still, my father placed me nominally at the head of the family — a continual weight and pain which wore my health and spirits. I never again had the joy and glee of youth."

However that might be, joy and glee were frequent in that abundant household, still colored by the receding eighteenth century when the pattern of life seemed in England fixed by heaven forever and ever.

Sometimes they ran out into the fields and made a fire and roasted potatoes; or rode down into Norwich and drank syllabubs through straws, and listened, thrilling, to the military band. Or "in the evening a blind fiddler came and we had a most merry dance and ended with a violent romp."

What a house it was for hide-and-seek, with its many irregular rooms and passages and its cupboards and nooks, endless, inexhaustible.

Another time, driven wild by madcap spirits, Richenda and the rest of the Four went on the highroad for the purpose of being rude to the folk that passed. "I do think being rude is most pleasant sometimes," records Richenda, heartily unrepentant.

It was the Gurney sisters who in their girlhood were the sensation of the countryside. But Sam, that resolute child who was sent away to school at eight years old instead of twelve because of his strong will, is not to be overlooked. Observe him escorted by his seven sisters for the first stage of his journey, and then, embraced half to death by that fair bevy, taking his solitary place in the London coach to continue his journey entirely alone.

Sam, when told by his father, for some childish misdemeanor, that he was to go to bed at six for a punishment, put himself to bed at four, and assured his discoverers that he preferred bed to all other places. This was the boy who grew up to be the Gurney of Overend, Gurney and Company, "the banker's banker," one of the greatest financiers of a critical age.

But meanwhile he and handsome Joseph John and the less distinguished though older John were away at school, and Daniel was too small to count, and his sisters held the field. Earlham hummed with them.

"Prince William has been here with a great deal of company; I like him vastly. There was amazing fuss made about his coming," writes the saucy Louisa.

This prince was the Duke of Gloucester, nephew, and later son-in-law, of King George III, stationed at Norwich with his regiment in 1797. He no doubt found the Gurney household quite a new thing in the way of enjoyment, seven fair maidens all in their early bloom, with lively, free, yet well-bred manners, and a simplicity not to be found in the houses of fashion.

The first time he called on them, he kept his carriage waiting two hours while he sat enchanted by their singing. On another visit, a livelier mischief was afoot. They all bore him, on some challenge of his, to "Betsy's room," away from the Great Parlor and the possible censure of advanced maturity, and there travestied for him a Quaker meeting at which the lovely Rachel acted as preacher.

"Rachel gave a most capital sermon. I never saw anything so droll as it was to see the Prince and all of us locked up in Betsy's room, and Rachel preaching to him, which she did in her most capital manner, giving him a good lesson in the Quaker's strain, and imitating William Crotch to perfection.

"The rest of the day was truly pleasant," runs on Richenda, eldest of the Four, "I never saw the Prince so sociable and agreeable as at this time. Cousin Mary and he had a long talk at dinner all about religion. After dinner we began to sing. Rachel sang delightfully; I don't know when I have heard her sing so well. After the Prince was gone we had a dance; the finest dance I ever had: all joined, single and married, old and young, little and great. I had no idea that gay company could be as pleasant as it was."

The invasion of the military and royalty quickened the pace in Norwich. Richenda, sixteen years old and quite "out," was in heaven. There were three or four parties a week. "We danced from seven to twelve. I don't know when I enjoyed dancing so much, there were such beaux, so superior to the bank boys.[2] What a surprising difference rank and high life make in a person's whole way and manner, it is most pleasant being with people who have been brought up that way."

4

But Betsy, after a spell of this kind, felt uncomfortable reaction. "I feel by experience how much entering into the world hurts me." It made her feel that competitive self lively in her heart, the desire to excel and to shine; "it excites a false stimulus." Vanity is awakened and fed, and envy is both felt and observed. Where are the high thoughts of a noble life, a stern sincerity of conduct? They are displaced by careless chatter, by the exchange with partners of flirting banalities. "It leads to think of dress and such trifles." And the effect does not end with the evening. There is a hang-over for days. One cannot get back to one's

[2] Clerks from her father's bank.

real self. The excited mind flies to "scandal and novels" for entertainment.

But at the same time how absorbing those lively emotions were that were excited at a dance! How admiration inflated one and made one feel — oh, wonderful! And when combined with music, which even by itself could move one so, the resulting state was practically one of intoxication. "Music has a great effect on me, it at times makes me feel almost beside myself." Betsy takes out her book, which is by now "quite a little friend to my heart," and struggles to subdue herself. "Without passions of any kind how different I should be. I would not give them up, but I should like to have them under subjection; but it appears to me, as I feel, impossible to govern them. I believe by not governing myself in little things I may become a despicable character and a curse to society. . . . I must beware of being a flirt, it is an abominable character; I hope I shall never be one, and yet I fear I am one now a little. Be careful not to talk at random. Beware, and see how well I can pass this day without one foolish action." But stern self-knowledge comes quickly on the heels of resolve, and she adds with naïve sincerity: "If I do pass this day without one foolish action, it is the first I ever passed so."

Of course young men buzzed around all this honey. Not only the bank boys and the officers and the superior beaux of rank and high life, but men of the Gurneys' own world, friends and comrades and, if permitted, serious suitors. There was Sam Hoare, who waited loyally for young Louisa; there was James Lloyd, who was almost engaged to Betsy; there was romantic, passionate, fascinating Henry Enfield; and there was Pitchford, the young Roman Catholic, whose chivalry passed every test.

The last two were Rachel's slaves, and found more intimate and poetic opportunities of associating with the Gurneys than were afforded by the dance or the candle-bright assembly. John Pitchford left on record a full account of one idyllic day at Earlham Hall, a day containing the very cream and essence of the dying century. It was July the twenty-seventh, 1797, that chance had chosen for this kind of immortality, and it comes to our hands, not like a pressed flower without color or perfume, but like a rose fresh-gathered with the dew still on it.

"This is a day which I shall ever remember with delight. I have spent seventeen hours with my seven most enchanting friends. I rose at 4 A.M. and walked slowly to Earlham, as I did not wish to disturb them too soon. I had partly made up my mind not to throw pebbles at their windows (the preconcerted signal of my arrival) till six, but I found them already risen. The morning was clear and brilliant. Rachel saw me first and knocked at the window. Then Richenda and Louisa came down, and soon all the rest except Betsy, who does not rise as soon on account of her health. After a short walk, the four were sent to the schoolroom to do their lessons. Kitty, Rachel, and I seated ourselves in the shade. I had brought *Peregrinus Porteous* in my pocket, and read the beautiful description of the farm at Pitane; they completely enjoyed it. Rachel left Kitty and me alone together for a few moments, when we talked of her brother,[a] and concurred completely in our opinion of him — that he is at present very amiable and interesting, but that he is in great danger of receiving bad impressions.

"We enjoyed a charming breakfast together, Betsy having joined us, and then we went into the kitchen-garden to eat fruit. After this, we selected a shady spot on the lawn, where the whole party reclined upon a haycock, while I read to them part of my journal, omitting certain passages which avowed my attachment to Rachel. Three or four times, however, I stumbled on passages of this kind, and was obliged to interrupt myself. I am not clear whether the

[a] John, second of the name.

sharp-sighted Rachel did not suspect the truth, but her behaviour during the rest of the day was full as kind as ever. They were all interested with my journal. 'Now we really know you,' they exclaimed, 'let us join hands and vow an eternal friendship.' This we did with rapturous feelings and glowing hearts. Rachel now read some of Henry Enfield's journal, which he regularly sends her, and Betsy read part of her journal, in which she acknowledges all her faults with the most charming candour. Finally, Kitty read part of her journal, which consisted chiefly of reflections. We talked afterwards of my visits. They thought I might come once a week, but on consideration it was agreed to limit it to once a fortnight.

"While they went to dress for dinner, I amused myself with looking over Bowyer's splendid edition of Hume's *History*. After dinner we went to the pianoforte, and Rachel and I practised some songs. I taught her the 'Stabat Mater,' which she much liked. We then went in the boat, and had some most interesting conversation, and after tea chose a delightful spot in the garden facing the setting sun, where Kitty read the poetry of 'The Monk,' and I the 'Deserted Village.' Then we went to the village church, where I read Gray's 'Elegy' by twilight with great effect. Kitty said, 'We will be your seven sisters.' When we got to the river-side, we again had enchanting singing, finishing by 'Poor John is dead,' and, as we returned, promised each other that any of us in danger of death should be visited by the rest. Then we extended our views beyond the grave, and enthusiastically sang till we reached the house 'In Heaven for ever dwell.' It was with difficulty that I tore myself away after supper. It was a day ever to be remembered with transport."[4]

It was a day which all of them may well have remembered, with that delight that is the sharper for regret.

[4] A. J. C. Hare, *The Gurneys of Earlham*, I, 84-5.

It was the climax of the Gurney youth. Never again would they gather on the sunny lawns at Earlham with nothing to divide heart from heart, sharing each other's journals, swearing eternal friendship, full of hope and gayety and warmth.

By the next summer, dawning maturity had wrought its inevitable changes, more drastic than usual. Pitchford had been banished on account of his religion, Rachel's heart had been broken by Enfield, her gayety quenched forever.[5] And Betsy's life had taken on so strange and new a current that it not only caused a great rift in the family but brought a powerful alien element into their hitherto close-knit group. God is a dread neighbor.

[5] John Gurney, at Uncle Joseph's instance, had dismissed Enfield because he was a Deist or Unitarian. The effect on Rachel was so serious that after a year's probation — during which Henry Enfield sent her certainly installments of his journal — an interview was allowed. What passed was only known to the participants. It was stormy; Enfield rode away in a passion. And when, after a few weeks, John Gurney sent a servant on horseback to the Enfield house with a relenting letter from himself to be delivered only if the circumstances seemed to warrant it, he found that the young man had contracted a hasty marriage.

II

BETSY

1

ONLY on Sundays they remembered they were Quakers, and were forced to sit, fidgeting in their gay attire, through a long and dismal two-hour meeting in the Friends' Meetinghouse in Goats Lane, Norwich. They all wrote frequently in their journals, "disgusting." Or briefly, "Goats was dis."

When illness prevented going, they thanked their stars. "We three have been blessed with staying at home lately because of our coughs." Betsy was the most fortunate in this respect.

The young meeting-goers did not feel themselves morally benefited by the discipline. "Sometimes I think I will make better use of my time at Goats, but when I get there I seldom think of anything else but when it will be over, unless perhaps some little foolish circumstance happily engages my attention," says Louisa. And Richenda, who grew up to join the Church of England and marry a Vicar, is even worse. "I had a truly uncomfortable cloudy sort of meeting. It was real bliss to hear the clock strike twelve. What an impatient disposition is mine! I sometimes feel so extremely impatient for Meeting to break up that I cannot, if you would give me the world, sit still. Oh, how I long to get a broom and *bang* all the old Quakers, who do look so triumphant and disagreeable."

Their amiable father did not suspect what skeptical hearts beat violently under the scarlet cloaks. Even in the afternoon, when safe at home again in the spacious luxury of Earlham, one still could not throw it off. One felt "rather goatified and cross."

John Gurney was a Quaker by ancestry, birth, and habit rather than by choice. His easy-going disposition inclined him to enjoy open-house hospitality, and the romps and music of his girls. He admired the scarlet cloaks. And surely he had done his duty when he took his bevy to meeting. They brightened up the meetinghouse.

Friends were tolerant to a man of Gurney's birth, wealth, and standing. Some Friends were plain Quakers and some were not. But remonstrance did, after a patient space, rise to a head regarding the dangers to which his growing girls were exposed in their intimate association with the Enfields, who were Unitarians, and the Pitchfords, who were Roman Catholics. And on those matters John Gurney reluctantly took a stand, although with great pain to himself and them.

Remonstrance chiefly came through Uncle Joseph Gurney of the Grove, a plain Friend and an elder of the meeting. He even went so far as to deal with his nieces personally about their going to dances, although with no result but hurt feelings and tears.

If poor John Gurney was stirred up to attempt a little religious education now and then, remembering that his girls had no mother, it was far from being welcomed by them. "I read half a Quaker's book through with my father before meeting. I am quite sorry to see him grow so Quakerly."[1]

Their own usual reading was very different. They read Rousseau, Voltaire, Godwin, and Tom Paine, and discussed them with their non-Quaker friends, finding their most re-

---
[1] Louisa's journal. *Gurneys of Earlham*, I, 66.

ligious feelings in the fashionable romantic love of nature. The most genuine religious influence in their young lives, if the scandalized Quakers could have known it, was young John Pitchford, a sincere Catholic. Chivalry and good-breeding prevented him from the faintest hint of proselytizing in an intimate acquaintance that had lasted for a period of years, but religion to him was too real and important to be ignored, and he spontaneously and simply turned the thoughts of his seven lovely friends toward God as his own turned there. They admired him and were affected by him up to a point. Catherine, especially, felt her conscience stirred, and made spasmodic efforts to do her duty to the younger ones along her mother's pious lines. Alas, poor Kitty! "Kitty read the New Testament to us, which I was unusually interested in, but at this time I do not believe in Christ."[2]

2

When they drove or rode into the city, they left their little River Wensum behind at Earlham to pick it up again at Norwich, a charming, meandering stream "so wanton that it knoweth not its own mind, which way to go." It was from the river shores within the city that one saw best the whole outline of the Cathedral, immersed as it was in the crowd of houses. Yet the vista of every winding street seemed to be closed by a black church tower or the Cathedral spire. Coming in to do their shopping or to pay calls, the Gurney girls, leaving the leafy lanes, would pass under the dark thick portal of a mediæval gateway, part of the old town walls, and now ride between the timbered fronts of overhanging Tudor houses, pillared Queen Anne portals, and flat, solid Georgian façades. The shady narrow street would turn abruptly, and behold a patch of sunshine on the cobblestones released by the opening of a walled garden between the houses. Trees

[2] Richenda's journal. *Gurneys of Earlham*, I, 79.

leaned over the wall and flecked the sunshine with a pattern of shimmering shadow. "Either a city in an orchard or an orchard in a city" boasted the citizens of Norwich. The Bishop's gardens, around his palace near the Cathedral, kept a particularly large space of air and beauty, like a lung in the midst of the town. And a few little hills, seeming immense in the surrounding flatness, provided pleasant Sunday walks and "prospects" at a convenient nearness for healthful diversion. Just a little part of this crumpling of the earth's surface came within the city, and the remains of the old castle, with the keep hideously and efficiently restored, stood proudly upon a rump, dominating the town, symbol and barracks of the garrison that marched and drilled upon the meadows in 1797.

All around was the open country, the flat sparse meadows, the sea-deserted marshes of Norfolk, with the wide, wide skies that could be both so cheerful and so bleak.

In spite of the ecclesiastical atmosphere that had emanated from the Cathedral since the days of William the Red, Norwich in the eighteenth century was a city of the middle class. It was a centre of the woolen trade, and had been so ever since the exiled Flemish weavers had fled there on a religious quarrel in Queen Elizabeth's time. The Gurney clan were among the wealthiest of the woolen manufacturers. This was partly due to the sheer accumulative inertia of an inherited family business, and partly to the energy and ability which had enabled them in latter years to add banking to their other enterprises. The Gurney Bank was the chief bank of Norwich, with a branch at the neighboring town of Lynn and a headquarters in Lombard Street, London.

The power of money is irresistible. By its gradual encroachment three of the most attractive estates in the neighborhood of Norwich had fallen from the hands of impoverished country gentry into those of the enterprising traders. Keswick Hall, near the village of Runcton, had been purchased by John Gurney's father and inherited by the eldest brother, Richard — heronry, rookery, gardens, woods, and sixteen summerhouses all complete. The Grove, "a house," said William Savery, "quite in the Stile of a nobleman," had been bought by John Gurney's brother Joseph. And John Gurney himself had moved out from Norwich with his young family three miles along the gently rising slope toward Lynn, to the beautiful estate of Earlham Hall. The house was entailed in the Bacon family and could not be sold, but was obtainable on so long a lease that more than five generations of Gurneys were able to dwell in it and set the stamp of their memories upon it. And John Gurney was able to purchase some sixty acres of adjoining land, so that in any accident his family had at Earlham at least a secure foothold.

John Gurney's older children could remember other homes. But they had taken root in the congenial soil of Earlham. They loved every brick and every brush and tree of the place as if the portraits that hung on the walls of the long gallery had been not those of past aristocratic Bacons but of their own sturdy weaver and mill-owning ancestors. Perhaps the fair and ruddy Gurneys, occasionally glancing, in the course of hide-and-seek, at those dark alien faces, felt a tie with them in the common love of Earlham as deep as that of blood.

John Gurney's deceased wife, Catherine Bell, had been on her mother's side a member of the great Barclay clan, also bankers, chiefly resident in London. Robert Barclay, the Quaker apologist, was her great-grandfather.

One way and another, the Gurneys had an air, a sort of dashing grace that was more aristocratic than blue blood itself. It was a Gurney, the founder of the bank, who had early in the century gone up to London to plead the cause of the woolen industry before the House of Lords. His theme was an argument to prohibit the import of calico and manufactured cottons, because they competed with the sale of woolens. His ability in this bad cause was such that Sir

Robert Walpole, the Prime Minister, offered him a seat in Parliament. But at that time, though seats could be given by the hand of authority, they could only be given to members of the Established Church. And Gurney was a Quaker. So he returned to attend to his business and to leave his four sons, between them, one hundred thousand pounds. But he was ever after called "the weavers' advocate."

Cotton came in, in spite of him, and his grandchildren wore it with enjoyment. But wool flourished, and banking perhaps still more. The eighteenth century was the heyday of the private banks, all issuing their own private notes.

Gurney's notes were currency wherever Gurney's name was good. The science of banking was in its infancy, and was to go through violent convulsions before attaining an international stability. But meanwhile it paid very well. So John Gurney of Earlham walked through Norwich with a brisk step and a face that betrayed a man of happy life.

On Sundays, rumor has it that the Bishop on state occasions borrowed John Gurney's striking team of four matched black horses for the episcopal coach, sending his inferior bays to draw the Earlham chariot to meeting.

3

John Wesley had died in 1791, leaving the impress of his personality in every part of England. His peculiar creed, which he summarized as "justification by faith" and called "the plan of salvation," became with extraordinary rapidity the fundamental tenet of orthodox Protestant Christianity for the next hundred years or more, and had already changed the religious tone of Great Britain far beyond the circle of his own converts.

But in 1789 the fall of the Bastille had thundered throughout Europe with a symbolic force, and young Coleridge, at Cambridge University, had used gunpowder to emblazon the words "Liberty and Equality" on the lawns of St. John's and Trinity. His friend, William Wordsworth, had declared: "Bliss was it in that dawn to be alive, but to be young was very heaven!" Dreams of freedom, of the ideal life and the perfect State, fermented in men's minds. Bonds of all sorts, religious, political, social, were seen as cramping limitations to vigorous personal growth. Young people who were footloose went to France to drink in the new elixir at the fountainhead and poured forth a heady literature as a result, among them Wordsworth and Mary Wollstonecraft. Voltaire's *Lettres Philosophiques* became popular reading in English cultured circles. They were mainly about the English, written after his stay in England in '32; and they began with five letters on the religious sects — Quakers, Anglicans, Socinians, and Arians. Clear, pungent, and witty, they appealed to the lively intellectual taste of the eighteenth century, and led men to conclusions more daring than they expected. At the same time, they were flattering to the English pride, in their assumption that the English had managed better than the French. It is indeed curious, and has a certain touching quality, to see the friendly reactions, the mutual admiration and reciprocal influence, of these two nations only a few years before they were to engage each other in a wearing and wasteful war.

The city of Norwich was by no means outside of the stirring currents of the day. Jane Austen, in her country parsonage in Hampshire, might not at the age of fourteen take notice of the French Revolution, but the grown-up ladies of Norwich, young and old, held salons, read everything, entertained at one and the same time French émigrés and republican opinions, and set their own pens busily to paper in outpourings of prose and verse. Norwich was the "Athens of England." Amelia Alderson, later Mrs. Opie, was writing sentimental novels that drew tears from Walter Scott. Mrs. Barbauld left her mark on the mind of Hazlitt.

"The first poetess I can recollect," he says, "with whose works I became acquainted before those of any other author when I was learning to spell words of one syllable in her story-book for children." Old Crome had made Norwich the centre of a vigorous and indigenous school of painting. The Martineaus were growing up — Harriet not yet born. And Nelson was a child of Norwich; though Betsy's only contact with him was in later years to see his funeral cortège pass along the Thames.

Such was the spirit of tolerance that Roman Catholics, Unitarians, Quakers, Episcopalians, and Dissenters mingled comfortably in the same social circles. The Aldersons and Barbaulds were Presbyterians. The Martineaus were Unitarians. There were so many Quakers that Norwich could support two meetinghouses, one for general use in Goats Lane, and one for larger special occasions, called the "Gildencroft" from its ancient Flemish owners. "Goats" was entirely surrounded by houses, but the Gildencroft made one of the green oases of the city with its burying ground, where grass and trees made a gracious resting place for Quaker generations.

The "plain Quakers," by their principles, were debarred from easy mingling with general society, but the "gay Quakers" were just like other people, except for a stern barrier against intermarriage with "the world."

The Earlham girls, going to spend the afternoon in the cheerful city house where their friend, Amelia Alderson, was hostess and housekeeper for her widowed father the doctor; or taking dinner with the Enfields, that fascinating and cultivated family; or with the sons of Dr. Taylor, the famous German scholar; or entertaining these and other fashionable friends in their own home, were everywhere exposed to very free, lively, and speculative talk. Catherine Gurney later described it as "the infidelity that prevailed in the place at that time." Deism was the favorite frame of their religious thought, based on the dictum of Voltaire: "The great name of deist is the only one that should be borne; the only book that should be read is the great book of Nature. The sole religion is to worship God and to be an honourable man. This pure and everlasting religion cannot possibly produce harm."

Neither, of course, could it produce comfort. The Gurneys were not of the cool philosophic temper that could do without an emotional element in religion. For a few years only, of their happiest youth, could this cold and glittering air sustain their spiritual life. The first of the family to find it unsatisfactory was the one for whose sake the others have preserved their identity among the vast anonymity of the prosperous, cultivated citizenry of the eighteenth century. Betsy, the ugly duckling, was the one.

4

The impulse toward religion may be given by the desire to escape from pain. Or it may be given by the desire to escape from mystery, and to find a comfortable and reassuring explanation of the daunting and hitherto indifferent universe. Both these elements were present in the early mental set of young Elizabeth Gurney. The immediate provoking cause was a love affair.

When she was at the mere age of a Shakespeare heroine, less than sixteen years old, a young man had come and fired her quick blood, stirred her vanity, won her flighty beginning of a heart. He was one of the sons of the large Lloyd family of Birmingham, and his father was the founder of the still-existing Lloyds' Bank. The Lloyds were Quakers, and their home, Bingley Hall, was another Earlham, but more scholarly: Wordsworth, Southey, Coleridge, and Charles Lamb were all, at times, their intimates.

There had been what amounted to an engagement between James Lloyd and Betsy Gurney. Then it had been broken. The young gentleman had gone away on his fast and loose career, later to repent at leisure. "I dare say he might be said to have treated me badly," Betsy allowed herself to remark, in retrospect.

She recovered rapidly. The hurt healed. She was fundamentally unharmed. But she was changed. A touch of bitterness, of disillusion, had crept in. There were some symptoms of nervous breakdown. Life was hollow at the core. She began to struggle to get back to the feeling of solid reality and satisfaction in living. How indeed did people achieve the good life? She was hungry for the real secret of happiness. James Lloyd had not had it — no, not at her best moments with him.

The development of every person of genius requires a period or periods of solitude. If circumstances or education do not provide it, the growing spirit must be protected in some other way from the constant pressure of the commonplace and the too-great magnetism of more aggressive personalities. Betsy's protection lay in her physical delicacy.

Neither Betsy nor her sisters had the slightest suspicion that she possessed that uncommon extra quality, that mysterious something more, which achieves greatness. But the destiny watching over her demanded for her room to grow. In the late seventeen-hundreds, the need of a healthy person to be occasionally alone had not yet been recognized. A room of one's own was rare. Jane Austen was writing her masterpieces in any odd corner of the drawing-room, in the company of her sisters. Young Florence Nightingale was soon to be fretting and fuming at having no time and no place to herself. And still, in Betsy's lifetime, the girl heir to the English throne grew up in the stuffy safety of her mother's bedroom, to make her first command as Queen, "Then may I be alone for half an hour?"[3]

[3] Lytton Strachey, *Queen Victoria*.

Betsy shared a bedroom with three other sisters. By day or night, in that abundant family circle, she was seldom alone for a moment. But there were excursions which she was unable to share, and there came long Sunday mornings when everyone else had been driven reluctantly to Goats, when Betsy experienced the delight, the rest, the mental and spiritual *stretch* of solitude.

At times neuralgia prevented these hours from being more than an exercise in endurance. Then Betsy would fall back upon her grim little motto, "Come what, come may, Time and the hour run through the roughest day."

But at other times, the maturing girl examined her life as she seemed unable to do in the dead atmosphere of Goats Meetinghouse.

"*Monday, May 21st. 1797.* I am seventeen to-day. Am I a happier or a better creature than I was this time twelve-months? I know I am happier; I think I am better, I hope I shall be much better this day year than I am now. I hope to be quite an altered person, to have more knowledge, to have my mind in greater order; and my heart, too, that wants to be put in order as much, if not more, than any part of me, it is in such a fly-away state.

"*August 12th.* I do not know if I shall not soon be rather religious, because I have thought lately, what a support it is through life; it seems so delightful to depend upon a superior power, for all that is good; it is at least always having the bosom of a friend open to us, to rest all our cares and sorrows upon, and what must be our feelings to imagine that friend perfect, and guiding all and everything, as it should be guided. I think anybody who had real faith, could never be unhappy; it appears the only certain source of support and comfort in this life, and what is best of all, it draws to virtue, and if the idea be ever so ill-founded that leads to that great object, why should we shun it? Religion has been misused and corrupted; that is no reason why religion itself is not good.

"I feel I am a contemptible fine lady. All outside, no inside. May I be preserved from continuing so, is the ardent prayer of my *good* man, but my *evil* man tells me I shall pray in vain.

"I feel in the course of time I shall be all outside flippery, vain, proud, conceited. . . . But I am good in something, it is wicked to despair of myself, it is the way to make me what I desire not to be.

"I wish I had more solidity and less fluidity in my disposition. I feel my own weakness and insufficiency to bear the evils and rubs of life. I must try by every stimulus in my power to strengthen myself both bodily and mentally, it can only be done by activity and perseverance."

She suffered from dreadful dreams. All her life she had had three great fears, of the dark, of death, and of the sea. Night after night in childhood she had sobbed herself to sleep in terror for the want of a light. Day after day, in family holidays by the sea, she had almost died of horror when the strong bathing women seized her and ducked her three times in the icy waves, to be released shivering, gasping, choked, and in her mind half-drowned.

And the fear of death had haunted her so much that often as a child she had crept up to her delicate, beautiful mother, asleep, and listened anxiously for her breath. Her mother really had died when Betsy was twelve years old, confirming all these anxieties as reasonable, and setting a dreadful seal upon that fear.

So in the dark night adolescent Betsy dreamed of dying in the sea. The terrible tide rose higher and higher, the waves beat upon her, she struggled but was at last submerged, and woke in an agony, sweating and shaking. This dream was often repeated, night after night.

But by day the buoyant Gurney temper and her own strong common sense wrestled with her devils. She strove to rise out of depression. "In a valley" she called her down moods; "off my centre," her moods of wild gayety; she longed to be, she strove to be, in a "good mind." But, never ceasing to miss her mother, she struggled alone.

In December 1797, her ardent spirit and her clear, cool mind, not intellectual but vigorous, struck together into a deeper stratum. "A thought passed my mind, that if I had some religion, I should be superior to what I am, it would be a bias to better actions; I think I am, by degrees, losing many excellent qualities. I am more cross, more proud, more vain, more extravagant. I lay it to my great love of gaiety and the world. I feel, I know, I am falling. I do believe if I had a little true religion, I should have a greater support than I have now; in virtue my mind wants a stimulus; never, no never did mind want one more; but I have the greatest fear of religion, because I never saw a person religious who was not enthusiastic."[4]

January set its dreary grip upon the landscape. Pushing back her fair hair, she looked out of the window at the leafless trees, the bare lawns, the dead garden, and meditated upon death.

"I must die! I *shall* die! Wonderful, death is beyond comprehension. To leave life, and all its interests, and be almost forgotten by those we love. What a comfort must a real faith in religion be, in the hour of death; to have a firm belief of entering into everlasting joy. I have a notion of such a thing, but I am sorry to say, I have no real faith in any sort of religion; it must be a comfort and support in affliction, and I know enough of life to see how great a stimulus is wanted, to support through the evils that are inflicted and to keep in the path of virtue. If religion be a support, why not get it?"

This frame of mind is what William James later called the "will to believe." It rapidly increased in intensity.

[4] The word in the eighteenth century had a connotation of extravagance, fanaticism.

Like a person lost and wandering in a dark cave, she saw light in that direction; or at least a possibility of escape from darkness. "I think it almost impossible to keep strictly to principle without religion; *I don't feel any real religion; I should think those feelings impossible to obtain, for even if I thought all the Bible was true, I do not think I could make myself feel it;* I think I never saw any person who appeared so totally destitute of it."

Her sense of need deepened. She was aware of "that dim capacity for wings" that stirred beneath the hampering female dress, the hampering female life, and made her feel at one and the same time her ambitious nature and her present futility. She had no special talent to direct her line of march. She only had a sense of latent power, needing direction and development. Young ladyhood stultified her.

She was not of a studious or bookish temperament. Reading was no relief. She saw her days drifting by in a futile struggle with luxurious circumstance and aimless occupation. Indolence and dissipation ate up her time. She had desperate moments. "I am a bubble, without reason, without beauty of mind or person; I am a fool. I daily fall lower in my own estimation. What an infinite advantage it would be to me, to occupy my time and thoughts well. I am now seventeen, and if some kind and great circumstance does not happen to me, I shall have my talents devoured by moth and rust. They will lose their brightness, lose their virtue, and one day they will prove a curse instead of a blessing. Dreaded day. I must use extreme exertion to act really right, to avoid idleness and dissipation."

The solution was ready for the crystallizing agent; and it appears at least a singular coincidence that the appropriate agent should arrive so pat to the requirement.

5

An American Friend named William Savery reached Norwich on February 3, 1798. He was a well-to-do Philadelphia tanner, traveling in the ministry. To "travel in the ministry" is a term used by Friends to indicate the activity of one of their number who feels a strong concern, tantamount to a command from God, to visit Friends in other places. A certificate from the Monthly Meeting, the local church executive, is necessary to give such a concern proper backing with the strangers who are to be visited. These visiting Friends in the eighteenth century made very strong links between one meeting and another at a time when communication was slow and difficult, and corporate feeling weak. The very survival of the Society of Friends probably depended upon these individuals in whom the spirit of adventure and devotion was strong enough to stir them out of their ruts and send them abroad. And probably no church has ever fought its way to survival by so apparently free-and-easy a method. Traveling Friends mostly paid their own expenses, but received a great deal of hospitality on the way.

In the case of William Savery, his concern was not limited to the people of his own persuasion. He had had missionary journeys in his own country among the Red Indians. And in 1795 he applied for a certificate "liberating him for service in Great Britain and elsewhere in Europe."

Stephen Grellet, the French émigré to Pennsylvania who had joined the Quakers, was a close friend of Savery's, and probably stimulated his impulse for European service.

At all events, Savery's warm temperament and knowledge of French and German [5] soon urged him onto the Continent, and he had traveled extensively in France, Germany, Holland, and Ireland before he began his English itinerary.

[5] Francis R. Taylor, *Life of William Savery*.

In England, as he moved from meeting to meeting, it was marked that he would often sit silent in gatherings which consisted of Friends only. He felt "nothing to constrain me to minister. . . . Few besides Friends attending I had not occasion to appear in the ministry." This peculiarity is even more clearly noted by him in his journal after attending Westminster Meeting. "I had thought I should have been silent as usual, but divers men and women of other professions dropping in, I had a little matter for them at the close, in which I found peace after meeting."

It was a temptation to the most sincere Quaker to find for himself a "leading to speak" when he saw large numbers of Friends gathered for the tacit purpose of hearing him. But it was a temptation to which Savery seemed immune. Toward the end of his time in England, a woman called Barbara Drewery told him that she had heard he had only preached five times in Friends' meetings since he came to England. Savery looked thoughtfully back over his journeys, and replied that he believed the report exaggerated. "I could recollect," he wrote, "but four, and two of them would hardly bear the name of preaching."

But at meetings open to the general public, either in a Friends' meetinghouse or in some larger public place, he drew large crowds, and addressed them with singular charm. At Carlisle, "the house, which holds about one thousand, would not contain the people"; at Deptford, seven or eight hundred people piled themselves upon the hop bags in a malt house; at Stockwell, he had five hundred in a corn store and many could not get in. A barn at Stoke Newington held eight hundred. Doorways, window sills, and passages were packed to suffocation. Savery was always exhausted after a meeting by the stuffiness and press.

A contemporary newspaper report [6] describes his fascina-

---

[6] The *Norfolk Chronicle or Gazette* of February 3, 1798, quoted from the *Bath Chronicle*.

tion. "Monday evening, the Quakers' Meeting-House at Bath was crowded to an excess, for the sake of hearing a celebrated preacher from America, who for good sense, fluency, and even eloquence, formed a singular and very agreeable contrast to the usual style of religious address existing in that community. . . . His name is William Savery. . . . He is a man of prepossessing appearance and address, mild and persuasive in his language and manners, and unusually liberal in his sentiments. If the Quaker preachers were to imitate the example of this extraordinary brother, instead of distilling a sentence once in five minutes, many an orthodox and dissenting pulpit that is now held in admiration would be powerfully rivalled." Savery was this year forty-eight years of age.

The morning of February 4, 1798, dawned bright and clear. Betsy Gurney was not feeling very well, but she decided to go to Goats that day with the others. For one thing, Uncle Joseph Gurney was beginning to protest against her frequent absences. For another, the famous American Friend was to be there and might possibly afford a little change.

The seven gay sisters crowded into the chariot and chaise, and presently bustled like bright birds into the meeting-house. They sat in the front row, facing the minister's gallery. Oh, do look at Betsy's new boots — purple, laced with scarlet! Oh, the rascal! They nipped each other and smiled before settling into their usual decorous fidgetiness. Another two hours of Goats! Ah, me! How dis!

As for Savery, sitting with Uncle Joseph Gurney and other grave Friends in the gallery, he was profoundly shocked. With that bright row just beneath him, and few enough in strict Quaker garb among the two hundred Friends present, he "thought it the gayest Friends' meeting I Ever sat In, and was grieved to see it." All sense of a message was stifled within him. It was true that he preferred, or was mostly inspired in the presence of, non-Quakers. But these were not non-Quakers, they were "pretend" Quakers. They had thrown off the traditions of their fathers, they were not taking up the fiery torch. Not ignorant of the Truth, but indifferent to it, they selfishly and indolently came to meeting in the mere pursuance of a habit which they did not care to break.

If Savery had maintained, as often before, an unbroken silence in that unpromising meeting, rustling with silks like a field of corn, would it have mattered? Would it have made any difference in the end? He could hardly have supposed it.

But the powerful Hand seized him, to supply the one necessary ingredient to a prepared and now seething solution. "I Expected to have pasd the meeting through in Silent Suffering, but at length believed it most for my peace to stand up with 'Your Fathers, where are they, and the Prophets, do they Live Forever?'"

Betsy's smooth fair hair drooped forward over an oval cheek as delicately tinted as an apple blossom, appearing all the fairer between the warm auburn colorings of Rachel and Louisa. She was looking down at her pretty boots, turning her foot gently this way and that in a purr of pleasant vanity. Then suddenly the dull silence was broken, not by the usual drone of Quaker preaching, but by a voice resonant and musical, with something definite to say and great feeling in saying it. "Her attention became fixed."[7]

It was, in sober fact, the crisis of her life.

6

It was the crisis of her life, but one of the cultivated, skeptical Gurneys was not going to submit to a lightning, methodistical conversion, displaying all the dreaded quali-

[7] Richenda's journal.

ties of "enthusiasm." In the waves of emotion which assailed her, she struggled to keep a cool head, above all to guard her sincerity from assault.

Savery's late utterance considerably delayed the rise of meeting. There was then a large dinner party at the Grove [8] in his honor. Betsy was there, and her uncle, seeing that she was in a sensitive state, sent her alone with William Savery in the carriage to the evening meeting. After the evening meeting she returned to the Grove in the same manner, and from there returned home to Earlham Hall in the carriage with her sisters. "Betsy sat in the middle and astonished us all by the feeling she showed. She wept most of the way home." [9]

The evening meeting, held not at Goats, but "in a large meeting-house in another part of town" (namely, the Gildencroft), was open to the public. It was attended by John Pitchford and by the Press.

Pitchford, invited by Uncle Joseph into the gallery, where he had a favored position above the crowd, notes in his journal, "The name of the speaker was Savery, and his sermon the best I have ever heard among Quakers, so full of candor and liberality. My only objection to it was its excessive length — two hours and a half."

The *Norfolk Chronicle*, a weekly paper, published a full report in the next issue, February 10. "On Sunday evening last Mr. Savery, from America, commanded the attention of a very crowded and respectable audience, at the Quakers' Meeting, for above two hours. The subject was

[8] Uncle Joseph Gurney's house.
[9] Richenda's account in later life, quoted in various memoirs, is not to be taken literally. It is clear by her contemporary statements that Richenda was not even present at the meeting which she describes many years later with well-meant but inaccurate detail, for in her journal of February 11, 1798, she states that she has not been to meeting for a fortnight. "I went to Meeting in the morning and I was very sorry to see that place again after a separation from it a whole fortnight." Betsy herself says that in the morning meeting she "laugh'd at what passed." However, she was an April girl, and might easily have done both.

generally interesting, founded upon the maxim that the society which did not revert to first principles was liable to decay, which he with considerable address and seriousness applied to the individual professors of religion, observing that the innovation of creeds and articles, framed and imposed by human authority or cunning, had produced much infidelity, and arose from a want of adherence to first principles. That the creed of the great founder of Christianity was simple, being directed to promote 'Peace on earth and good will towards men'; he expressed his hope that the turnings and overturnings of the present time [10] would end in restoring the primitive union of Christian fellowship, and that countries assuming the appellation of Christians would no more delight in War, adding, he could not think it an acceptable service to thank God for victory over an enemy. He related with great advantage and perspicuity the advantage he had enjoyed in finding amongst what are called Heathens, men of piety and goodness, who, though they were destitute of a written law, were a law unto themselves, and favored with the assistance of the spirit of the Almighty; very happily illustrating that the salvation published by the Gospel would be participated by numbers in the extensive nations of the earth, who never possessed the means of knowing it, while those who rejected its great advantages would be exposed to just condemnation.

"It is computed that there were near 2000 persons present in the Meeting, and the serious part of the auditors appeared highly gratified with his discourse, which however was much too prolix, and consequently tautological."

To the twentieth-century reader of this report it is extraordinary evidence of the eighteenth-century tolerance of ideas that such remarks on the unchristian character of war and of victory could pass without protest, and even with-

---

[10] The American Revolution, French Revolution, Industrial Revolution, etc.

out comment, in the midst of the Napoleonic Wars. Only the year before, a panic, caused by fear of French invasion, had caused a run on the country banks barely averted by drastic measures on the part of the Bank of England. And the subsequent naval victories of June the first and of Camperdown in October, clearing the Channel temporarily of hostile fleets, had caused national rejoicing, and thanksgiving in all the churches. That God-be-thanked victory was only four months old. Napoleon was now busy conquering Egypt, with an eye to India. Recruits for the army and the fleet were being kidnapped every day. Yet the serious part of the Norwich auditors could appear highly gratified with a discourse which included the most uncompromising pacifism.

Savery himself remained chiefly affected by the gayety of the Norwich Friends, and though he became aware, during the late evening drive, that he had made an impression upon one of them, he hardly hoped that the seed could take root among so many distracting tares. Even good Aunt Jane Gurney, Uncle Joseph's wife, appeared to him "a dressy woman." And beside a group of Friends at dinner, few indeed of whom seemed to him to be "upright standard-bearers" (though to Betsy Gurney they seemed a very sober crowd), he was again scandalized by the young ladies.

"After dinner I Retired to my Room & staid till tea-time. Several Gay Girls, Daughters of John Gurney, and their father with them, gave us their Company, and I Rode with Elizabeth to meeting."

It is a singular light upon human fate, and the difficulty of discerning for himself the relative worth of a man's own actions, that, of all William Savery's arduous journeys on two continents, his crowded meetings and liberal if tautological discourses, what keeps his name now chiefly in remembrance is that he rode with Elizabeth to meeting.

7

For it was the private conversations in the carriage rather than the public discourses which indelibly impressed the sensitive girl.

She wrote two accounts of this momentous day in her journal, one brief and hasty, the other carefully and seriously composed. They were not apparently written on the same day.

The question at once arises, why were there two? The need of confiding her mind at once to her diary had become imperative, and by this time many little books had been filled. Sometimes she ran short of books, and while waiting for a good one would get on with a little temporary one. When the good one arrived, some overlapping might ensue. As she says in one place, "I have been waiting for my book a day or two and as I cannot get it I have made myself a small one just to express my ideas in for my mind is full and wants relief."

One of these "small ones" may have traveled with her in her pocket to Goats on a Sunday when she was planning from the start (Richenda to the contrary notwithstanding) to be away from home all day. And her first account was probably scribbled in it while waiting for the carriage to go to the Grove after the evening meeting; the merest hasty outline of the day.

At home, in a collected frame of mind, the next morning she stole away to the anteroom, often called "Betsy's room" because she liked to sit there, and sat long with her real journal, analyzing and recording the events, thoughts, emotions, hopes, and fears that had beset her, and the extraordinary *experience* through which she had passed.

"*Sunday. Feb. 4th. 1798.* This morning I whent[11] to Meeting though I had a very bad pain in my stomach be-

[11] Betsy's spelling.

cause I wished very much to hear an American friend who was there preach. His name is William Savery. I was engaged to spend the day at the Grove and after a meeting of three hours I whent with Aunt Jane. All the friends dined there. I felt rather odd as I was the only gay person. There was a soft, pleasing manner in friend Savery, but I thought he had something of the totem of quakers about him. The meeting was not till six in the evening and Uncle Joseph came to me to say he wished me to go with friend S. alone in the carriage to meeting. We had much talk but not much *concerning* conversation. We whent to meeting which lasted very long and he preached a very excellent sermon."

This far from fervid account was evidently written at the meetinghouse, immediately on the close of the meeting, while the huge crowd slowly emptied out, and friend Savery was engaged in talk with many congratulatory hearers. It was the return drive with him to the Grove that clinched matters for Elizabeth and accounts for the different tone of her second writing.

"*Sunday. Feb. 4. 1798.* To-day much has passed of a very serious nature. I have had a faint light spread over my mind, at least I believe it is something of that kind owing to having been much with and heard much excellence from one who appears to me a true Christian. It has caused me to feel a *little* religion. My imagination has been worked upon and I fear all that I have felt will go off. I fear it now, though at first I was frightened that a plain Quaker should have made so deep an impression on my feelings, but how truly prejudiced in me to think because good came from a Quaker I should be led away by enthusiasm and folly.

"I have *felt* there is a GOD. I have been devotional and my mind has been led away from the follies that it is mostly wrapped up in. I loved the man as if almost he were sent from heaven. We had much serious conversation, in short what he said and what I felt was like a refreshing shower upon parch'd up earth that had been dried up for ages. It has not made me unhappy. I have felt ever since *humble*. I have long'd for virtue. I hope to be truly virtuous, to let sophistry fly from my mind, not to be enthusiastic and foolish, but only to be so far religious as will lead to virtue. There is nothing seems so little understood as religion.

"This morning I went to meeting though but poorly because I wished to hear an American Friend. His name is William Savery. After a meeting of three hours (where I laugh'd at what passed), I then went with Aunt Jane to the Grove. All the Friends dined there and I felt rather odd as I was the only gay person there. However I liked the manners of the Friend. He was kind and pleasing. He had a meeting at six and Uncle Joseph wish'd me to go with Friends to it. We had much conversation as we went to meeting but not much serious. Meeting lasted very long. He preach'd a very excellent sermon. I was very low almost all meeting. I don't know why. I could not help considering how near my mother was in the burying-ground, which led me to think of death. After meeting I rode home to the Grove with friend S. We had a *sort of meeting* all the way. As soon as we got to the Grove he had a regular one with me. When I got home I mixed too much the idea of growing religious and growing the Quaker. I had a painful night. I dreamt nor thought of anything but this man and what had passed. W. S. came next morning. He no longer preach'd but was kind and affectionate."

Richenda's inaccurate account, written from memory many years later and colored by Betsy's established fame, says, "The next morning, William Savery came to breakfast, prophesying of the high and important calling she would be led into." But Richenda's own journal at the time gives no such impression.

"*February 5th. 1798.* Friend Savery has been here, who

seems a charming man and a most liberal-minded Quaker. Betsy, who spent all yesterday with him, not only admires but quite loves him. He appears to me a truly good man, and a most upright Christian and such men are always loved. To me he is quite different from the common run of disagreeable Quaker preachers. In every society and sect," adds Richenda with unconscious irony, "there is always something good and worthy to be found." [12]

But no indication of any public singling out of Elizabeth. Savery, indeed, was quite unconscious of any such intention. His own journal reads impersonally: "J. G. is a Widower. His Children seem very kind and attentive to him, and he is very Indulgent to them; has provided them with an Extensive Library and every Indulgence that Nature within the Bounds of mere morality Can desire. They were very Respectful and kind to us, and very much Regretted, I Believe Sincerely, our being Like to Leave them so soon. They are a family very Capable of distinguishing, through the Grace, what the truth is and Leads to, but whether, with all the alluring things of this world about them, they will any of them Chuse to walk in it, time only must determine."

8

Betsy would have warmly concurred in that last sentence. Time only must determine. Was her experience real and lasting, or would it wear off? She watches herself closely, and her journal enables us to do so. We look through clear glass at this period and watch her busy thoughts in their hive. She could not spell, but her style remains for some time yet lucid and free.

Sunday had been wonderful, and Monday she had written it all down and so relived it again, but Tuesday began everyday life. "I rode to town and had a very serious

[12] *The Gurneys of Earlham*, I, 75.

ride, but meeting some one and being star'd at with apparent admiration by some officers brought on vanity, and I rode home as full of the world as I had riden to town full of heaven.

"My feelings toward friend S. are unintelligible — a strong and odd impression he made upon me. I could almost have gone to America with him. I felt no fear, not the least, in his company as I do with most plain Friends. I loved him as a messenger of glad tidings. He felt as if he overflowed with true religion and was so humble, yet a man of great abilities and he having been gay and unbelieving only a few years ago made him better acquainted with the heart of one in the same situation. If I were to grow like him a preacher, I should be able to preach to the gay and unbelieving better than to any others for I should feel more sympathy for them and know their hearts better than any others."

Then Sunday came round again, too soon for most of the Gurneys, and, alas! Goats proved as uninspiring as usual. Betsy makes no pretenses.

"*Sunday. Feb. 11th.* It is very different to this day week (a day never to be forgotten while memory lasts). I have been to meeting this morning. To-day I have felt all my old irreligious feelings — my object shall be to search, try to do right, and if I am mistaken, it is not my fault; but the state I am now in makes it difficult to act. What little religion I have felt has been owing to my giving way quietly and humbly to my feelings; but the more I reason upon it, the more I get into a labyrinth of uncertainty, and my mind is so much inclined to both scepticism and enthusiasm, that if I argue and doubt, I shall be a total sceptic; if on the contrary, I give way to my feelings, and as it were, wait for religion, I may be led away. But I hope that will not be the case; at all events, religion, true and uncorrupted, is of all comforts the greatest; it is the first stimulus to virtue; it is a support under every affliction. I am sure it is better to be so in an enthusiastic degree than not to be so at all, for it is a delightful enthusiasm."

A family so affectionate, outspoken, and united as the Gurneys could not fail to be aware of the turmoil of one of its members. Uncle Joseph Gurney had his opinion — one of hope; the sisters had theirs — one of apprehension; and John Gurney felt that, for good or ill, Betsy must have a change. In fact, Betsy had better go to London and see the world.

Well, certainly London was the world; but at the moment London was also William Savery.

Betsy's diary breathes her wild excitement.[18] "My mind is in a whirl. In all probability I shall go to London. Many, many are the sensations I feel about it, numbers of things to expect." Savery and all those plain Quakers to the right, and balls and theatres to the left — how will she keep to her instinctive ideal of the golden mean? "One will, I do not doubt, balance against the other; I must be careful not to be led away; I must not overdo myself. I dare say," she warns herself with a flash of insight, "it will not be half so pleasant as the Earlham heartfelt gaieties in the Prince's time. I must be careful not to get vain or silly, for I fear I shall. Be independent, and do not follow those I am with, more than I think right. Do not make dress a study, even in London." She adds, "But if I see William Savery, I shall not, I doubt, be over fond of gaieties."

[18] Augustus Hare in *Gurneys of Earlham* says: "The request which Betsy — Elizabeth Gurney — made at this time to her father, astonished her sisters more than anything else. She begged that she might be allowed to visit London and examine for herself into all the fascinations and amusements of the world." But this does not tally with Betsy's own account.

III

LONDON

1

A BRIGHT frosty morning was a good one to choose for travel. Off they set, father and daughter and a female attendant, the anxious six gathered in the hall doorway to wave farewell, and the seventh looking back at them through the window, her eyes blurred with tears. It was the first separation of the kind, and, as Betsy wistfully reminded herself, they were "sisters formed after my own heart."

But once beyond the village and fairly launched upon the great highway, bumping and banging along over the frosty ruts, the exhilaration of travel banished regrets. The roomy chaise, lined with fawn-colored watered silk, was well-sprung and cushioned, and contained great pockets for books, refreshments, and the odd impedimenta of travel. The steps, carpet-covered, were folded up inside the carriage. The party were well wrapped up, with a warm sheepskin over their feet and tins of hot water to place their feet upon.

Betsy every now and then rubbed away with her mitten the mist that formed on the inside of the window and looked out upon the winter landscape, intersected by the new-grown hedges that were beginning to change and beautify the face of England, upon bare trees, and lonely farms, and flocks of birds feeding in the ploughed fields.

Before one was too fatigued with the rattle and jolt, it was time to stop at an inn to bait, and to change horses. One's own beasts only took one to the first post; after that it was necessary to hire both horses and armed postilions.

Thetford, the halfway halt, was reached before dusk. Here at the good old inn, the White Hart,[1] the Gurney party was to spend the night. What roaring fires before which to stretch limbs somewhat stiff and chilled; what a pleasant, low-ceiled parlor, bright with candles and firelight, and presently what a dinner for hungry travelers! Betsy and her father, very cheerful at their *tête-à-tête* meal, were served with "a broiled chicken, a plover, plate of sturgeon, tarts, mince-pies and jellies," and all for eighteen pence a head. They drank beer with their dinner, and when the cloth was drawn, coffee was brought in for them to sip luxuriously beside the fire.

They were a fine pair to look at. John Gurney's red hair was hardly touched with gray, and his handsome figure was well set off by the current fashion of knee breeches and stockings, light waistcoat, dark buff tail coat, and a high white stock, burying the firm chin in its soft folds.[2] Betsy's hair was a fine flaxen, parted simply on the brows and done rather high in a knot behind. Muff and cloak and poke bonnet laid aside, she wore a white muslin dress of semi-classical simplicity, cut low in the neck, with a pale blue sash tied under the armpits. It was a fashion hard indeed on the billowing outlines of middle age, or on an angular, flat-chested woman, but designed perfectly for the enhancing of every beauty of rounded, long-limbed, supple youth.

John Gurney, who had married a dowerless girl for love,

---

[1] See Woodforde, *The Diary of a Country Parson.*
[2] Portrait by John Opie. And Percy Bigland's picture of the "Quaker Wedding," in which is portrayed our great-grandfather's suit of this period.

against the opposition of his family, was secretly of the opinion that if a young person of either sex showed signs of serious disturbance, marriage was the best remedy. He had more irons in the fire than one on this trip to London. And as he watched his daughter's lithe grace, bringing him with care the brimming coffee cup, he said to himself with fatherly pride that she was eminently marriageable.

He began to talk to her about her mother, as he often did, renewing his memory of the dark beauty that Gainsborough's canvas keeps forever young. Before long the dreamy talk and the warmth and food had their effect. John Gurney lit her candle for his daughter, and Betsy said good-night and went upstairs with her woman to lavender-scented sheets, made snug with a warming pan. "My father has been truly kind to me as he always is, but sometimes a little attention from him is quite delightful, he does it in so nice a way."

The next day's journey was even more exciting, passing more numerous towns and villages and more travelers upon the road, until at sunset they entered the hurly-burly of London. The lamplighters were just going their rounds, running quickly up and down the ladders and lighting the oil lamps which made London the best-lighted, as it was the best-paved, city in Europe. All the main thoroughfares were flagged and had curbs. The side streets were paved with cobblestones, and had no sewers with gratings to let off the rain, as the main streets had. The sedan-chair men were plying a lively trade, and a few sturdy women clicked past stiffly on pattens, splash, splash, splash.

The Gurneys drove to the solid and comfortable mansion of kindly Cousin Barclay, where welcome and warmth and food took off the strangeness of arrival to shy Betsy. She fell asleep to the unfamiliar cry of the watch — "Ten o'clock! Ten o'clock of a cold, wet night, and all 's well!"

The next day her father left her there, with her servant, and for the first time Betsy found herself out on her own.

2

The London to which Elizabeth Gurney was introduced was a strange mixture of refinement and brutality. Manners were elaborate and polished, morals were lax and loose. It was the London of the dandies and the wits and the Blue-stockings, and the three great clubs, Brooks's, White's, and Boodle's. High play was a fashion led by the Prince of Wales, whom the King's attacks of insanity occasionally made the Regent. His brilliant friends were Sheridan and Charles James Fox. Beau Brummel, that strange fellow of plebeian birth, was cock of the walk of fashion. Courage is so rare a quality that his extraordinary social daring set him on an eminence from which he could snub duchesses and censor the modes of royalty. Moreover, his serious and dazzling discourse on the tying of a stock, the placing of a button, created for the Prince and his circle a comforting artificial world of pleasant trifles, in which the guns of the French sounded muffled, and the intimate horrors of the Irish rebellion seemed like an unpleasant fairy tale.

George III was a man of quiet and domestic tastes. The Prime Minister, William Pitt the second, was even austere in his conduct and his single-minded devotion to his country. The war with France was sinking the country deeper into debt and causing prices to rise every day; but no example of sobriety or fear of national disaster could check the extravagance of society. Items appeared in the press constantly on gains and loss by gambling. "A lady of high title is reported to have lost at play more than £200,000; her Lord is very unhappy on the occasion."[3] "The Marquis of A. this season has cleared £60,000. The Earl of B. £50,000."[4] "The Marquis of X. lost £13,000 at one sitting."[5] The turf and the ring provided their usual stimulus.

[3] *Morning Post*, April 5, 1805.
[4] *Ibid.*, June 30, 1806.
[5] *Ibid.*, July 8, 1806.

A government lottery encouraged the gambling spirit among the very poor. And cockfighting and bullbaiting were vehicles not only for heavy bets but for the lust of cruelty present in the brutalized, uneducated, and underfed lower classes.

It is impossible to blame the lower classes for cruelty in an age when the government still used the stocks and the pillory, public hangings, and public whipping as instruments of order; when the army and navy were notorious for brutal punishments; and when harmless men in the lower ranks of life were liable to kidnapping by the press gangs for army or navy service.

As late as 1800 a man was whipped two miles through the streets of London for purchasing trusses of hay which he knew to be stolen goods. And in 1810 four men in the pillory were almost destroyed by missiles.

There were no factory laws or trade-unions, and the Industrial Revolution was bringing in an era of overdriven labor. Long hours, low wages, rising prices, and inability to read and write reduced the laboring population to a wretched level of existence from which drunkenness was almost the only relief. Gin shops in London openly invited the passer-by to get "drunk for a penny, dead-drunk for tuppence."

Children under ten were being cruelly driven to work in every mine and every steam factory in England. The workhouse and the debtor's prison were waiting for the pen of Dickens.

Meanwhile the upper classes led a life apparently unaware of all these things. In the journals of the young Gurneys, in Jane Austen's novels, in the plays of Goldsmith and Sheridan, there is not the faintest hint of them. One would gather that the military only existed in the country towns of England for the sake of providing dancing partners and disturbing maiden meditation with their admiring stares.

Even at that, they are all officers! The problems presented on the stage are the problems of manners and wit, possible and interesting only to the cultivated few. Jane Austen, the most intelligent woman of her time, tells in one of her novels of a family of gentlefolk reduced to such poverty that they could only keep three servants.[6] And the conversation of her very best, most sincere, most wise and lovable men and women never touches on any public matter of more moment than the relative merits of Cowper and Pope.

It is true that this era of extraordinary detachment was passing. The great-souled Wordsworth was just about to dawn; the first edition of *Lyrical Ballads* came out in this same year. And a great, though obscure genius had already become articulate: one who knew about the sorrows of the little sweep and all harassed and neglected children; who had seen God looking in at the window when he was four years old. Not a large public read *Songs of Innocence* and *Songs of Experience,* and not many people knew of William Blake. It was impossible, in the wilderness of London, that his wild, plebeian path should cross the sheltered path of young Elizabeth Gurney. But all these currents were abroad; together they made up the atmosphere of London. It is impossible to say that any of them did not subconsciously touch an electrically sensitive soul.

Betsy's first aim was to taste the world. Under the guidance of her fashionable relative she went to theatres, dances, routs, dinners, and every offered gayety. She had always been fond of dress, and it proved impossible, in London, not to make dress a study. Ah, vanity! Make-up was in style, and Betsy submitted to it. Her mirror approved. "I looked quite pretty, for me!" But to have her hair coiffured, with a Grecian mop of fashionable curls and a tall plume or bunch of feathers in front, that was

---

[6] *Sense and Sensibility.*

another matter. "My hair was dressed and I felt like a monkey."

Dancing she loved — the lively, spirited exercise of the square dances. But the partners were strangers, it was not so much fun as at home. The banality of conversation at the routs quite stunned her. To what purpose all this crowding together and exchange of sharp glances and quite meaningless remarks? And the theatre was a sad disappointment. She mentions Drury Lane and Covent Garden, but not the names of many plays. Did she see *The School for Scandal* or *The Rivals* or *She Stoops to Conquer?* Whatever the plays were, she gazed at the hollow glitter of eighteenth-century drama with her serious, sincere young eyes, and found her imagination unstirred. "I must own I was extremely disappointed. I had no other feeling when there than that of wishing it over. . . . I still continue not to like plays. I think them so artificial that they are to me not interesting, and all seems so far from pure virtue and nature."

She saw *Hamlet* and *Bluebeard*, apparently both in one evening, and was somewhat impressed by the latter. Current advertisements describe it as "the grand Dramatic Romance of Blue Beard; or Female Curiousity. The words by George Colman the younger, the music composed and selected by Michael Kelly." Betsy comments: "I suppose that nothing on the stage can exceed it. There is acting, music, scenery to perfection, but I was glad when it was over." What version of *Hamlet* she saw it is impossible to conjecture. And she does not say whether or not she ever saw Mrs. Siddons act; or John Kemble.

But there was an evening when she felt the world's fascination. It was when she went with Amelia Alderson and her fiancé, John Opie, to the opera. Then she did taste a new and strange savor and delighted in it with her whole youth. Was it the music? Or was it because with

John Opie and Amelia she was more inside the magic glittering circle than when with her wealthy Quaker cousins?

Amelia Alderson, at twenty-six years old, was about to make a very surprising marriage. The Cornish peasant genius, John Opie, had met her at a party in Norwich, had fallen stormily in love with her, and had actually succeeded in bearing off the prize. They were married in Marylebone Church, London, in May 1798, shortly after Betsy's visit. Dr. Alderson was not entirely free from the selfishness of the parent of an only daughter. He would, Amelia believed, have opposed any marriage. But he particularly disliked this one. Amelia herself had considered it something of a come-down. In her hesitation before it she had written: "There are moments when, ambitious of being a wife and mother, and of securing to myself a companion for life, I could almost resolve to break all fetters and relinquish too the wide and often aristocratic circle in which I now move, and become the wife of a man whose genius has raised him from obscurity into fame and comparative affluence; but indeed my mind is on the pinnacle of its health when I thus feel; and on a pinnacle I can't remain long."

However, the resolve once made, and the great leap taken, she found matters far otherwise than she had supposed. Instead of relinquishing aristocratic circles, she found the one that she had moved in before narrow indeed compared to that which the wife of Opie could command in London. Her rough-mannered but intrinsically noble husband was the fashion. His sincerity was as impressive in its way as that of Dr. Johnson. Mrs. Inchbald reported that she "found a kind of joyful astonishment in his habitual ruggedness of address." He had been introduced to the capital seventeen years before by Dr. John Wolcot, who wrote essays and criticisms under the pen name of Peter Pindar. The young peasant's success as a portrait painter had been immediate. There had been ups and downs, as the fickle tide of fashion ebbed and flowed. But in good fortune and ill, Opie cared only for one thing. As Northcote said of him, "Other artists painted to live, but Opie lived to paint."

Amelia Alderson had not only to overcome her middle-class prejudice against Opie's low birth. She had also to swallow the fact that he was a divorced man. His first wife had eloped with an army officer, and Opie had divorced her. She was still alive, as another man's wife.

None the less, when the second Mrs. Opie bravely took up her abode at Opie's house in Berners Street, she found herself at once in the swim. Sir Joshua Reynolds was her husband's friend and admirer. Sir James Mackintosh held that if Opie had not been an artist, his original and powerful mind would have made him one of the first philosophers of the age. Mrs. Siddons, Lady Caroline Lamb, painters, writers, musicians, and aristocrats, flowed in and out of the modest house, and Amelia quickly became the lively centre of a stimulating and delightful life.

So when Betsy Gurney was in the company of the Opies, she was really in the world. And when they took her to the opera she went as one of the *beau monde*. Sensitive as she was to music and to the society of the great, the combination of fine music and fine company quite bowled her over. Even there, however, the acting left her cold. She was fascinated by a near view of the Prince of Wales, who held her attention more than the stage. She deplored her love of grand company; but there it was.

Amelia, however, did not give more than the good-natured minimum of attention to the young *ingénue* from Norwich. The time was yet far distant when the strange spell of Quakerism should reach her also, or when the boy Joseph John Gurney should become a man powerful enough to lay a heavy hand upon her mental life. Her future husband was urging her forward with her writing, as earnest about her art as his own. And she was tasting the sweets of the successful author. Her days were full, with literature, with preparation for approaching domesticity, with social engagements. Betsy Gurney was caught briefly in her current, swept along, and left again upon the shore.

A fortnight with her connections the Hoares, at Hampstead, gave Betsy a breathing spell. Life in the cheerful, opulent Hoare house, surrounded by large gardens and wide views over London, recalled the life at Earlham Hall. Savery's description of the Hoares' place is extant in his journal.

Betsy was there this time in March, the windy month, with crocuses short and bright under the yet naked trees. Savery was there two months later, in the very crown of May. "Rose Early [May 28th], it was a delightful morning, walked in the Grounds and Garden of S. H. [Samuel Hoare] which were in high stile much beyond the Symplicity of a frd. His son and Daughters Came to me and though they are quite in high life and gay in their Appearance were as loving and kind as possible. From hence we Could see over great part of London abt 6 miles of; and several Villages and a most Delightfull Scene of Gardens etc. around us. The Castle at Windsor 12 or 14 miles of etc. The house stands on one Side of Hempstead heath which also makes it a fine open Situation. Here seemd to be almost Everything this world Could wish and an open Reception for frds; but more Conformity to the Simplicity and ways of truth Would have made it still pleasanter to me."

To Betsy, however, it was familiar and jolly, a second home. The parties of young people, cousins and cousins' cousins and intimate friends, who gathered for her entertainment were just the sort that she was used to. She made several new friends, among them a girl of about her own age, dark-eyed Hester Savory. The tie of kinship between Hester and William Savery, in spite of the change of spelling caused by transplantation of the family stock, made a quick attraction between the brunette Savory and the blonde Gurney; and, true to herself, Betsy was absorbed.

But there were one or two remoter cousins who were pressing the claims of relationship rather hard. Hudson Gurney was the most attractive, a man older than herself with a bit of an edge to him. He gave éclat to her second visit to the opera, which she actually begged on her return to Uncle Barclay. It was wonderful, when people around in the brilliant crowd were paying and receiving visits between the acts, to have Hudson Gurney come up to her, with the self-possession of a man of the world. "I was charmed to see him; I was most merry."

And Frederick Bevan, a duller fish, was finding less conspicuous opportunities. "Frederick Bevan was here this morning, stay'd with me alone. We had much talk. I don't dislike him so much as I did, but I don't like him to behave to me as if he liked me very much." Her pen leaves poor Bevan for Savery, and she writes a great deal respecting her feelings toward him. "May I never forget the impression he has made on my mind."

But Hudson also had made an impression. "I got out of the carriage before we got to the gates and *met* Hudson. It gave me quite a *glow* to see him. How very much I do like him, I think I would do anything to make Hudson happy. I quite long to tell him my change of opinions. I dislike to have any great change without his knowledge. I always feel so much confidence in him."

But London was not all grand company and gayety and "H——" and "B——." There were Quakers. There were meetings. She went to Westminster Meeting and saw William Savery. Again she fell under his spell. "He said the deist and those who did not feel devotion looked at nature, admired the thunder, the lightning and earthquakes, as curiosities; but they looked not up through them to nature's God. How well," she adds, "he hits the state I have been in." It is impossible not to be strongly persuaded that on this occasion at least Savery spoke direct to a particular heart. He was now thoroughly aware of her. She was his "dear E. G." They met not only at meetings but at various Quaker homes. The chief Friends of London gave hospitality to William Savery; and the chief Friends of London were friends of the great Gurney clan. The Savory family, being his kinsmen, were his principal hosts, and the daughters, Hester and Anna, frequently invited Elizabeth Gurney. And there was an even wealthier family called Fry.

3

Meanwhile Elizabeth struggled. "May I never forget the impression William Savery has made on my mind. As much as I can say is, I thank God for having sent at least a glimmering of light through him into my heart, which I hope, with care, and keeping it from the many draughts and winds of this life, may not be blown out, but become a large, brilliant flame. . . . May I never lose the little religion I now have; but if I cannot feel religion and devotion, I must not despair, for if I am truly warm and earnest in the cause it will come one day. . . . I feel there is a God and immortality, happy, happy thought. May it never leave me; and if it should, may I remember I *have felt* that there is a God and immortality."

She called on Mrs. Siddons, who was not at home, and on her friend Amelia Opie, who was, so justifying the statement made by one of her biographers that she mixed, at this season of wild oats, with "actresses, novelists, and others of a similar character." Visits and parties were numerous. Then on Tuesday her father returned to London and took her out to dinner and to a rout; and on Friday "I had a pleasant, merry day with Peter Pindar"; on Monday, to Sir George Staunton's.

"Some more visits," some to people of the world, and others to plain Quakers, and then father and daughter and female attendant resumed their places in the fawn-colored chaise, and rattled home to Earlham through the opalescent world of mid-April.

The experiment was over. Betsy had had her test of a variety of experiences. And her own prognostication had turned out to be correct. She had seen William Savery, and it had prevented her from being overfond of gayeties.

4

It was natural to write to him for advice. Four days after her arrival home she received a long, supporting letter from Savery, warning her against being led away by gay companions, holding up before her the ideal of religious peace and power. It is a warm letter, but a wise one. The closing paragraph reads: "My dear child, my heart is full towards thee, I have written a great deal more than I expected; but I fain would take thee by the hand if I were qualified so to do, and ascend, as our Heavenly Father may enable us, together, step by step, up that ladder which reaches from earth to heaven; but alas! my weakness is such, I can only recommend both myself and thee to that good hand that is able to do more abundantly for us than we can either ask or think; and bid thee, for the present, in much christian affection, farewell."

Betsy comments on this letter: "I feel he gives me a stimulant to virtue; but I fear by what I expressed in my letter he suspects I am turning plain quaker. I hate that he should estimate me falsely." Her abhorrence of the "plain quakers," and the "enthusiasm," or lack of moderation, which their ways seemed to her to express, is very hard to get over. Even Savery, with all his charm, had something of the totem of Quakers about him which had put her off at first. She asserts her strong native independence, even against his powerful influence. "I must look to One higher than he; and if I feel my own soul satisfied I need not fear. Look up to true religion as the very first of blessings, cherish it, nourish and let it flourish and bloom in my heart; it wants taking care of, it is difficult to obtain. I must not despair or grow sceptical, if I do not always feel religious. I felt God as it were and I must seek to find him again."

The next day she writes at greater length than usual in her journal, reviewing several years, reasoning herself into religion. "We are all governed by our feelings; now the reason why religion is far more likely to keep you in the path of virtue than any theoretical plan is that you feel it; and your heart is wrapt up in it; it acts as a furnace on your character, it refines it, it purifies it; whereas principles of your own making are without kindling to make the fire hot enough to answer its purpose."

Savery's influence is on every page. "I am so glad I do not feel Earlham dull after the bustle of London: on the contrary a better relish for the sweet innocence and beauties of Nature. I hope I may say I do look 'through Nature up to Nature's God.'"

But she fortifies her halting faith with a remarkable piece of pragmatic evidence. Her dreams have stopped. On the night of February the fourth, "that night I dreamed the sea as usual was coming to wash me away, but I was beyond its reach; beyond its powers to wash me away; since that night I do not remember having dreamed that dream. Odd! It did not strike me at the time so odd; but now it does. . . . It ought, I think, to make my faith steady; it may be the work of chance. But I do not think it is, for it is so odd not having dreamed it since. What a blessed thought to think it comes from heaven!"

Sixteen-year-old Richenda's journals reflect at this time some of the outward effects of her sister's inward ferment.

Betsy's letters home from London had a moving quality. Says Chenda: "We have had a long letter of advice from Betsy. I fully intend to profit by it. I am determined henceforth to conquer the foolish weakness I have when Master Sammy begins to bellow and I can hardly keep myself in patience, I am so angry with the child; and when Cilla [1] comes forward in her pert way, and I feel the inclination to give her a good beat."

When Betsy came home again she was under that close, critical examination which only sisters can supply. Too absorbed in her own growing pains to be aware of it, she passed the test with honors. "Betsy is come back," writes Richenda; "she has been a good deal improved by her journey; she has seen a good deal of William Savery, whose whole soul seems formed and made for true religion and perfect faith. From the workings of her own mind and her acquaintance with him, Betsy seems to be changed from a complete sceptic to a person who has entire faith in a Supreme Being and a future state, and I should suppose she feels all the delight which such a belief must bring with it."

She did feel some of that delight; and with the energy and frankness characteristic of the Gurney temper she at once passed it on to a dying servant. "I told him I felt such faith in the blessings of immortality that I pitied not his state; it was an odd speech," she muses, ever conscious of death's terrors, "to make to a dying man."

But though Betsy's advance was undeniable, it was not received by her lively sisters with unqualified approval. Was there, could there be, something of the totem of the Quakers appearing about their Betsy? Was it merely one of her headaches that made her reluctant to join the dance? Or was it her toothache that made her less eager to sing duets with Rachel? She had made no marked change in her dress, to be sure, but she was dressing as plain as she could. "We all feel about it alike, and are truly sorry that

[1] Priscilla.

one of us seven should separate herself in principles, actions and appearance from the rest." On the other hand, there was a something appearing in Betsy which was extraordinarily attractive; one felt in her a great increase of vitality as well as sweetness. One could not but admire. "In short, if it were not for that serious manner which Quakerism throws over a person, Betsy would indeed be a most improved character."

However, she thought and spoke and wrote a good deal about and to William Savery, and Savery was a man whose charm they all recognized. These frequent references, these letters, what could they mean but one thing?

The sisters talked together among themselves, and presently Rachel, as nearest Betsy's confidence, challenged her direct. It was now late June, and the garden at Earlham was full of the scent of roses. Betsy, rosy herself, turned her startled attention away from the problems of belief, from F. B., and from H., and from her old flame J. L. (who had recently reclaimed her attention by becoming seriously ill), and gave it entire to this new and extraordinary idea. Indoors, in privacy, she got out her diary and her pen to help herself to think better.

"*June 23rd.* Rachel has just said she thinks I am *in love* with W. Savery. I answer'd I did not think I was but I own I felt not clear in my own mind respecting him. I think I may love a person as I love him without *being in love*, but I doubt it. I first loved him for his religion, but the feelings of human nature are very apt to join in with the superior feelings of the heart. I don't think I am in love with him. I should be grieved to think I was. I think it a rong suspicion to enter my mind but I fear I shall never no never see him again."[8]

Her candor broke down in a burst of tears.

[8] Savery was married. His journal often refers to his wife. "In London at J. Savory's, 2nd Day 1st mo. 29. 1798. Evening Recd a Comfortable Letter from my Dear Sally though not so much so as some I have had."

5

John Gurney did not need the warning of his daughters. At the beginning of July a visitor arrived in the house, one of Betsy's new friends from London. He was a well-set-up young man, with a steady eye, but he had not the polished manners to which the Gurneys were accustomed. He was shy, not ready of address, and had a loud hearty laugh. They thought him rather uncouth, and a plain Quaker at that. From the marriageable point of view, however, he was one of the richest matches in the Society of Friends, being the son of William Storrs Fry, whose estate at Plashet, near Epping Forest, is described in Savery's journal as "sumptuous."

"I reminded him of not setting his heart too much upon it," he writes, with kindly anxiety. Savery was so far out of his time as to believe in his heart of hearts that riches and Quakerism were an ill-yoked team. But English Friends thought otherwise.

The Frys, like the Gurneys, were bankers, and their banking activities had, as in the case of the Gurneys, arisen out of a successful and well-established business. But instead of being wool staplers they were importers of tea and spices. The headquarters of both businesses was at St. Mildred's Court in London, and it was at the London house that the youngest son lived with his brother William.

Joseph Fry might lack elegance, but he was not wanting in discernment, nor in a certain sturdy power of making himself felt. He knew well how to engage the interest of his fascinating friend. "*July 2nd*," writes Elizabeth, "this afternoon I have been entertained by an account of animal magnetism from young *fry*. J. Fry has been telling me he saw W. Savery not a week ago."

A few days later she is rebuking herself for vanity and

"being a long time dressing." One cannot but feel that "young fry" has made some progress.

The visitor gone, John Gurney presently broaches another plan. He will take them all seven on a trip south, to see Wales and the South of England. What a family for bustles ours is! On July the twenty-first they set off, with the chariot and the chaise. And so it came about that Betsy Gurney was at William Savery's farewell meeting at Gracechurch Street on July 25, and was able to give him with her own hands a girlish keepsake. It was sad, but not too sad.

"All J. G.'s and R. Barclay's familys there and a number of high friends," writes William Savery. "Numbers came and took the most affectionate leave of me. Dear E. G. was much affected."

E. G., shaky as usual in her spelling, hastily scrawls: "*Sunday 25th*, I whent to meeting this morning and was sore that what I felt for W. Savery was not love as I felt the same towards Mary Watson, who I was quite grieved to part with. . . . My dear, dear William Savery is I think only five miles off *me this night*. Perhaps we never again shall be so near each other, but I *firmly believe we shall*. I long to know how he liked my pocketbook that I gave him this morning."

Three days later the Gurneys had left London, and Savery and his companions were on the sea.[9] "I think a good deal of W. Savery and I do not much feel for him though he is on a small and old vessel."

She was right. Not privateers or icebergs or leaks could bring that liberal if tautological soul to the bottom. They never met again. But Savery's work was done.

[9] In a very unseaworthy boat called the *Washington*, which, however, although sailing with a convoy, herself carried no guns. It was the best Savery's staunch pacifism could accomplish at that season; and he had already delayed his start three months in the hope of avoiding any protection by arms.

IV

THE CHANGE

1

THAT summer was a very happy one. The journey itself through the South and West of England was full of interest and beauty. They stayed at a number of places, met friends and relatives, made new acquaintances, had adventures, and enjoyed youth's chief pleasure, variety. There was the time when Betsy almost fainted with terror climbing down the steep rocks by the Devil's Bridge.[1] "If I had I must have fallen to the bottom." And the happy evening at the inn, where, "arriving wet, we were obliged to put on our dressing gowns and sit over a fine turf-fire in the public-house, singing and being sung to by the interesting Welsh inhabitants."

But above all there was the visit to Colebrook Dale, which marked another milestone on Betsy's road. There she formed another of her ardent friendships, this time with her cousin, Priscilla Gurney; and there she attracted the discerning and enthusiastic interest of a notable plain Friend, Deborah Darby.

---

[1] The bridge over the Severn, near Colebrook Dale, Shropshire, the first cast-iron bridge ever built, a span of 100 feet, rising 40 feet. Date, 1779.

"*Sept. 3rd.* Cousin Priscilla and I got up late, but I heard that Deberough Darby was here and went down during breakfast. I felt my *heart beat much.* As soon as it was over D. D. preached in a deep, clear, and striking manner, first to us all . . . and she then addressed me in particular. I do not remember her words, but she express'd first that I was, as I am, *sick* of the *world,* which is true indeed."

"This afternoon I was at the Darbies, and the love they all express for me is *great.* I fear my kind dear friend D. D. is rather to encouraging to me but I do not think," she adds with a touch of wistfulness, "I shall after meet with such encouragement." As for Priscilla, she has become a confidante, as good as or better than the little book. "Prissy Gurney I feel my constant little friend, dearly do I love her indeed."

In such an atmosphere of sympathy and warmth Betsy's heart expanded, her pulses quickened, her confidence increased. "I look upon this as one of the happy and bright seasons of my life." In this mood, open, confiding, understanding, and understood, she went to Deborah Darby's house on September 4, a day afterwards to be ranked in her memory as of equal importance with the Norwich Sunday fourth of February.

"After we had spent a pleasant evening, my heart began to feel itself silenced before God and without looking at others, I felt myself under the shadow of the wing of God, and I soon found the rest dropp'd into the same state. I felt that there must be a meeting. There was: after seting a time in awful silence, Rebecca Young did speak *most beautifully.* She did retch my heart. D. D. then spoke. I only fear she says too much of what I am to be — a light *to the blind,* speech to the *dumb and feet to the lame.* Can it be? . . . After the meeting my heart felt really light and as I walked home by starlight I looked through nature up to nature's

God. Here I am now in Cousin Prissy's little room — never to forget this day while life is in my body.

"I know now what the mountain is I have to climb. *I am to be a quaker.*"

As she lifts her pen to consider that word she realizes, with her honest logic, that it connotes, among other things, willingness sometime to speak in meeting. Alas! Down she comes from the heights of high resolve and exaltation. There are certain odd little difficulties in the way. She soberly notes them and their remedy.

"There is another little matter that I *do wish* most hartily I could obtain which is to write and speak english better. My want of percevearance is my only objection."

Thirty years later, recalling her early education and its defects, she wrote: "I was considered and called very stupid and obstinate. I certainly did not like learning, nor did I, I believe, attend to my lessons, partly from a delicate state of health that produced languor of mind as well as body; but I think having the name of being stupid really tended to make me so, and discouraged my efforts to learn. I remember having a poor, not to say low, opinion of myself, and used to think that I was so very inferior to my sisters Catherine and Rachel."[2]

Harriet Martineau suffered from similar feelings, and it is interesting to recall that Mrs. Sidney Webb's mother wrote of that most distinguished of her daughters when she was a child, "Beatrice is the only one of my children who is below the average in intelligence." Beatrice Webb also suffered from chronic ill-health and writes of herself, "My childhood was not on the whole a happy one." She speaks of "ill-health, sharp pains of mortified vanity, remorse for untruthfulness," and mentions her adolescence as characterized mainly by "the search after a creed by which to live."

[2] *Memoir*, I, 21.

2

"I am to be a quaker." Feet to the lame; speech to the dumb. . . . That was it. That was what she wanted, what she had been waiting for. Something to *do*. She sought a way of putting her new experience of religious feeling into touch with the world of reality. And the harder the better.

By September 9 the Gurneys were home again, and Betsy eagerly set to work. First she plunged into a course of grammar study and stiff reading; but self-improvement and self-discipline were not enough. She looked around to see if there was no one whom she could help, even with her small qualifications, — help *now*, to-day, — and her eye at once fell upon the salient spot. The countryside swarmed with children, totally untaught. Her very desire to educate herself taught her the value of education, and the crippled state of life without it.

Young Miss Gurney, measuring herself beside her cultivated friends, might "wish hartily to write and speak english better," but these poor children could neither read nor write. Their parents could neither read nor write. They had no one to tell them stories, to open to them the world of books. Even that most accessible library of all, the Bible, was closed to them. "We saw but one Bible in the parish of Cheddar," said Hannah More, "and that was used to prop a flower-pot."

Timidly Betsy took one little boy and read to him and taught him Bible stories, on Sunday evenings. He responded. He told his little friends. More wanted to come. Betsy took them up into the eleven-sided attic and taught them. The avidity of the poor little wretches was touching. The threat of banishment maintained discipline. Betsy, thrilled at her success, came out of the attic and took them into the laundry, where they did not need to enter the house. From fifty to seventy children, of various ages, gathered there weekly, some of them already weazened and distorted by work in the factories of Norwich. Yes, at her very first halting step upon the new road of a useful, a dedicated life, she had become feet to the lame, eyes to the blind, speech to the dumb, although she did not notice it, and looked forward to that as to an entirely future state. Joy and energy filled her. Like Florence Nightingale when she went to Kaiserswerth and found for the first time "a better life for women, a scope for the exercise of morally active powers," Elizabeth also felt what it was "to love life, to find life rich in interests and blessings."[3]

She followed the children into their homes, and found hunger, found sickness. She ministered to both, up to the top of her girlish capacity. On October 16 she wrote: "This afternoon I have been to see some one. May I one day be capable of virtue. May I realy be able to lessen the sorrows of the afflicted. . . . *November 19th.* I rode to Norwich after some poor people; I went to see many and added my mite to their comfort. . . . *December 29th.* I have many things rather weighing on my mind — first the poor, next my french, next my logic, next to write to W. Savery."

The new year dawns, and February comes again. Absorbed in her new interests she writes, half-absently: "*February 14th. 1799.* It is more than a year since I first knew W. Savery and I think it was through him I first was made acquainted with the doctrines of religion. . . . I have one remark to make — every step I have taken towards quakerism has given me satisfaction."

Her new content brims over. "I thought what is it I want — how I overflow with the blessings of this world. I have true friends as many as I wish for, good health, a happy home with all that riches can give, and yet these are nothing without a satisfied contience."

[3] Sir Edward Cook, *Life of Florence Nightingale*, I, 111.

There seemed enough work in her school and in the village and city near her home to keep her busy the rest of her life. Strange! It had been there all the time and she had never noticed it. None of her sisters or friends had noticed it. All these neglected children, growing up like savages, losing even the little primitive culture of the home as their mothers and fathers were caught in the new industrialism and snatched into the factories,[4] who was caring for them? Simply no one in the neighborhood but young Elizabeth Gurney.

"Betsy's Imps," her sisters called them, and were thankful to have no such concern. After all, even if seventy children were learning something here, look at all the thousands who were not! It was a mere drop in the bucket. Some great reform was needed, some government measure; new laws, and so on. Just what, no one could say. Meanwhile, the family gathered cosily in the Great Parlor with their music and their books, in the pleasant glow of candlelight and a bright fire. It was forlorn in the laundry. And with all that crowd of dirty, ill-fed little bodies — Phew, my dear!

So they did not help; but they did not hinder. They indeed respected. But there were other, more personal, results of Betsy's new point of view that they resisted with all their might.

3

The Quakers of the strict type, the "plain quakers," had always seemed to Betsy and her sisters too drastically severe, absurdly narrow. They wore the special Quaker dress, used the special Quaker speech, and condemned the four chief social pleasures — dancing, music, cards, and the theatre.

---

[4] By 1786 one partner could write to another that people were "steam-mill mad." Quennell, *A History of Everyday Things in England*, III, 80.

Even when first under Savery's spell Betsy had dreaded "confusing being religious with being the quaker." One could be the first in a moderate and pleasant manner without falling into the uncomfortable extremes of the second.

But as the months passed, she began to see their point. To see it not only caused her pain, but would, she knew, cause friction in the family. She might have said, as Florence Nightingale later said to her own puzzled and estranged relations: "My beloved people, I cannot bear to grieve you. Life and everything in it that charms you, you would sacrifice for me; but unknown to you is my thirst, unseen by you are waters that would save me!"

What Elizabeth needed was concentration. As she found scope for morally active powers, she felt those powers increase with use. And she longed to bring her whole life into training, as a musician is constrained to devote himself to his instrument, or a painter to the constant exercise of brush and pencil. "Of late I do not think I have been sufficiently active, but have given rather way to a dilatory spirit. . . . I want order." She valued religious emotion, but she feared it, too. Action was her refuge and her ultimate satisfaction. She had suspicion of her "enthusiastic and changeable feelings." Her temperament was not mystical, and she speaks in a very low tone of her inward, personal assurances. "For a few days past I have at times felt much religion for *me*," she says. And in December 1798, "True religion is what I seldom feel." She felt that she needed every possible protection and incentive for the living of the good life. Where a Roman Catholic would have joined some secular order such as the Third Order of Saint Francis, Betsy felt herself drawn toward the outward and visible signs, the protective habits and manners, of the plain Quakers.

"I still continue my belief that I shall turn plain. . . . I find it almost impossible to keep up to the principles of

Friends without altering my dress and speech. . . . They appear to me a sort of protector to the principles of Christianity in the present state of the world."

She did not, however, do it easily — no, nor quickly. "*October 1798.* I have now two things heavily weighing on my mind: dancing and singing, so sweet and so pretty do they seem. It is not only my giving up these things, but I am making the others miserable and laying a restraint upon their pleasures. . . . *December 12th.* This day finished with a dance. If I could make a rule never to give way to vanity, excitement or flirting, I do not think I should object to dancing, but it always leads me into some one of these faults; indeed I never remember dancing without feeling one, if not a little of all three, and sometimes a great deal. But as my giving it up would hurt many, it should be one of those things I part with most carefully."

John Gurney had thought his daughters very well as they were, and now all the trouble he had taken to restore Betsy to the family groove — to what a modern father would call "normality" — appeared to have been fruitless. As Florence Nightingale's parents later found, it was vexatious.

"*Jan. 8th.* My father not appearing to like all my present doings has been rather a cloud over my mind this day," says Betsy to her book; "there are few if any in the world I love so well; I am not easy to do what he would not like, for I think I could sacrifice almost anything for him, I owe him so much, I love him so much."

It was for many months, however, that Betsy had been asking herself, "Is dancing wrong?" She tried to balance its good and ill: ". . . It animates the spirits and produces good effects. I think dancing and music the first pleasures in life." But she had to reckon with her excitable, sensitive temperament: "The danger of dancing, I find, is throwing me off my centre; at times when dancing I know that I have not reason left, but that I do things which in calm moments

I must repent of." Singing, too: "How much my natural heart does love to sing! But if I give way to the ecstasy singing sometimes produces in my mind, it carries me far beyond the centre. It increases all the wild passions and works on enthusiasm." Even so, Wesley and his followers had taken that ecstasy of singing and used it as a great engine of religious feeling. In Betsy Gurney's journal can be seen the difference between the Quaker genius and that of current revivalism. "Many say and think," she continues, "that it leads to religion. It may lead to emotions of religion but true religion appears to me to be in a deeper recess of the heart where no earthly passion should produce it."

She cannot bear, however, to condemn what was so joyous. "Music may sometimes be of use; and I think our earthy feelings are made use of to lead us much to better things."

"Young fry," whose knowledge and love of music was much deeper than that of any of the Gurneys, was not there to advise, and might have carried no weight if he had been.

Betsy falls back on her natural pragmatism. "I think the only true standard I can have to direct myself by is that which experience proves to give me the most happiness, by enabling me to be more virtuous. I believe there is something in the mind or in the heart that shows its approbation when we do right. I give myself this advice: Do not fear truth, let it be ever so contrary to inclination and feeling. Never give up the search after it: and let me take courage, and try from the bottom of my heart to do that which I believe truth dictates, if it lead me to be a quaker or not."

4

Her steps, though slow, were definitely in one direction. First she used the plain language, saying "thee" to a person.

"It makes me think before I speak, and avoid the spirit of gaiety and flirting."

Then she relinquished, painfully and slowly, music and dancing, and last, as her wardrobe needed replenishing, gradually replaced her fashionable gowns by others made after the Quaker style, and adopted the kerchief and cap. Common-sense reasonings attended all these changes. "When the cap is once worn," she notes, "the fasson of the head does not require so much attention."

And though there is a great deal in her journals throughout the year 1799 concerning her prolonged struggle in regard to being "plain" or not, she never once loses her sense of the fundamental unimportance of all these things. "I used to think, and do now, how very little dress matters." Her idea was the concentration and simplification of life. For one thing, it reduced the number of decisions to be made. A person who had adopted Quaker dress would not even be asked to go to a ball, to a theatre, to a card party or an opera; would not even be expected to stand up and dance or to stand up and sing. To go plain was for Betsy not to escape from sin, — she never used the word, — but to prune off the unessential. The cutting hurt. That which she cut off was bound up in the lives of others, and their pain doubled hers. But once the effort was made, she felt release. Pragmatically she was justified.

John Gurney again administered a dose of London. This time Rachel went too, Betsy's nearest and dearest sister, with whom as a child, in their mother's lifetime, she had shared the pleasures of a shell cabinet and dolls' things, and who now was showing her the most sisterly sympathy possible without full approval. Rachel's tenderness had recently been developed in the hard school of sorrow, through her painful love affair with young Enfield. But Betsy too at this period was particularly winsome. She went out of her way constantly "to keep truly intimate with them all [her brothers and sisters] — make them my first friends. . . . I should fully express my love for them, and how nearly it touches my heart, acting differently to what they like."

London, however, was a relief from various strains, and Betsy's human femininity felt an elasticity of rebound. The entry in her journal for "*Sixth day evening. London. March 22nd,*" beginning "I am once more at Brick Lane," is very girlish in its vivid portrayal of a debate between "cap, turban, turban, cap," before appearing in public at a party at the Hoares'. Not only vanity and the dread of being conspicuous, but whether the cap would embarrass Rachel, all enter into the question. "However, after much uncertainty, I felt most easy to appear like a quaker and wear my cap, which I did."

That settled the "fasson of the head," but not the "fasson of the heart." Alas, for the volatility of warm-blooded nineteen! "The Roaches were there, who I admire, particularly Banjamin who reminded me of William Savery. I think I felt rather too flirty with him, partly because I was told he was a flirt."

The Hoares, "who understand better than almost any people I ever saw the true method of being kind; they seem to me to feel for others and therefore understand what will most please them," had no doubt included in their parties other friends of the Gurneys, especially one who did not know how to flirt but wished to promote a plain and honest courtship. Betsy was perhaps hardly aware of his wooing, being accustomed to swains with more address and polish. But it was not long before "young fry" was to force himself solidly upon her attention.

5

It might be well at this point to consider the change in the appearance of a young girl who adopted Quaker dress at the turn of the eighteenth century. Instead of a semi-transparent gown with a high waistline and low neck, she donned a dress with a natural waistline, made of silk or print, and with a white kerchief folded softly around the throat. This kerchief was sometimes partly covered with another cross-over in silk of the same tone as the dress. Instead of a turban in the daytime and a feathered headdress at night, she wore on all occasions a white lawn cap. It was, as a matter of fact, a very charming costume, and one far better fitted to the English climate than the current styles. Choice of color was left to the wearer, and though pastel browns and grays were popular, especially in silks, we hear of Elizabeth after 1800 in a colored print, a "pink acorn gown," and in 1828 a young Preparative Meeting Clerk in Dutchess County, New York State, is described as presiding at the meeting dressed in "a painted muslin with a very large figure, almost white, a cape with a small transparent handkerchief round the neck and a bonnet of white silk in the English fashion. . . ."[5]

The Gurneys, including Elizabeth, did not see the beauty of the Quaker costume. And possibly no Quakers did. It was one of the faults of the Quakerism of the period that they spent their time fussing about details of dress from the point of view of "mortifying vanity" instead of putting their energy into practical religion.

But an outside observer of taste, such as Charles Lamb, could appreciate the charm of Quaker fashion to the full. "Every Quakeress is a lily; and when they come up in bands to their Whitsun-conferences, whitening the easterly streets of the metropolis, from all parts of the United Kingdom, they show like troops of the Shining Ones."[6]

It is not always known that Lamb's admiration of the Quakeress was not only general but particular, and that

[5] Amelia Gummere, *The Quaker: a Study in Costume*, 170.
[6] "Essay on a Quaker Meeting." *Essays of Elia*.

the love of his maturity was that very Hester Savory who was Elizabeth Gurney's friend and William Savery's kinswoman.

In that memorable spring of 1798, whenever Elizabeth Gurney went to spend the day in Chapel Street, Pentonville, with her friends the Savorys, she passed the house in which dwelt Charles and Mary Lamb. And when she and Hester walked abroad together up the street, on a little errand, or to take the air, they were watched, all unconscious, from the window by the eyes of that acute observer, that most delicate receiver of impressions. Betsy had at that time no marks of a Quaker, but her friend was the lily par excellence, the supreme quintessence, to the lonely genius, of Quakerly and womanly charm.

Lamb was living there to be near the Islington madhouse, on his sister's account. His tragic story was known to his neighbors, and though he and the Savorys were not "acquainted," glances passed, looks were exchanged, of interest and pity on the one hand, of earnest and simple adoration on the other. In 1802 Hester Savory married, and in 1803 she died of her first child. Lamb wrote to Manning, "I send you some verses I have made on the death of a young Quaker you may have heard me speak of as being in love with for some years while I lived at Pentonville, though I had never spoken to her in my life. She died about a month since": —

> A springy motion in her gait,
> A rising step, did indicate
> Of pride and joy no common rate
>   That flushed her spirit.
>
> Her parents held the Quaker rule
> Which doth the human feeling cool,
> But she was train'd in Nature's school,
>   Nature had blest her.

THE CHANGE

A waking eye, a prying mind
A heart that stirs, is hard to bind,
A hawk's keen sight ye cannot blind,
    Ye could not Hester.

My sprightly neighbor, gone before
To that unknown and silent shore,
Shall we not meet as heretofore,
    Some summer morning,

When from thy cheerful eye, a ray
Hath struck a bliss upon the day,
A bliss that would not go away,
    A sweet forewarning? [7]

So, if a Quaker girl could strike so deep into a receptive heart through the eyes alone, it is clear that her dress was no nun's garb. It preserved her woman's power to attract.

[7] E. V. Lucas, *Life of Charles Lamb*, I, 327–8.

V

JOSEPH FRY

1

Joseph Fry had carried in his heart for many months a picture of a tall girl in a brown silk dress, the fairness of her hair and skin enhanced by a black lace turban, the ends of which were pendent at one side. But when he saw her in London, at the Hoares' or the Bevans', with her white Quaker cap upon her hair, she looked to him sweeter than ever and more accessible.

He had had occasional contacts at Earlham in time past as a school friend of John Gurney, Jr., and had sometimes ridden over from the house of John Holmes, in Norfolk, where he had spent some months from time to time to learn the management of an estate, a necessary skill for the heir of Plashet. The easy abundant life at Earlham was very attractive to him. It was no wealthier certainly than that which he was accustomed to at Plashet, but it was much, much jollier.

On those occasions, however, hunting and coursing with John and John's friends, he had seen little of the ladies of the house, and they had scarcely been aware of seeing him at all. He was a "plain quaker," therefore very dull, an outdoor man with no great indoor ease, and his shyness was quite eclipsing in the formidable brilliance of the seven sisters.

But when Betsy began to show signs of Quakerism, a thoughtful father recollected this eligible "plain" acquaintance, and had him as at least one of the irons in the fire on Betsy's first visit to London.

Betsy, out by herself, was far less alarming than as one of the bright bevy. As Hester Savory's friend, as the Hoares' and Bevans' cousin, circles in which Fry himself was familiar and at ease, he could at least watch her without becoming overwhelmed with blushes, he could even exchange a word or two with her in the course of an evening, and he could listen to what she said to other people. So he had ventured to pay a very definite visit to Earlham in the summer of '98, on John Gurney's invitation, and to engage Betsy's attention upon matters which he had noticed interested her — animal magnetism, for instance, and William Savery.

So far, so good. She had sweet manners, and, when her interest was engaged, how sincerely she listened, with her grave, candid eyes sometimes lifted to his.

Now this London March there was the Quaker cap. And he made up his dogged mind.

In July 1799, he made formal application to John Gurney for permission to seek Elizabeth's hand in marriage. The permission of William Storrs Fry had already been granted. Everything was in order, according to the stately custom of the time. And Fry was invited down to Earlham to speak for himself.

Elizabeth, in the meanwhile, had hardly given that "young fry" a thought.

The first entry in her journal on her return from London, April 28, is about her obstinate and sturdy little brother: "I had a very interesting evening with my dear Sam. How much I love that boy. May he do well."

She becomes absorbed in home affairs: her school, her

poor, her "french lessons — so boring." "I expect Lesage this morning and I do think it a duty to speak french to him when I consider the expence my father is at in his teaching me, and I should in gratitude try to profit by it."

Her knowledge of life is enlarged, in the frank eighteenth-century atmosphere, among young married friends and servants. "I went to H. Scarnels[1] where we had a long gossip about the Enfields, her laying in, and realy," she confesses to her book, "it was an interesting time."

Her nineteenth birthday arrived on May 21, and passed without much comment. In June she had a great excitement, a new friend. One Mary Anne Galton came for a visit, and proved "one of the most interesting and bewitching people I ever saw . . . *most attractive, most flattering* . . . she appears to me *realy* clever. . . . I think I hardly ever remember," adds Betsy, with short-memoried enthusiasm, "any *person* attracting me so strongly." But discomfort soon crept into their relations. A sense of strain, a tinge of insincerity, destroyed the enchantment. Betsy's hearty honesty notes with disgust what it does to a person to be flattered by the "realy clever." "I find it difficult to keep strictly to truth with her. I pretend to know what I do not, which is silly. This evening she was talking to me about some characters in history. I had twice courage to tell her I did not know them, but the third time I pretended I did."

So down goes Mary Anne, and Betsy's school and "schollers" again claim her book's attention. To-day "there were in all 56. It was to be sure a pleasing sight to me, particularly as my *father and all* seem'd to enjoy it."

John Gurney had indeed come to perceive in Betsy's Imps more than either a passing whim or a sign of ill-health. Looking in now and then at the laundry, he had seen a surprising sight, and a rather lovely one. He began to bring

[1] A former housekeeper at Earlham Hall.

ELIZABETH GURNEY (LATER FRY)
AGED ABOUT NINETEEN

Reproduced from the drawing by Amelia Alderson (later Opie) with the kind permission of the owner, Quintin Gurney, Esq., Norwich, England

his friends to see it. Betsy might be weak in historical characters, but she was developing a gift for easy narrative and clear, straightforward expression. She was educating her "schollers," and her "schollers" in return were liberally educating her.

And then that "young fry," from the very edges and fringes of her consciousness, walked right into the middle of her ordered world. Not only was he there, as her father indicated, a very solid and inescapable fact, but he threatened to disrupt the whole of it.

Betsy was so taken by surprise that at first she could only give way to a girlish curiosity, not untinged with vanity, as to how and when she would be proposed to.

"*July 25th.* I am much occupied with an affair of consequence as the present happiness of an individual seems much concerned. Joseph Fry is come here. . . . He has not yet made *me an offer*.

"*5th day July 26th.* This morning Joseph Fry made me an offer in a long talk with him. I discouraged the affair but fix'd not to give him a final answer till 6th day. [Friday.]

"*6th Day.* Though I fully see the many good things I give up in not having him and perhaps may never have another chance of marrying so well, yet I believe all in all I am wise in my determination of giving it up."

Joseph Fry withdrew, the sisters rejoiced heartily, and Elizabeth set herself to read Hume's *History of England*, so as not to be caught out so easily again by "realy clever" people.

But the harm was done. There was Joe Fry, large and solid, in the middle of her consciousness. Do what she would, her thoughts kept bumping up against him.

2

John Gurney's theory was, give no time to brood. J. F. was hardly out of the house, Elizabeth had hardly opened her history book, before a great bustle of preparation for travel pervaded Earlham Hall, and the family were whirled off on one of their sudden journeys. This time it was to the North. They visited the Quaker Boarding School at Ackworth — where embarrassed Betsy was asked to examine some of the children in spelling and grammar, and afterward "I was pointedly asked what I thought of their spelling, which I said; and also that I did not think they attended to the words of one as well as to those of many syllables." Did they have some trouble with that tiresome word "whent"?

They drove on to York and Newcastle, and spent some happy, outdoor days riding about an estate of John Gurney's at Sheepwash "on the beautiful banks of the Wanspeck," probably a sheep farm in connection with his woolen mills at Norwich. Betsy found her courage rather tested by riding an unruly horse. But she was not a timid horsewoman. The whole experience was delightful, except for toothache and a certain strange flatness of the mind.

They wound up at Edinburgh, and were back at Earlham by the end of August. It had been a pleasant journey, but it was not quite so easy as usual to pick up the home threads. In September Betsy noted that she "awoke with a cloud over me"; in October, "I feel in a state of real and true discouragement; I have little faith and little hope." Her happy energy seemed lost. She began to feel flurried, with her home duties, her lessons, her "schollers," her poor.

"*October 24th.* I feel this morning as I have felt lately, quite in a hurry about what I have to do; and I do not think that that is the way to do it well; it is better to go soberly and quietly to work about it, and not to flurry and bluster. . . . I put some things in proper order, read history and grammar, wrote letters and worked." But, alas, pull oneself together as one may, it cannot be denied "I feel in rather a flat silent state of mind."

3

The autumn leaves that had bowled so merrily about the Earlham lawns had been swept up. The untidy bunches of the rooks' nests showed in the bare trees. The farm fields were neat and bare, the water meadows grew dun, and a film of ice formed on the little River Wensum. Winter shut down upon Earlham. It was a time to ride out in one's scarlet cloak and be busy about the poor, it was not a time for lovers.

But to young Joe Fry it was good hunting weather, and he came down into Norfolk after more than foxes. His friends the Holmeses offered a good base for a new campaign. Elizabeth had had a decent minimum of delay, and now his decisive movement dealt her another shock.

"*12 mo. 12.* This day my father had a letter from Joe Fry saying he intended being here next 2nd Day."

All the hidden thoughts and feelings that had been playing havoc with her work and her peace were dragged out into the open to be examined, as far as she was able, in justice to an honest man. "I believe the true state of my mind is as follows: I have almost ever since I have been a little under the influence of religion rather thought *marriage* at this time was not a good thing for me as it might lead my interests and affections from that source in which they should be centred and also if I have any *active duties to perform* in the church (if I really follow as far as I am able the voice of truth in my heart) are they not rather *incompatible with the duties of a wife and mother* and is it not safest to wait and see what is the probable course I shall take in this life before I enter into engagements that affect my future life. So I think and so I have thought, but to look on the other side, if truth appears to tell me I may *marry*, I shall leave the rest and hope whatsoever my duties are, if I am willing I shall be able to perform them. But it is now at this time the prayer of my heart that if I ever should be a mother, I may rest with my children, and realy find my duties lead me to them and my husband; and if my duty ever leads me from my family, it may, it may be in single life. . . .

"I see part of what I have written may be wrong and perhaps are realy the inclination of my heart not to have domestic and duties of the Church unite, for with God all things are possible." [2]

On Tuesday afternoon, when they came in fresh and rosy from a ride for their three o'clock dinner, Joe Fry had arrived, rather red in the face, perhaps, obviously embarrassed, a little awkward in his manners, but with a certain sturdy intention to be himself.

It was a difficult ordeal for a rejected suitor, even had he been conscious of polished self-possession, to be the centre of attention of that too lively group, to know that they all knew why he had come, and to be gruelingly aware that he stood publicly at Betsy's mercy. But he had a stubborn consciousness of worth. He knew himself able to offer even one of the rich Gurney girls a home suitable to her upbringing. Other girls had set their caps at him, ere now — aye, even Quaker caps. He refused to be put entirely out of countenance by these brilliant Gurneys.

He forced himself to greet Elizabeth as he would have put his horse at a difficult fence, and it encouraged him to see that it was her self-possession that was shaken. She blushed, she was confused, she could not look him in the face. It was very lovable.

He accepted John Gurney's invitation to stay several days at Earlham.

[2] Betsy was nineteen years old.

Elizabeth to her journal: "*3rd day. 12th month.* When we got home Joe Fry was here, and it has been to me ever since rather a more agitating time, at least an *awkward* time. I have had a great deal of serious conversation with him. It puts me most in mind of my feelings to James Loyd's affair.

"*7th Day.* This morning I awoke in a harrassed nervous fatigued and unsatisfied state of mind and body. . . . I had a long concluding talk with *poor Joseph* and *refused his offer*, but I was not at liberty to say to what the future might produce. . . . The day may come that I may feel willing and at liberty to marry, and whenever that is the case I am sure I cannot tell who it may be, for at *this time* I am not inclined to marry anybody, and am not in love with any person."

So once more Joe Fry was forced to retire, but this time he left very different feelings behind him. The critical sisters were not glad to see him go, they were sorry. His love of music and his skill as a performer had made him a welcome addition to the evening circle in the Great Parlor. Although he was not a ready talker, they perceived, as they became better acquainted with him, that it was the result of repressive training, and not of an empty or ill-informed mind.

And though a Quaker coat did not set off a young man's figure, and Fry had not the grace of build of the Gurney men, he had an admirable seat on a horse. The two John Gurneys, father and son, were his firm friends. As for Betsy, she alone knew what inroads he had made upon her. It is true that she was not "in love with any person," but then she was always justly suspicious of enthusiastic and changeable feelings.

In those five days of walks and rides and long talks, Fry had possessed himself in an amazing way of her confidence. Not even Priscilla Gurney had proved such a friend. Her dawning sense of vocation, her delight in work, her "children," and her poor, her half-formed ambitions toward a full use of her powers in such a great cause — she did not know how to express it — dared she — well, truly, in the service of mankind, in the service of God — he drew all this out of her. She told it all to him, as she had told it to no one before. Then they discussed marriage from that angle. Could a married woman have any other vocation beside the duties of her home? Joe Fry said yes, if she were *his* wife.

She refused him at last, but timidly, hesitatingly, and with regret. She shed tears for his pain, and when he rode away she felt she had lost a friend. But no, she was not ready yet; and she was not "in love"; but as to the future — well, as to that she could not say. The day might come . . .

4

The morning after Fry's departure was a Sunday, and Goats was as unhelpful as usual. "I had a rather volatile meeting." But her work steadied her. "I had a satisfactory evening with my children." And on Monday better still: "I spent most of the morning in nursing, as H. Scarnell was very poorly and so I went to attend to her and the little baby — a job I rather liked."

But when not absorbingly occupied she was depressed and restless. "*January 1st. 1800.* This has not been one of the clear and bright days of life: little has been done, and that little as in a nightmare; not feeling able to get forward, and discouraged. . . . I had my children and found them a great burden."

She tries to discipline herself by struggling with her fear of the dark, forcing herself by will power to go into dark rooms in remote parts of the house. She rides to Norwich in the bitter winter weather to "pay visits to some in affliction." She reads in her Ackworth grammar, the gift of its author, Lindley Murray. She receives a letter from William

Savery. But all efforts to distract her thoughts fail. She has lost her peace.

"*1st mon.* (*Jan.*) ³ *31st. 1800.* My father returned home just before supper and sent a letter to the supper-table directed to Miss C., R., & E. Gurney." (Catherine, Rachel, and Elizabeth.) "We thought at first it was from the Galtons, but what was our surprise to find it from *James Loyd*. I felt quite agitated, it was so odd. . . . I think and hope I *never* shall be his.

"*1st Day. 2 mon.* (*Feb.*) *2nd.* As usual I can say little for my attention at meeting — sadly volatile. How exceedingly difficult if not impossible it is to settle the mind into a silent waiting upon God.

"How much the family are altered about Joseph Fry. All now seem to *wish* for the connection."

But John Gurney had a careful eye upon Elizabeth. He arranged that she should go to London again at the end of March. London had never yet failed to do her good. And besides, if young Fry will only be patient and use his opportunities there as they come . . .

Young Fry, however, is far from patient. Those long talks with Elizabeth have given him food for thought, and he believes that now is the time for action. He therefore acts, with delicacy but with directness. "*2nd Day. 24th. 2nd mo.* (*Feb.*) My father received a letter from John saying poor Joe Fry hoped to pay *another visit* here. . . . I think he had better not come as I think of soon being in the neighborhood of London."

But when she gets there, what then?

"*26th.* To-night I am in mind a little occupied about Joe Fry's coming. I don't quite like the thought of what I am to do about him in London."

³ The plain Quakers always referred to the months of the year and to the days of the week numerically to avoid using their "heathen" names. The insertion of the latter in parentheses is therefore the author's.

John Gurney wrote to his son John to advise Fry not to come to Earlham at present. And Elizabeth got what respite she could from that. Her sisters were tactful and gentle in her unexpressed trouble. They ceased to worry about her dress and other trifles. She understood and appreciated their forbearance. "It is a fine sight to observe their tenderness towards me and sympathy in my feelings."

But solitude was what she really longed for, a little time to think and feel without even the kindliest observation. And accident gave it to her. Everyone but herself went off on March 9 on a trip to Clare to stay overnight. She confides to her journal: "I intend to sleep alone to-night, which is a thing I hardly ever *remember doing in this house*. It is lovely to me their being from home, particularly of an evening being by myself."

Twenty-four hours of peace. And no doubt she roamed in luxury through the empty rooms; sat snugly all alone by the fire when evening fell; ate in great quiet her solitary supper; did not even trouble to write up her journal, or to wrestle with her fear of the dark; had candles aplenty; and rested, relaxed, sank down into that deeper self beyond thinking where she believed that truth was to be found.

A week later Joe Fry, having received the kindly rebuff via the hand of his friend John, returned again to the attack, threw aside the delicacy of the indirect approach, and wrote a manly letter of entreaty to his lady's father. In that letter Elizabeth felt again the sturdy shock of his presence.

"*3 mo. (March) 19.* My father shewed me a letter from Joe Fry to beg he might come. I think that has brought me to see the affair in a better light."

John Gurney had, however, refused the request before showing Elizabeth the letter. Her visit to London was almost due; and she had expressed herself most clearly and decidedly in respect of Fry's coming at the time of John's letter in February. John Gurney had never felt less optimistic as to Fry's prospects than he did in March 1800. He wrote him as follows: —

"*March 16th. 1800.* I can do no less than recommend thee, at least for the present, to waive all thoughts of a visit to Earlham. I am of opinion it is in no respect likely to further thy wishes, and if so, then it must have a contrary effect, because it must call upon Betsy, if she cannot return thy affection for her, to take a line of absolute prohibition as to casual intercourse. She will have to consider that young women suffer a disadvantage in character when there shall be any appearance of allowing a young man to remain in the character of a suitor when there is no inclination or intention to give him a future encouragement. . . .

"For myself, I am vastly at a loss how to act, for unless thou couldst summon resolution to relinquish thy views towards her, I feel it a hardship upon thee to have her in the neighborhood without holding intercourse; and with the sentiments which I am aware she holds, I could not think an intercourse could be allowed with satisfaction to thee, or propriety to herself."[4]

But Joseph Fry had seen her blush before him, had seen her weep, and was doggedly determined of the contrary.

5

In other visits to London, Joseph Fry had been hardly noticed, but now he held the centre of the stage. He brazenly took every advantage of the liberal opportunities afforded him of casual intercourse. At least she should know him, risk or no risk. He had more ardor and determination than tact. But perhaps after all he was the best judge of his own business.

Meanwhile beleaguered Betsy had no real confidante but her journal. "*April. In London.* I feel oddly and very

[4] *Gurneys of Earlham*, I, 108.

changeably toward him, but I know I always feel emotion, either dislike or really like. I cannot well describe how I am with him but now the remembrance of him is very pleasant to me — the other day it was truly disagreeable — *so I go on.* . . .

"I much wish to know his family, for I think that an important thing in forming such a connection. . . .

"This has once more been a day of absolute trial about Joseph Fry. He came early . . . vexing to me he stayed so late. . . . I like him as my friend but dislike him as my lover.

"After meeting [at Gracechurch Street] I was introduced to Eliza Fry and her father, and although I longed to have the matter ended, I felt a little drawn toward them. . . .

"Went to Joe Bevan's. I was *low, tired, nervous,* and vexed a little when I heard them say Joe Fry was expected to supper. I was rather cross with him but as the evening advanced I grew more comfortable — things brightened and I enjoyed his company.

"*I dreamed pleasantly* about him. I mention that because I think dreaming agreeably or disagreeably of a person has its effect in such a tossed-about mind as mine."

John Gurney brought Kitty and Rachel with him when he came to fetch Betsy, and William Storrs Fry promoted friendship between the families by inviting them to Plashet. It was a pleasant and hospitable time. Everyone enjoyed it, and the sisters spoke cordially of the house and family to Betsy.

Returned to Earlham, Betsy received a letter herself from Joe Fry, and returned a kind reply. It was more than kind. But had she forgotten her lover's temper? Never had that young man been given an inch that he did not take an ell. It brought him down to Earlham as fast as horses could perform the journey; and it brought him in a mood of ultimatum. He carried with him a gold watch. His interview with Betsy that evening of May 24 was brief and almost stern.

"*Fifth month (May) twenty sixth. 2nd Day morning before breakfast.* I went down to breakfast — my heart was full.[5] I could hardly keep from crying before them all. I was so oppressed with the weight of the subject before me, natural inclination seemed to long to put the hour of decision afar off, but he gave me the watch last night with this engagement. If I gave it back to him by nine o'clock this morning he *never more* would renew the affair. If I kept it after that hour he never would receive it back. I found inclination, reasoning and imagination so fickle that I saw my best plan was to leave them all and in humility to try to do the will of God, who alone was able to carry me through. . . .

"I did not feel *at liberty to return the watch.* I cryed heartily. *Joseph felt much for me.*"

It boded well for their future relations that their candor was from the first complete. It was to him alone that she could confide her tremors, and it was on his comfortable shoulder that she sobbed her indecision away. Once he had established himself as her friend she had no other confidant. She turned to him unconsciously, instinctively, with childlike trust. She had no reserves with him.

"*3rd Day.* Last night before I went to bed painful feelings towards Joseph began to enter my mind and this morning I woke with them strongly upon me. I went to him and told him alone what I felt and soon began to recover them only great trepidation [?][6] remained which I did not mind in comparison to painful feelings. Now and then my painful

---

[5] Yesterday is understood. It is evidently an account of the day of the twenty-fifth. The watch story told by Augustus Hare in *Gurneys of Earlham*, I, p. 111, and repeated indefinitely in slightly varying versions by other biographers, is legendary.

[6] Timidity? Word indecipherable in MS.

feelings towards him returned a little — a sort of distance and almost dislike, but as we spent some very pleasant time together in the afternoon and parted comfortably, I trust all things will in the end work together for good."

It was very unlike the proud misunderstandings between Rachel and the passionate Enfield, who had ridden away and incontinently married another. "I cryed and cryed for her in the night," wrote Betsy, who was in a state to understand deeply and suffer sharply for her sister's pain.

A few days of their new, close association, and Joseph had steadied her. She felt safe with him. Her skies cleared.

"*6th day. 5th mo. (May) 30.* My feelings toward Joseph are so calm and pleasant, and I can look forward with so much chearfulness to a connection with him."

William Storrs Fry presently came down to Earlham, and marriage settlements were in order. None of the three men concerned was a favorer of delay. Joe Fry was already established in business, with an ample house at his command. And the wedding was set for August.

6

Elizabeth's days became full of winding up her work and preparing her trousseau. In less than three months' time all that she had begun to do, with so much zest and with so much success, must be left behind forever. "It overturns all my theories," she had written when beginning to succumb to Joe Fry's addresses in London. "The idea of leaving my station at home is to me surprising, as I had not thought that it would have been the case."

But her surprise at her decision does not weaken it. Her tossed-about mind is at rest.

On her seventeenth birthday she had said in her journal that not only her mind but her heart needed to be put in order, her impressionable heart that was in such a fly-away state. "But I think if ever it were settled on one subject it would never, no never, fly away any more; it would rest quietly and happily on the heart that was open to receive it, it will then be most constant; it is not my fault it now flies away, it is owing to circumstances."

So now she settles like a butterfly on a honied flower, and spreads her peaceful wings in the sun.

"*Sixth month (June) sixth*. I received a letter I liked from Joseph, and answered it this afternoon. I felt unwilling to represent my own faults to him, although I told him how faulty I was.

"*9th*. I have been busy to-day without doing much. They all went out about twelve. I then put my poor people's things in a little order, and cut out linen till dinner, and from dinner to tea. I am slow in what I do. I have thought rather seriously upon becoming mistress of a house. The preparations of clothing etc as they lead me into the little things for which I have a taste, if I do not take care may hurt me, and yet they are both pleasant and interesting to me." So she moves dreamily about her unexacting tasks, turning and folding the smooth linen, sewing the quiet seam, while the scent of roses blows in at the open window and the pomp of summer rustles in the Earlham garden. For a while there is a respite from the responsibility of high resolve. She is nature's child. A spirit, yet a woman too.

"*17th*. My state is a truly comfortable one this morning, such peace of mind and body. I seem to have at present no cloud over me — so calm, so easy."

Some of her stricter friends felt there was a little falling off.

"*30th*. Crissy Gurney has a dull effect upon me and leads me to feel as if she *thought* me a luke-warm quaker. I believe I am in some respects," confesses Elizabeth hardily, "because deeply as I feel interested in the Society ⟨*⟩ and much

⟨*⟩ Of Friends.

as I feel some of its scruples, yet my limets are great and I do not feel little scruples of that importance other people do."

For instance, there is now always conspicuous upon her Quaker dress an incongruous ornament, a gold watch chain. Uncle Joseph's eye upon it can make her abashed and self-defensive, but nothing can make her remove it. She murmurs to her diary that it is not "quite consistent with my dress," that it is "almost an unnecessary ornament." But she concludes obstinately, "it has its uses."

So August comes, with deeper sunshine. *"Eighth month (August) 4th.* This has been a comfortable day to me. I have been busy, and a little gone on in my old plans; I have great hopes of leaving all things in good order, which is a relief to me. It is a blessing indeed to feel thus healthy in mind and body: for I think we are subject to mental diseases that are not in our power, any more than bodily ones, and that require our patience: although it is our duty in both mental and bodily maladies to do our utmost to overcome them."

A week before her wedding she gathers her little "schollers" for the last time. *"Eighth month (August) 13th.* Nothing particular happened till evening, when all my poor children came: It was rather a melancholy time to me. After having enjoyed themselves with playing about, I took them to the summerhouse and bade them farewell: there were about eighty-six of them, many of them wept . . . when they went away I shed my tears also."

On August 19, 1800, the old Meetinghouse in Goats Lane was crowded to the doors for the first wedding in the Earlham family.

Apart from an occasional gentle rustle, a hardly perceptible sigh, or the quiet tread of a late-comer passing quickly to his seat, a profound silence lay over the gathering. Not a whisper, not a glance of recognition, from one to another. Each sat wrapt, if not in meditation, at least in hush, men on one side of the aisle and women on the other. The sunbeams themselves were not more quiet.

Into that deeply silent gathering entered at last the wedding procession, walking slowly and softly. Young Fry, sitting on the facing benches beside his parents, with folded arms and a blush that brought tears to his eyes, saw them enter the door and got to his feet. A slight wave of movement went over the congregation, as all heads turned, but all remained seated.

Betsy came up the aisle on her father's arm, rather pale and tremulous in her quaint Puritan dress, followed by her six sisters and four brothers in fashionable array. The wedding train placed themselves in the front benches reserved for them, and John Gurney and Catherine sat down with Betsy on the facing seats. Betsy now sat facing the meeting, between her father and her bridegroom; and Joe Fry sat with his mother on his left hand, and his bride upon his right.

Again a stillness settled upon the meeting, seeming to deepen as the moments passed. Joe Fry, clearing his throat uneasily, knew that everything now rested upon him. It was he, with unaccustomed voice, who had to break that profound stillness, to interrupt that unutterable worship. Panic-stricken, he stole a glance at Elizabeth. The transparent white kerchief about her neck was rising and falling over panting breath, and he saw a tear, like a fragment of rainbow, slip over the round curve of her down-bent cheek. It braced him. That flood of tenderness for her weakness that was at the very heart of her charm for him, when coupled with the deep respect he had for her, made him lose his own embarrassment in pity. He laid his hand firmly on hers. She started and trembled and looked up. Had the dreaded moment come? It had, his eyes answered, and reassured her. He rose and drew her gently to her feet. So the two of them stood alone before the congregation, she trembling madly, the throbbing of her heart vibrating to his, her hand clasping his hand like a drowning person. He held her fast, and said huskily and hastily: —

"In the presence of the Lord and of this assembly, I take

this my friend, Elizabeth Gurney, to be my wife, promising by divine assistance to be unto her a loving and faithful husband until it shall please the Lord by death to separate us."

A hush. He pressed Elizabeth's hand. She made a supreme effort, and her voice came out sweet and clear: —

"In the presence of the Lord and of this assembly, I take this my friend, Joseph Fry, to be my husband, promising by divine assistance to be unto him a loving and faithful wife until it shall please the Lord by death to separate us."

They were married. They seated themselves. There was a little rustle of relaxation through the meeting. A tension was broken.

John Gurney, Jr., and one of the young Gurney cousins carried forward a little table spread with the wedding certificate and ink and pens. Joseph Fry signed it, and then Betsy, writing for the last time her old name, Elizabeth Gurney.[8]

Then the certificate was handed to Uncle Joseph, the little table was carried away, the two young men took their seats, and with due deliberation Uncle Joseph Gurney read the marriage certificate through aloud to the meeting, word for word, including the signatures, as is still the custom of Friends.

The certificate was then returned to the table, to be signed after the meeting by all who cared to, and the meeting settled again into quiet. Uncle Joseph almost immediately broke the silence by a prayer for blessing on the young couple, and for an hour prayer and exhortation followed from both men and women Friends, speaking spontaneously one after the other without much pause.

The high-strung bride, who confessed that she "awoke in a sort of terror at the prospect before me," "wept a good part of the time" in the meeting, "and my beloved father seemed as much overcome as I was." But at length the elders appointed broke up the meeting, by shaking hands, Friends

[8] The custom now is for the bride to sign her new name.

THE QUAKER WEDDING

Painted by Percy Bigland

stirred themselves, straightened their bonnets and picked up their hats, and Betsy, leaving this time on the arm of her husband, led the procession out of the meetinghouse into the warm August sunshine.

There were the carriages waiting, and some of her children lined up throwing flowers. A confusion of faces. Carriage space was too valuable for the bride and groom to go alone. Here were Father and Kitty and Rachel, and who else Betsy scarcely knew. She hardly knew, either, how she felt. She was in April mood, a state of dream. However, she wrote, "The day passed off well . . . although cold hands and a beating heart were often my lot."

Homesickness was unconquerably rampant. Driving through Norwich for the last time as Betsy Gurney, "the very stones of the street seemed dear to me."

But when the wedding feast had been eaten, the last farewells exchanged, with wise Kitty, with John, with lovely Rachel, with the Four, with handsome Joseph John and dear, dear Sam, and little Daniel; when her father, unable to speak, had handed her into the carriage, while servants and guests crowded out onto the gravel sweep to see them go; and the carriage had passed the turn of the avenue, and then passed the lodge and the gates and was out and away and bowling merrily down the familiar London road — then how comfortable it was to find beside her no dazzling stranger, no formidable bridegroom, but her sturdy friend Joe Fry, with whom she was so much at ease, before whom she could, if she wished, cry "hartily," and who would patiently dry up her tears and feel much for her.

By December, their discerning and affectionate friend Amelia Opie could write, "Betsy Fry is settled down with everything requisite to domestic happiness. Mr. Fry pleases me very much."

VI

THE YOUNG WIFE

1

YES, but what is requisite to domestic happiness? When Amelia Opie alighted from her sedan chair at Joseph Fry's door in the late afternoon of the eleventh of December, 1800, a thick fog was blanketing the city of London. A warm glow shone fuzzily out from the windows of the countinghouse on the ground floor, and from the windows of the house in Mildred's Court above. Withdrawn a little from the traffic and noise of the street, there was the charm of a quiet harbor about the court. The Fry warehouse for tea, coffee, spices, and other imports of the East India trade formed one side, and an aromatic smell made of many mingled odors traveled through the air. The lantern over the front door of the mansion made a dim moon-like glow, but the link boy whose hire the fog had made necessary lifted his torch to each step in turn as Amelia clung to the curved iron railing and mounted the steps cautiously in her long furred pelisse. The boy pulled the big iron bell that hung outside the door and woke a jangling peal.

Almost at once the big door opened, and a neat footman ushered Mrs. Opie into the lighted hall. The hall, of course, was cold. But her card instantly admitted her further, into a room where warmth smote her in the face as she entered and made her cold nose tingle. There a great coal fire roared in the fireplace under the Adam mantel. Warm hangings at the windows shut out the fog and dusk. The young hostess, looking like a picture in her Quaker dress, rose with a glad little cry, embraced Amelia, took off her things, drew her to a cosy chair beside the hearth. Amelia, to homesick Betsy, was Norwich, was Earlham, was all her happy youth. But Amelia, although a novelist, did not perceive that. She was used to being welcomed. Was she not, in herself, a charming person? What she did see was that Betsy was thinner. "But the leanness is not unbecoming, my love. And now you are so very comfortably settled you will soon get fat again!" Firelight and candlelight gleamed cheerfully on polished oak and walnut; on fine napery and silver; on the most delicate of china cups. And no one in London could serve a better dish of five o'clock tea than Mrs. Joseph Fry, who got the pick of the market from her husband's warehouse. In all her appointments and furnishings the daughter of Earlham had confided to her journal that her inclination was to have "everything very handsome though nothing mearly for ornament." Amelia Opie began to believe that this perhaps was a part of Quakerism, a background and accessory to the picturesque dress. "In all Quaker houses," she wrote to Mrs. Taylor next day, "there is a most comfortable appearance of neatness, comfort and affluence."

Joe Fry and his elder brother, William, came up from the countinghouse for tea. Joe was in high spirits, his boisterous joviality suggesting rather the country squire than the city banker. He was pleased and proud that one of the old Gurney circle should see his wife in her new setting. He was proud of his house. And he was proud of the grace and order that Betsy had introduced there. Betsy felt him, in these moods, perhaps a little unnecessarily loud. His sense of humor was a little crude and hers entirely absent. But he pleased Mrs. Opie. She loved to laugh, and her own husband, who belonged to the Johnsonian school of force rather than refinement, could be even louder.

Returning to her more modest house through the deepened fog, she reflected on Betsy's condition as she joggled along in her chair, not with envy, — for she had a sweet nature and was very happily wed, — but with a maturer woman's appreciation of the worth of material things. The wife of a painter, whose income depended upon the caprice of fashion, and who had very little to fall back upon, she could not but be aware of the superior security of the wife of a wealthy young banker and merchant in these hard times. Why, look at Betsy Fry! She is young, she is healthy, she is loved, her husband is a kind, good-natured young man. It is an old established firm, with sound capital behind it. What has she left to wish for? Yes, really, she has everything, thought Amelia Opie, conscious that she herself had almost everything — except security. She did not know what disconcerting experiences Elizabeth was going through.

2

Security, yes. There were bread riots in the streets of Norwich the very August that Elizabeth was married. No sensitive person in the year 1800 could be unaware that to have a sufficiency of the necessities of life, not to say comforts and luxuries, was to be fortunate. But it is only to the starving that life consists of bread alone.

Elizabeth had not at all been able to foresee what it would mean to marry a younger son of a great mercantile house, and live at the seat of business. And she had not been intimately enough associated with the Frys before her marriage to realize the different standard of behavior to which they had been bred.

The house at Mildred's Court had formerly been occupied by Joseph's elder brother, William Fry, and his wife Eliza. When William Savery visited Newgate Prison in June 1798, he afterwards "took a Glass of Wine and some Cake at W. Fry's, Mildred Court."[1] It had been arranged that the house and its responsibilities should be handed over to Joseph and his bride. But it was perhaps typical of pretty Eliza's inequality to responsibility that she should take no steps at all to prepare the house for its new mistress. When the bride drove up on the afternoon of November 1, 1800, her right to joyous arrival was cruelly taken away. "I felt rather low at the prospect before me, and more so when I saw the state of the house; confusion in every part."

William Fry, it is true, was on the steps to welcome them, but domestic matters were none of his concern. He retired to the countinghouse, and left the weary and dispirited girl to deal with affairs as best she could. Joe showed compunction, indeed vexation, but he too was helpless. He had prepared her mind for the fact that life at Mildred's Court was not quite a bed of roses; but this was a rough start. After the order of Earlham, the familiar disorderliness of his sister-in-law smote him sharply. But fortunately the last three weeks of the honeymoon had been spent in a return to Earlham Hall, and when they had left after breakfast on October 31 in "my father's coach," good Nurse Barns had accompanied them. She was a tower of strength, a lively and bustling liaison officer between young, inexperienced mistress and strange domestics. Betsy took counsel with Nurse, gave orders, and they were carried out. "I had a bedroom turned into a sitting-room put in order; and then went and put myself in order for dinner; our brother William dined with us." And when William had gone home to Plashet and his own wife, it was cosy to sit with Joseph by the fire in the little

[1] Situated west of the Bank of England, southeast of Guildhall, nearer to the Bank; in the district called Poultry, now numbered E. C. 2.

oasis she had made in the desert of muddle. "Joseph and I had a comfortable evening. Both I believe feeling the true comfort, I may say blessing, of being at last quiet in our own house."

John Gurney had been right. Elizabeth was made for marriage. It was Joseph Fry's misfortune that in those early, malleable days he could not have her more to himself.

Of the two months' honeymoon, one month had been spent with the parent Frys at Plashet House. The first week even had been spent in visiting various relatives as they moved down England by easy stages from Norwich to London. "From continued change of scene, and the great deal that I am obliged to talk, I seem of late to be continually letting out and taking nothing in," the bewildered bride confides to her scanty journal. And even among the delights of Plashet House, with its fish ponds and woods, she finds herself weeping in meeting "with thinking of them at home."

The return home had been reviving. Every man who married one of the Gurneys of Earlham had to deal in turn with homesickness on the part of his bride, and each one without exception followed Joseph Fry's example and brought the bride back to spend part of the honeymoon at Earlham Hall. Then, cheered by the feeling that her old home was still accessible to her as a married woman, and reassured by her husband's consideration, each bride went cheerfully forward to establish her new home and create for herself a new centre of happiness. But Betsy alone, the first to marry, was handicapped by the active interference of her husband's relatives.

It was Saturday night when Elizabeth and Joseph were rejoicing all too soon, in the blessing of being at last quiet in their own house. On Sunday morning they went to Gracechurch Street Meeting, proud after all their fatigues at being "very punctual to the time." It seemed incredible that they should not be allowed to dine alone that day, when the conscienceless Frys were all too well aware that there had been no time to get straight. But Mildred's Court was so very handy to Gracechurch Street, and it had long been the custom to go there for a family Sunday dinner. The Frys took it for granted, on this day as on other days. Why not?

"I felt low when I got home and seeing the freedom of the family in the house was rather a trial to me. I think they could not be freer if it were their own, and also there was such a state of muddle."

Monday was almost as bad as Sunday. "I rose early — first set about reading a little without much profit. After breakfast I sat down to write my footman's business. Soon *they* came and after that I had not much quiet. . . . The bustle of today's dinner, all the family dining with us in spite of all our muddles!"

3

The house did get straight before long, with good Nurse Barns as Betsy's lieutenant. But worse problems bristled under the orderly surface. William Fry was obliged by business duties to be daily at Mildred's Court. He often had both breakfast and dinner with Joseph and Betsy, just as formerly Joseph had taken all his meals with William and Eliza. It did not occur to William that a husband and wife who had been married some years could adapt themselves more easily to the constant company of a bachelor brother than a bridal couple could adapt themselves to the constant company of a married elder. Besides, William Fry was accustomed to behaving as master of the house, and though he perhaps tried not to do so, it really seemed unnatural that Joseph should now be in that position. As to Joseph's wife, in spite of her Quaker cap, she was one of those stuck-up "gay Gurneys." William had no patience with the new formalities and ways of doing that she was introducing into the domestic routine. He lent an indiscreetly ready ear to the complaints of the old servant, Jane King.

Elizabeth's quiet, rather shy manners, and her soft speech, combined with that fair, feminine look of hers, had rather blinded William to her quality. He thought that he could run that young couple. He meant nothing unkind or unfair, he only had an elder brother's assurance of being in the right and speaking for their good and keeping them up to the mark. A surprise awaited him. Behind all young Mrs. Fry's softness was a firm resistance, a disconcerting dignity. William said his say and retired, but he had a feeling of discomfiture. Was it possible that he had been wrong?

Elizabeth flew to her journal. "*Nov. 7th.* I have had a rather trying afternoon. In the first place my brother William came in, in rather an angry tone saying something about *our* not wishing to treat the customers well. It is trying to be blamed for a thing I hope is far from either of us. I do pity Joseph — they all seemed so inclined to blame him and also since we have been in this house I believe there has been a mutual endeavour to act our parts well. I have *try'd* part of this afternoon to overcome my husband's vexation as well as my own and try'd to please him."

It is no wonder that later that evening tears of homesickness trembled on Betsy's lashes, and her heart ached sadly under her snowy kerchief. "At times like this how apt I feel to look at Earlham and its beloved inhabitants; but I should remember that every situation has its trials and I had mine there. What *sweet tempers* they all have. . . . When my Joseph is try'd I must endeavour to put on a cheerful face and do my part towards making him happy."

But morning dawned on a better day. The Frys might not be sweet-tempered, but they were honest and goodhearted. William found that his conscience was uneasy and he lost no time in trying to put himself right with his sister-in-law. He was met with Betsy's own candor. "William came and ask'd my excuse for what he said yesterday, and then I had a little talk with him about our present situation with the family. I do hope to correct my feelings about them," says Elizabeth, looking facts in the face as usual, "for I believe they want correction."

4

It took time. Elizabeth had taken such pains to turn herself into a "plain quaker" that she could not understand that the Frys regarded her as almost "gay." With her sisters she had been a dove among birds of bright plumage; but with the Frys she was a dove among crows. Her natural elegance would not be disguised. The supple figure that had so loved to dance could not move otherwise than with ease and grace. Her daintiness, her fastidious refinement, her charm, and the politeness in which she had been bred, made her seem to her blunt new relatives like a woman of fashion.

Mrs. Fry, senior, had not, like the late Mrs. Gurney, drawn up a statement of the aims and methods of the education of her daughters; and if she had, it would certainly not have included the axiom that "gentleness of manner is indispensably necessary in women; to say nothing of that polished behaviour that adds a charm to every qualification."[2]

Polished behavior made the Frys feel inferior and they resented it. Pressure was brought to bear upon Joseph to make his wife conform to the Fry pattern, on the grounds of Quaker sincerity. So Joseph's first expressed criticism of his wife was one of the strangest ever made by a bridegroom. She took it none the less deeply to heart. "I was told of a fault by my husband — he thought my manners had too much of the courtier about them, which I know to be the case, for my disposition leads me to hurt no one that I can easily help, and I do sometimes but just keep to the truth

[2] From fragment of Mrs. Gurney's journal. *Memoir*, I, 18.

with people from a natural *yielding* to them in such things as please them." But temperament and training revived her. "I think such things in moderation are pleasant and useful in society. They are indeed one of the things that produces the harmony of society for the *truth* must not be spoken at all times; at least not the whole."

She meditates perhaps upon what would happen in domestic relations with her new family if she should at all times speak the whole truth. And concludes firmly: "Perhaps I am wrong. I do not know if I am not, but it will not do always to tell our minds."

Father Fry had no such inhibitions, and very painful his daughter-in-law sometimes found it. "My father Fry said he would not have consented to Joseph's marrying me or one of my sisters as gay as we were, which made me angry. It hurts me much to have one of them spoken against in the slightest degree, for I know their virtue."

Yet if Elizabeth did in an indiscreet moment forget her courtierlike manners and speak her mind too plainly, it was strangely unappreciated. The results were not such as would seem to justify the experiment. There was the little matter of the Christmas turkeys. Elizabeth remorsefully enters in her diary: "I fear I behaved improperly to-day to my father Fry — he and my mother gave us the present of a turkey which did not appear a fine one, and my own father sent us a very fine one, and I think I drew a comparison between them, which I know was wrong."

A narrow path indeed, and full of pitfalls. But an English winter provides its own respites. "I think I have tried to do better to-day, and a bad cold has prevented my saying much."

5

The exactions of hospitality extended beyond the family. Not only was her day's programme shattered by the incursions of invading and pervading Frys, but Elizabeth soon found that to be mistress of Mildred's Court was a career.

She and Joseph had planned that their first overnight guests should be the eldest and the youngest of the seven sisters, Kitty and Priscilla, who were to come on the nineteenth of November to stay for a week or two. But on the seventh of November, the traditions of Mildred's Court compelled them to receive a traveling Friend from Philadelphia, who was to make their house his headquarters for six weeks. It was a little soon to begin with that kind of visitor. And American Quakers of the period were not an unmixed blessing. Fresh from a rougher way of living, their manners were often crude, their denunciation of even the comforts of civilization formed a large part of their conversation, and their table habits were unpleasant. Savery's good manners had excited universal remark.

George Dilwyn soon made the sensitive Betsy "feel almost ashamed of the handsome things I have." His presence spread an air of solemnity over the house, and of restraint. At Earlham the air had been full of laughter and lively quarreling and eagerness. But even Kitty and Priscilla, when they came, could not bring the atmosphere of Earlham into Mildred's Court. Perhaps they were the wrong two to do it: Kitty, already a little withered on the stalk, a little too much the anxious motherly sister; and fifteen-year-old Priscilla, too young and too shy — "our little rosy Priss." They were overborne by the atmosphere of Mildred's Court, like birds who settle unexpectedly in oily water and find their wings made too sticky to fly.

Often of an evening Betsy, having made the parlor cheerful with candles and fire, looked forward to a snug and cheerful time with Joseph and her sisters. William gone home, dinner cleared, several hours to spend luxuriously in reading aloud over sewing, in pleasant desultory chatter, in showing and telling, before the supper tray rattled through the hall on the stroke of nine. And then to find George Dilwyn had been "led" to spend this evening at home, with the inevitable result that several Friends dropped in there to visit him. Away with sewing and books and careless chatter. The young hostess, ignored for the sake of her weighty guest, sat silent with folded hands. Her sisters escaped, if they could, to their bedroom. Joseph stifled yawn after yawn beside his wife. A heavy silence fell. As fresh arrivals were shown in, they shuffled as quietly as possible to a seat. The bright room was banked around with sombre garments as if the fog had leaked heavily indoors and congealed upon the chairs and sofas. It was a "meeting." So they sat, and Joseph replenished the fire very cautiously from time to time as if in a sickroom. Until, after a while, Dilwyn felt his message rise within him and delivered it at length, with ungrammatical unction, but with unaffected fervor; and other Friends, both men and women, would also lift their voices in exhortation or in prayer.

When the clock struck nine, if a suitable rustle seemed to indicate that the session was over, the unimportant young hostess had to pay an anxious visit to the kitchen to see that there was supper enough provided for ten or twelve more people than she had originally catered for.

Such occasions with Savery or with Deborah Darby had seemed to be an entering of a supernatural realm, hushed with awe. But now Betsy secretly records, "They begin I think to lose their solemnity from their frequency."

It occurred to her that one way to achieve a little space of peace would be to read a short passage out of the Bible after breakfast, before they separated on the day's affairs. She broached this startlingly original idea to her husband. To be sure, it was not "done" among Friends. Perhaps it savored a little of the Church of England. But was not the Bible after all a source of food for the soul? Joe was willing to humor her. She was never more lovable than when she was diffident. He agreed to the proposal, and forgot all about it.

Breakfast time came, and Joe said nothing. No Bible appeared. George Dilwyn and William Fry were both present; and Betsy could not screw up her courage. William was a special stumblingblock. "I felt doing it, particularly as my brother William was here; not liking the appearance of young people, like us, appearing to profess more than they who had lived here before us. However, I put off and put off till both William and Joseph went down; I then felt uneasy under it, and when Joseph came back I told him, as I did before, what I wished; he at last sat down, having told George Dilwyn my desire. I began to read the 46th Psalm, but was so overcome that I could hardly read, and gave it to Joseph to finish." But the ice once broken, Betsy got her shyness under control. "I again felt some difficulty in reading the Bible, however I got through well. George Dilwyn encouraging me by saying he thought I portioned the readings well."

George Dilwyn went away at last, leaving behind him an impression, on the whole, of a helpful and sincere person. But in March came the Quarterly Meeting, and Elizabeth found that she must keep open house for Friends at Mildred's Court. And even that was only working up to the grand climax of the Yearly Meeting in May.

6

The first census of the population was taken in a haphazard way in that December and January, and it was discovered that England contained at least fifteen million people, four million more than the boldest guessers had estimated. Elizabeth suspected that the population would be presently increased by at least one, and by March this was an open secret. But the pace did not slacken on that account. The ordinary social obligations of a bride marched abreast with the extraordinary obligations of a Mrs. Fry of Mildred's Court.

And it is not as if she had been naturally domestic. Far, far, from it! "Household matters are to me a real trial. I feel so incapable of commanding my servants from a foolish weakness and fear of them. Company days, even with those I like, are quite worrying to me; inclination I believe would lead me hardly ever to go out or have company. I feel so flat with people."

She tried to fortify herself, with childish pathos. "I doubt whether I can speak to William the footman about his not having meals ready by the right time."

In April she had the respite, not before it was needed, of a visit to Earlham. "I felt leaving my dearest husband." But apart from that even the journey itself was full of joy, through the countryside of spring. "Violets and primroses quite decorated the hedges."

Dear Earlham was just at its best, with greening lawns, birds building, trees tasseled with green, and the merry little Wensum running with spring freshets. The tender care of Kitty and Rachel and the respectful interest of the Four wrapped her about in comfortableness. She rested in the deep self-content of maternity, and wondered why she had minded so much about Brother William and William the footman and Jane King and all the flurries of domestic life. "Of late I have felt cumbered with the little things in life that are not worth worrying about."

But her detachment could not last. She hardly had time to resume control of her household and adjust herself once more to London life before the May Yearly Meeting was upon her. These meetings went on for about a fortnight, and Friends came up for them from all over the country. It was necessary for the Fry tradition that Mildred's Court, so handy to the Devonshire House buildings where the meetings were held, should keep open house all day and every day as long as the Yearly Meeting lasted. Saverys, Hoares, Barclays, and others did the same, but distance relieved pressure.

At Mildred's Court, forty hungry Friends might come in to dinner, or sixty. Hospitable Earlham itself had never had to deal with such problems of catering and accommodation. And though disagreeable Jane King proved a tower of strength, having had experience of the Yearly Meeting crush in former years, the responsibility rested on the inexperienced shoulders of the young wife, and that at a time when any extra company, "even those I like," was a burden.

Nor did Friends hurry away when they had eaten. Dinner for such numbers, even in a large house, had to be served in two or three shifts, and those first through swarmed upstairs to "take a lay."[8] Beds and floors disappeared under billows of resting Friends; every article of furniture was submerged in the tide of thrown-aside bonnets and shawls; snores and stuffiness and confusion filled the house. The domestic staff were thoroughly overworked. All water for washing had to be carried by servants to the bedrooms in pitchers. And it might be mentioned in passing that the servants had to perform other and less pleasant tasks. Sanitation at the close of the eighteenth century was as primitive as in the days of good King Alfred.

When at last strangers and acquaintances alike surged out of the house to attend the sessions of the Yearly Meeting, Betsy herself was sucked along with the tide to do her duty by sitting weary hours on a hard bench in a crowded room and listening to lengthy sermons or the conduct of tedious business.

The women and the men met separately in their business meetings at this period, and the interesting work, if any, was all done in the Men's Meeting. Deputations passed on occasion from the one meeting to the other, to communicate

[8] Mrs. Greer, *Quakerism or the Story of My Life.*

items of business or to exchange religious concerns. Much loss of time was involved, and much dullness endured. Savery recorded that at the Yearly Meeting he attended in 1797, the Men's Meeting spent some three hours in discussing whether or not to receive a deputation from the Women's Meeting; and when at last the deputation was received it had nothing particular to say. Another day was mainly taken up with a discussion on men's hat brims. The "plain dress" not being a uniform, variations of it were constantly under discussion.

But habit, and the pleasure of gregariousness, gave the Yearly Meetings of the "dead period" a value to most of the Friends. They were uncritical of the ministry offered, so that it was well interlarded with texts and delivered in the proper singsong. And they did not desire to share in the stirring public questions of the day.

One Joseph Woods wrote a descriptive and revealing letter to a friend in the nineties. "Our Yearly Meeting has been conducted with much moderation and harmony. Luckily we had no Americans to tell us what the practice is in their country, and our Irish brethren seemed contented to eat the fat of the land without murmuring. The women (I ask pardon, I mean our women Friends) sent no proposals of innovation. They told us however, as usual, that the Lord had owned them, an expression which, being so oft repeated, seems to imply a fear that they shd find no owner."

Charles Lamb gives a picture of the affectation and hollowness which had befallen Quaker preaching. In a letter to Coleridge, 1797, he says, "Tell Lloyd[*] I have had thoughts of turning Quaker, and have been reading or am rather just beginning to read, a most capital book, good thoughts in good language, William Penn's *No Cross, No Crown*; I like it immensely. Unluckily I attended one of his meetings, tell him, in St. John St., yesterday, and saw a man under all the

[*] Charles Lloyd the poet, brother of James.

agitations of a fanatic, who believed himself under the influence of some 'inevitable presence.' This cured me of Quakerism; I love it in the books of Penn and Woolman, but I detest the vanity of a man thinking he speaks by the Spirit, when what he says an ordinary man might say without all that quaking and trembling."⁵

Elizabeth Fry's journal for May 29, 1810, reads: "After dinner we attended our Women's Meeting at four o'clock which lasted till nearly eight o'clock; it was to me very long and very tedious; indeed it may be and I doubt not is in great part my own weakness, but to hold fast my faith I found in this Yearly Meeting no instrument ought to be looked to."

It was very odd. Betsy was plunged into the most "religious" circle she had ever lived in, and yet she was already having to struggle to hold fast her faith. The overwhelming burden of the domestic situation was one thing. But this boredom with meeting was another. Fatigue perhaps entered into it. But it lay deeper than any physical cause. "The state of deadness to religion that has lately been my experience," she honestly records. Where was the girl who had received such inspiration from William Savery and from Deborah Darby, and who had been able to maintain her own line against the lack of sympathy, and even opposition, of those she loved the best?

Now she lived among those who thought and talked much of religion. But they regarded religion as a state of mind, manifested in certain peculiar habits of dress and speech and in avoidance of frivolous and worldly things. They did not, like Savery, and like Elizabeth herself, find in it an irresistible impulse toward activity.

Savery had had such a passion for international peace that he had lost no opportunity of interviewing the rulers of Europe on the matter, including the King and Queen of England. He had had such an ardent sympathy with human suffering

⁵ Lucas, I, 155.

that as a young man, visiting a wealthy family in the Southern states of America, he had rushed from the breakfast table on hearing the distant cries of a beaten slave, and had stood between the victim and the whip until he had obtained the rescinding of the punishment. And he had worked to abolish slavery from that day.

But the rank and file of English Quakers were turned in upon themselves. Their utmost effort was to travel in the ministry to other groups of Quakers.

Yet in 1801 there were many conditions in England which might well have attracted their attention. Street riots of the starving in London and other large cities kept people in mind of the French Revolution and the danger of its repetition. Elizabeth of course was new to housekeeping, had ample funds, and never seemed to notice the price of food. But the cost of living had multiplied itself five times since 1773, and bread, the staple of the poor, was costing seventeen-pence for a quartern loaf (thirty-four cents). The London mob, attributing all rise in price to greed, would surround and yell at the King's coach, and would pelt merchants and brokers in the streets. But when they found a man in a Quaker coat they would roll him in the mud. Such was the reputation of Quakers for being selfish, close-fisted, and hard.

Among such a gathering of prosperous merchants, attending closely and cannily to their own business and practising only negative and domestic virtues, Elizabeth's spirit, too much alive to be satisfied with husks, was suffering a sort of starvation. "I attended both Meetings; what wishes I had at moments for good! and how surprisingly inaffectual they were."

Yearly Meeting was over at last, and the mere relief felt for a short time like peace. "*June 5th.* I had most of this morning in quietness, which was quite a treat to me. I wrote my journal, settled my accounts, and was not destitute of a wish to do right."

But quiet intervals were few. Days were hot and languorous, and her child was heavy and quick within her, but she wrote in July at Plashet: "We are so much from home and in such continued bustles I just have time enough to keep things in order; engagement follows engagement so rapidly, day after day, week after week, owing principally to our number of near connextions, that we appear to live for others rather than ourselves: our plan of sleeping out so often I by no means like, and yet it appears impossible to prevent it. To spend one's life in visiting and being visited seems sad."

7

And that most delicate relationship of all, the relationship between husband and wife, was endangered by lack of privacy. It is a marked tribute to Joseph Fry that his wife was happiest when alone with him, and increasingly so as their first year of marriage drew to a close. "I value being alone with my husband; it is a quiet I have not lately enjoyed and it does seem to me, at this time, one of the great blessings of life." But it was his lasting misfortune that when his influence with her was at its height, her softness toward him greatest, he could not perceive his opportunities. The fog of continual company confused them. And he lost the chance he might have had to share with her, and to win her sympathy in, some of the things he cared for most.

But Joe Fry had not the patience or the temperament to look into his wife's heart, even through the pages of her journal, always open to him. And his very admiration for her blinded him alike to the extent of his power with her and the dangers to his peace that were latent in her character.

"It is quite a serious thing," wrote Betsy, "our being so constantly liable to interruptions as we are. I do not think, since we were married, we have had one-fourth of our meals alone. I long for more retirement, but it appears out of our power to procure it, and therefore it is best to be as patient under interruptions as we can; but I think it a serious disadvantage to young people setting out in life."

One of the disadvantages was the lack of opportunity to practise the technique of happy, daily relations between just those two. Intimacy without the art of mutual perception and understanding in hour-by-hour trifles leads to carelessness, and little misunderstandings. "I rather fear'd my beloved husband and myself had not been on those sympathetic and happy terms I feel so desirable, almost necessary, to the comfort of married life. His reading and continual humming vex'd me when we were so seldom alone."

And there were worse causes of friction than humming. Some of William's remarks could not but rankle in the mind, because they had an occasional irritating appearance of truth. It could not be, could it, that Joseph was lazy? Certainly he was not fond of early rising. And he had a tendency to headaches and to making rather a fuss about them, a way of "thinking himself a little poorly" which tried her patience. She could not make them an excuse for so many hours off as Joseph seemed to think they justified. Stick up for Joseph as she may, she is impatient with dilatoriness, she has an irresistible desire to urge him along the energetic path. "I am sorry to say," she ruefully admits when only two months married, "that I might take an improper part in pressing him to go down to business, for after all my endeavours to please him this afternoon he realy seemed vex'd with me for having asked him to go down. I know he has often said to me he thought my urging him to business a comfort."

There is a curious illumination in that word "often." It could not be said that Joseph Fry was lacking in essential energy. His courtship of Elizabeth is enough to deny it.

But he was a man of outdoor tastes tied to an indoor trade, a man of jovial and rather careless habits forced into the meticulous cares of the countinghouse. He was also a man in love. And there was more than one breeze between them on account of her stirring him to duty.

Joe Fry would not have chosen to live at Mildred's Court had he been a free agent. It was Plashet that had his heart. The life of John Gurney at Earlham, farming one hundred and sixty acres as a hobby, and riding into Norwich to direct the bank and the woolen mills, seemed to him an ideal life. Short of being a country gentleman out and out, that is what he would have liked to do. The daily tedious round of business irked him. And at Mildred's Court there was very little respite.

Yet he and Betsy weathered that first difficult year. After all, however interfered with by day, they were alone together at night, and all misunderstandings were brushed aside, all pains and fears comforted, in the affectionate simplicity of their mutual relation. How quickly she turned from irritation to soft, wifely resolve. "May I give up every earthly consideration to please my husband and to render ours an increasingly happy union." Joseph also had his resolves, expressed in action, not words. "One of my first sensations was very pleasant to me this morning. It was an admiration of my dear husband for getting up a little after six of himself to get forward with business. It appeared," says the daughter of the Gurneys, with simplicity, "like an energy in a good cause that was truly pleasant to me to observe, as I have thought he used to want it. I have thought him lately altogether improved." No patronage in that remark. She measures his improvement as she would measure her own.

As for herself, she analyzes her condition with her usual skill. "How hard is it deeply, strictly, and for a long time together, to have as our first object to serve our Creator: for at first there is a natural glee, as for something new, and then we have to pass through lukewarmness, which is a dangerous state. May I be carried through it." [6]

And with her steady common sense she cheers herself up. "If I can with truth acknowledge it to be my first wish to do my best, although I may not feel the sensible gratification of doing my duty, I may yet be really doing it."

Part of her present duty is to love her relations-in-law, and her sweetness and justice have by this time got over the first barriers. "I have on this visit [to Plashet] I think increas'd in love for my mother and Elizabeth,[7] particularly my mother, in whom I see much to admire, although she may want a softness and refinement in her character."

Betsy had buried the hatchet with Father Fry long since. He had taken them on a delightful trip to Richmond Park, at Betsy's request, although it had rained and almost stopped them. Betsy's eagerness could not brook disappointment, though she "hardly expressed it enough, because I make myself appear almost weak by my fear of other people." And especially, "I feel with my father [Fry] almost always a difficulty in boldly doing what I think right." But she had prevailed. Father Fry had been indulgent and obliging and was rewarded by fine weather and the affection of his open-hearted daughter-in-law. The views and the country and the little lambs were all very pleasant and refreshing after the drab streets of London, but "one great pleasure in the day has been being so much with him, and I have quite enjoyed his company."

There is no doubt that from this time on Father Fry loved his daughter-in-law with increasing tenderness.

[6] *Memoir*, I, 122.
[7] The unmarried daughter. William's wife had the same name, but is always called Eliza to distinguish her.

8

It might well seem in all this overwhelming mass of womanish duty that Elizabeth's destiny had abandoned her; but it was not so. Hardly had she "fixed dinners for the Yearly Meeting with Jane King" than some unnamed friend or relative, remembering her interest in education, invited her to see an educational experiment that was going on in Southwark, and was beginning to attract attention. On May 15, 1801, Elizabeth casually records, "We went in the evening to see a Friend [Joseph Lancaster] who kept a school for poor children."[8] She did not realize that this date was to mark another milestone on her definite journey. Her first impression of Lancaster was that he was rather cocksure, and that the flattery and interest of his numerous visitors had gone to his head. But as their acquaintance progressed she recognized the mere assertiveness of a man with an enthusiasm, and in time she caught the contagion of his theory.

Lancaster was setting on foot an educational movement of such importance that before 1835 there were "Lancasterian schools" in all parts of England, and when the National Schools at last came into being they were started on the methods of Lancaster and Bell.

In evidence to the Parliamentary Committee on Education in 1835, a contemporary says: "Mr. Lancaster had a notion if he could allow boys to make a noise they would never consider it drudgery to be taught. I believe he was correct; there is in the school a perpetual noise; strangers find it confusion, but it is perfect order; the boys get the power of abstraction so as to go on with ease notwithstanding there is noise from the process going on."

The kernel of Lancaster's idea was the monitor system. He divided his horde into small groups of about a dozen,

[8] *Memoir*, I, 119.

each with a monitor to keep order, collect and distribute lesson material, and hear lessons recited; and the actual teaching of the younger children was partly done by the older, who first learned a lesson, and then taught it. The method was both enlivening and economical. Elizabeth, remembering her undivided class of seventy, saw a great light.

As long as she lived in London, she kept in touch with Lancaster's work, and helped him both by friendship and by financial aid when he was in sore straits. His contribution to her has never yet been acknowledged. We shall see later what it was.

9

But something all the time was drawing nearer, of which Elizabeth only knew by hearsay, and of which she now would rather not hear too much. August brought the year full circle, and her time was near. Even now, no peace. The heats of a London summer added to her fatigue. But no one saw how to help her best.

"I muddled at accounts till one, when I wrote. B. H. and her two children, with Joseph Bevan, dined here. The children rather put me out, for I had no place for them to be in conveniently. I was worried by it, my spirits not being good."

Mother Fry did not take the best course to raise her daughter's spirits. On the anniversary of Betsy's wedding, "My mother Fry and Eliza both dined here. . . . We talked a good deal about labor etc as might be supposed until I felt tired of having the subject brought so home."

But she has had her own secret thoughts. "The thought of a little child of my own within me quite excited my feelings. . . . How I love it in prospect. I can but admire how providentially everything is ordered, that now my love and hope of having a child comes just at the time I may be looking forward to the trial of bringing it into the world."

Having to buy some flannel to send to Norwich to be made up for the layette, she went to a young Quaker merchant of her acquaintance, "thinking it would be kind to serve him." Her outgoing friendliness was warmly felt by the young man, and he poured out his heart to her. "When I got there I stay'd a *long* time to hear his love *tale*. I think he will have Anna Savory." Events proved her right.

"My thoughts are now very often in my nursery, fixing plans for children. I am very full of castles about my good management. . . . I am a great friend to close and constant attention to early education, even the very first years of a child's life."

But the day of trial, so long in coming, dawned at last, and its terrors surpassed imagination. Rachel was with her, and Hannah was in the house. All that love could do, all that money could do, was lavishly and fervently done. But chloroform was yet in the future. The cruelty of nature was unchecked. And when at long, long last her husband showed her the little newborn child, she could only answer by a burst of tears.[9]

[9] *Memoir*, I, 123.

VII

FAMILY MATTERS

1

SIXTEEN mail coaches left the General Post Office daily, and to see them start was one of the sights of London. They each picked up mail and passengers from an appointed inn along their way before they left the metropolis for the long country journeys. The Norwich coach started from the Swan with Two Necks, in Lad Lane. Four inside passengers and one out were the quota,[1] and each coach carried a guard who had his little seat at the back with a large blunderbuss and horse pistols to guard the mail from highwaymen. The coach spanked along at the excellent average rate, including stoppages, of eight miles an hour, and the immense sensation caused by its arrival at the final and most important destination did good to a coachman's heart. Norwich then boasted sixty thousand inhabitants — "which however I Rather doubt," said William Savery, and a goodly concourse was always assembled in the market place to await and to cheer the arrival of the mail. Gentlemen's carriages, citizens on foot, and many little boys to turn somersaults were there as usual on August 23, 1801, when the great coach came in

[1] The larger coaches, probably not so fast, carried six inside and four on the roof.

at a hand-gallop, horn blowing, horses foaming, wheels flashing intermittently in a glorious cloud of dust. The waiting Gurney chariot was conspicuous with a bunch of those charming girls from Earlham fidgeting in and out of it, consumed with anxiety and impatience. But a letter for them there was, thank goodness, a letter from London; and they could not wait to take it home, but read it there in the carriage, all their heads eagerly together to listen to the one who read it aloud. The first niece! They were all aunts!

Home again, they seized pens and paper. They must write to darling Betsy, to Rachel, to Hannah. Louisa's letter has survived: —

"*August 24, 1801.* Dearest Rachel and Hannah, I don't think I can write much to you, I feel almost too interested about the delightful news. . . . After Meeting yesterday we went into the market-place to wait for letters, and there — between great fear and great joy — Kitty read that the darling girl was born. I longed to fly out of the coach and tell everybody that knew us the news. Then we went round to tell Hannah Scarnell. . . . How I do long to see it! I think thee, Rachel, must feel so satisfied in having been with Betsy through it all, and I hope it has not been too much for thee or Hannah. What Hannah must have felt when she heard the sweet cries of the child! I long to hear far more — how dearest Betsy spends every hour, and what she says, and what she feels, and how you all do, now you have reaped the fruit of such pain as you must have gone through." [2]

But Betsy's exhaustion was more extreme than Louisa could imagine. Her hours were spent for many days in almost passionate rest. A whole year of accumulated fatigue was taking its toll, and her "weakness and low spirits" were such that when she heard the sweet cries of the child, she could hardly help crying too. It was a month before she

[2] *Gurneys of Earlham*, I, 113.

could write in her journal, "I have now pretty much recovered," and even then she was spiritless.[8] Little Katherine was indeed "a source of quiet pleasure," but there was a kind of anguish in the intense love of the depleted young mother. "My present feelings for the babe are so acute as to render me at times unhappy from an over-anxiety about her, such an one as I never felt before for any one."

Early in October, all Norwich had a great sensation in the arrival of the mail coach bearing a great placard "Peace with France," with the coachman wearing a sprig of laurel in his buttonhole. So, in days before the telegraph, the news was quickly circulated through the length and breadth of England in a highly satisfactory manner. The noise of celebration in London, with roaring crowds, rockets and pistols, was not at all welcome to a resting mother with a headache, and Betsy complained to her journal that this drunkenness was not the right way to show their joy. But Joe Fry and the others went out to see the fun. And Betsy probably felt more sympathy even with mob extravagance when she found that the price of bread immediately fell 50 per cent, and that all foodstuffs became cheap and abundant, owing to the opening of the Baltic ports. October 1801 was a fortunate month in England, a month of hope and cheer; and the Gurney family felt it to the full when on the nineteenth some of them drove to Thetford to meet Betsy halfway, and some of them remained to bustle about Earlham Hall and provide every comfort for the dear heroine and her marvel of a babe.

Among the party at Earlham were some new guests, a friend of young John Gurney's called Fowell Buxton and his sister Anna, already uncommonly at home in the Earlham circle. When the chaise was seen approaching up the avenue of golden limes in the mellow evening sunshine, the Buxtons courteously joined the excited group of welcome on

[8] *Memoir*, I, 123.

the doorstep. The chaise drew up, brother John sprang forward, opened the door, and let down the steps, and out first trod Hannah proudly, carrying the baby. There she stood, with her white dress, her blue pelisse, her pretty bonnet, unconscious of her own sweetness, looking down tenderly at the sleeping infant. Her sisters surrounded her with gestures of delight and cooing cries. Fowell Buxton, taller than anybody present, looked over their heads at Hannah and an almost intolerable emotion swept through his breast. He said to himself, "She shall be my wife!"[4] He was that year sixteen and looked nineteen, and Hannah was eighteen and looked sixteen.

But pale Betsy was now helped out by her husband and brother, and John Gurney pressed forward to take her in his arms, his little daughter, bringing the first grandchild to her father's house. And each sister wanted her cheek. And the servants were not to be forgotten, curtseying and greeting Miss Betsy, and wanting a glimpse of the precious lamb, the new little Miss Katherine. And dearest Kitty must now hold her namesake. And somehow the travelers were swept indoors to be fed and rested and petted and admired.

The Buxtons were presented. Hannah, making her courtesy to the tall youth with her absent mind upon the baby, looked up at his grave, intent face without in the least suspecting that she had met her fate.

Betsy wrote: "Our reception was delightful; my father and all so much admire our little darling and seemed to love her so dearly that it was delightful to me. It was indeed a striking sight to see them all meet her."[5] Though in all the sweetness there was a tiny drop of bitterness, and many a wounded sensibility philosophically endured found expression in a quiver of the lip with the reflection, "How much more I am made of here than in London!"

[4] Told by Hannah in later years to the "baby," her niece Katherine.
[5] *Memoir.* I. 124.

But this is not a reflection on her husband. She speaks of him presently in a very different tone of deep, heartfelt content. "I accepted my Joseph more from duty than anything else, and how much I now love him."

2

It was a delightful holiday. But it is impossible for a married daughter to fit again completely into the old home circle. As the color came back to Betsy's cheeks and the liveliness to her spirits, it seemed to her that they wasted a great deal of time. Her sisters were busy all day, and yet what did they do?

They got up early, and did some solid reading before breakfast. After breakfast, they strolled about the garden in the sunshine, and walked down through the little wood to see the autumn colors reflected in the stream. Then they separated for the morning, pursuing some favorite occupation in their different rooms. In the afternoon there was generally a walk. In the evening, Rachel, Richenda, and Anna Buxton would knot together to read Tasso, in which they were much absorbed.[6] And the others would work at their embroidery and chat, or someone would go to the piano[7] and start some music. Speaking of music, that was another thing. With so many people to practise their playing and singing, the piano was hardly ever silent all day long for five minutes together. And as Betsy sat in luxurious idleness under the trees of a sunny afternoon, or sewed at some trifle for the baby in the cheerful Great Parlor of an evening, surrounded by soft voices and laughter, she remembered with a pang the neglected houses of the poor

[6] Richenda's letter, *Gurneys of Earlham*, I, 114.
[7] The piano, invented by an Italian in 1709, had displaced the harpsichord in all well-to-do houses in England. John Gurney purchased one for his daughters around 1796. The harpsichord plucked at the strings, the piano hit them with little hammers.

with which she had once been so familiar in that neighborhood, and the sixty, seventy, eighty forlorn children into whose lives she had once shed a ray of cheerfulness and hope.

At Earlham now she too was idle. There was nothing for her to do there but care for her baby, and no one could pretend that that took up all of an active young woman's time. "I do not feel satisfy'd as if my time were usefully employ'd. Although attending my babe is one of my first duties, yet there are others to attend to."

Her sisters regarded playing the piano as a duty. Not one of them had ever thought of taking over Betsy's Imps. And Betsy was more than ever convinced that the "plain quaker" view of music was the right one. It distracted one's attention and took up one's time from things that really mattered.

Joe in the meantime had gone off with John and Sam and young Fowell Buxton on a shooting party to Cromer, all of them sportsmen and congenial with each other, to spend happy days in the bracing sea air with no customers and no brother William to worry him. It was exactly what he needed.

Betsy, of course, went to meeting at Goats, and her reception was very warm.[8] Many Friends called on her at Earlham, and she made a valiant struggle not to be a fatuous mother. "I heard my child much praised, which rather flattered me although I do not think it deceives me about her, for I imagine I look on her in her true light and do not see anything *so very particular*, although she is all that is dear and sweet to me." But her thoughts, as November drew on, began to turn happily towards London. Her necessary reorientation had at last taken place. She no longer said to herself "home to Earlham," but "home to Mildred's Court."

"I look forward with much interest and pleasure to the thoughts of being quietly and comfortably settled at Mil-

[8] *Memoir*, I, 124.

But this is not a reflection on her husband. She speaks of him presently in a very different tone of deep, heartfelt content. "I accepted my Joseph more from duty than anything else, and how much I now love him."

2

It was a delightful holiday. But it is impossible for a married daughter to fit again completely into the old home circle. As the color came back to Betsy's cheeks and the liveliness to her spirits, it seemed to her that they wasted a great deal of time. Her sisters were busy all day, and yet what did they do?

They got up early, and did some solid reading before breakfast. After breakfast, they strolled about the garden in the sunshine, and walked down through the little wood to see the autumn colors reflected in the stream. Then they separated for the morning, pursuing some favorite occupation in their different rooms. In the afternoon there was generally a walk. In the evening, Rachel, Richenda, and Anna Buxton would knot together to read Tasso, in which they were much absorbed.[6] And the others would work at their embroidery and chat, or someone would go to the piano[7] and start some music. Speaking of music, that was another thing. With so many people to practise their playing and singing, the piano was hardly ever silent all day long for five minutes together. And as Betsy sat in luxurious idleness under the trees of a sunny afternoon, or sewed at some trifle for the baby in the cheerful Great Parlor of an evening, surrounded by soft voices and laughter, she remembered with a pang the neglected houses of the poor

[6] Richenda's letter, *Gurneys of Earlham*, I, 114.

[7] The piano, invented by an Italian in 1709, had displaced the harpsichord in all well-to-do houses in England. John Gurney purchased one for his daughters around 1796. The harpsichord plucked at the strings, the piano hit them with little hammers.

with which she had once been so familiar in that neighborhood, and the sixty, seventy, eighty forlorn children into whose lives she had once shed a ray of cheerfulness and hope.

At Earlham now she too was idle. There was nothing for her to do there but care for her baby, and no one could pretend that that took up all of an active young woman's time. "I do not feel satisfy'd as if my time were usefully employ'd. Although attending my babe is one of my first duties, yet there are others to attend to."

Her sisters regarded playing the piano as a duty. Not one of them had ever thought of taking over Betsy's Imps. And Betsy was more than ever convinced that the "plain quaker" view of music was the right one. It distracted one's attention and took up one's time from things that really mattered.

Joe in the meantime had gone off with John and Sam and young Fowell Buxton on a shooting party to Cromer, all of them sportsmen and congenial with each other, to spend happy days in the bracing sea air with no customers and no brother William to worry him. It was exactly what he needed.

Betsy, of course, went to meeting at Goats, and her reception was very warm.[8] Many Friends called on her at Earlham, and she made a valiant struggle not to be a fatuous mother. "I heard my child much praised, which rather flattered me although I do not think it deceives me about her, for I imagine I look on her in her true light and do not see anything *so very particular*, although she is all that is dear and sweet to me." But her thoughts, as November drew on, began to turn happily towards London. Her necessary reorientation had at last taken place. She no longer said to herself "home to Earlham," but "home to Mildred's Court."

"I look forward with much interest and pleasure to the thoughts of being quietly and comfortably settled at Mil-

[8] *Memoir*, I, 124.

dred's Court. I do hope we shall remain at home and without company for some little time after our arrival, for I do long to be settled, which I have hardly been since we married."

They returned to Mildred's Court about the middle of November. And they returned to familiar situations with which she was now able to deal. A young mother had more right to privacy than a bride; and vaccination, teething, and winter colds make a protection against outside intrusion.

The full days flew by in a narrow circle, and she felt "Martha-like," but unable to be otherwise. After all, "I do heartily enjoy our being alone and falling into some plans. Not being interrupted I appear naturally to fall into employment, and it is so sweet to have quiet plans at my own dear home. How much I think my marriage tends to my outward comfort."

3

In March the Peace of Amiens was finally concluded, and the French prisoners, upwards of 20,000, began to leave England as fast as transportation would permit. In the old-fashioned courtesy of war they had been supported for several years by the French government, and great had been the outrage of the English government when one of Napoleon's reforms in economy had required the English to feed the prisoners themselves. The French had not been very well fed under either scheme, but they bore no malice. The *Morning Herald* of April 19, 1802, reports that about a thousand of them "embarked at Plymouth on Thursday aboard the coasters and trawl boats, and spent the night on shore waiting the tide and stayed up all night. This morning at 3 o'clock they sung in very good style through the streets the 'Marseillaise,' the 'Austrian Retreat,' with several other popular French songs, and concluded with the popular

British song 'God Save the King,' in very good English."

April 29 was set as the official day for the Public Proclamation of Peace — why hurry? — and illuminations this time were on a grand scale. Apart from the transparencies and set pieces, almost every window in England boasted a triangular wooden frame set with candles to make a brave show. It was indeed a great national rejoicing.

Elizabeth and her husband and baby were spending a week or so in lodgings at the village of Hampstead, near her beloved connections the Hoares, while the house at Mildred's Court was being renovated; and on April 22, when preparation for the great day a week hence was going on all over London, Elizabeth had a trying day. "I felt in a great muddle. My house at M. Court all in great disorder, company, toothache etc. etc. baby rather cross. I sometimes think leaving off malt liquor and wine might help me, but it appears almost impossible for me, if I do that, to be well." [9] So it was really the last straw to have almost a quarrel with Joseph. "Illuminating our lodgings [at Hampstead] was mentioned and my Joseph said if I would not let our landlady illuminate he would leave Hampsted. He spoke rather sharply and I felt rather depressed and said, partly in joke, none of the Frys are so ruled as I am by their husbands, and I was very sorry to have made such a remark. The subject of illuminations has been so much talk'd about." [10]

So the lodgings were illuminated, and there was peace at Hampstead also.

The year 1802, when the whole nation seemed to take breath, was a calm and happy year. The months were free, on the whole, from overstrain, and Betsy's journal reflects her increasing serenity. "To-day we have been married

---

[9] E. F. took these under doctor's orders, as was common at the time.
[10] Savery had felt very strongly that people who disapproved of war on principle should show no sign of rejoicing at victory.

two years. Time slips through quickly, trials and pleasures before unknown have indeed been felt by me, trials and joys of many kinds. The love of a husband, the unity experienced; the love of a child, the maternal feelings, are real and great sources of enjoyment. They are apt to occupy the mind perhaps too much. My family is to me in more comfortable order than it was, at least I feel more mistress of it." But oh, dear me, what a lot of bothersome small responsibilities there are, and how difficult it is to keep one's mind on them. "My forgetfulness I find a material hindrance to me in many such concerns."

In October, Joe took her on a delightful journey. Although the baby and nurse went along, and Betsy's second pregnancy was in its fourth month, it was much more like a honeymoon than their first journey had been. They visited Coventry, Stratford-on-Avon, Warwick, Wolverhampton, Colebrook Dale, Rock Ferry, Liverpool, Manchester, and Keswick. Joseph Fry was combining business with pleasure. They went to see Shakespeare's monument at Stratford-on-Avon, a sweet country churchyard. They had breakfast at Warwick and saw the castle and the church; "the outside of the Castle I like very much, the inside pretty well." Many memories were revived at Colebrook Dale. They admired Chester, "the town is so extraordinary"; and the views from the walls were beautiful. Bad weather delayed them at Rock Ferry; but the delay was jolly, in a cosy inn, with bright fire and candles, and windows closed against the wind and rain. Betsy welcomed the rest. "The quiet within was so pleasant, when the storms without were so violent, and I enjoyed my beloved husband's company. What earthly pleasure," says Elizabeth restfully, "is equal to the enjoyment of real unity with the nearest of all ties, husband and children?"

She was much delighted when, sailing across from Rock Ferry to Liverpool with the wind still high, she yet "hardly felt any fear. I do not think I am nearly such a coward about some little things as I was before I married."

At Liverpool and Manchester, business detained them some days. The chief event at Manchester to Betsy was tea with John Thorp. "I really admire and love that man, I think we seldom see so much of good united with a cultivated understanding and the sweet simplicity of religion as in him." [11]

Keswick, in the Lake District, was terribly wet. They rode about on horseback in the rain and looked at waterfalls; damp mists clung in veils about the hills, and when the wind blew the vapors aside for a moment, glimpses of shining lakes appeared. Betsy complains, "There is too much water in this place, too much lake, and too much barren mountain." [12] It was far from snug. But the young wife bore her husband valiant company. After the watery day, the weather having somewhat improved, "we first took a long ride, part of it over rather frightful roads, on the edge of a precipice without any wall or guard to it. This evening my husband and I climbed Skiddaw. When we arrived at the top after some pain and fatigue, we were almost in a whirlwind, and so extremely cold and damp, being in the midst of a cloud, and the wind so violent that it appeared almost impossible to stand against it; however we got down safely." It is again with much satisfaction in her own advance in matronly poise that she reflects complacently, "This would have appeared to me some time ago rather a frightful day."

After all these travels, how delightful it was to get back to her own now well-ordered house. "Mildred's Court. *Eleventh month (November) 18th.* We have had a prosperous journey and have at last arrived at our comfortable home. It really looks quite sweet and nice. It is a great thing to have gone so far and returned home safely."

[11] *Memoir*, I, 129.   [12] *Ibid.*, I, 129.

This was only the first of many journeys that Elizabeth took with her husband for the sheer fun and pleasure of travel and the enjoyment of his company. It was not for ten years that any other motive for travel emerged. And in these journeys, Fry certainly came into his own. He dictated the route, chose the inns, paid the bills. Elizabeth had nothing to do but to be a charming companion. How well she succeeded in this is proved by the fact that he never got tired of taking her.

The Earlham family also went to the Lakes that year, and stayed there long enough to get a less damp and barren impression. It was to them, as to anyone who sees it softly opalescent under the sun, a most delightful country. Hannah's letter to Elizabeth from Ambleside took Betsy vividly back into the frisky cosiness of the family group.

Old Crome,[13] the famous landscape painter, — the first landscapist to paint direct from nature, — was with them as tutor, sitting with them in rustic summerhouses and helping them to paint the prettiest views — really difficult things, like waterfalls. Long walks and picnics were the order of the day, with many vigorous quarrels as to plans — "but after a rough hour or two," says Hannah, "calm ensues and good minds reappear. We three, Fowell and Sam and I, had a very pleasant and droll ride home in a countryman's cart, which passed us on our return to Ambleside, after we had been climbing up a hill at Grasmere and walking a long way when there. We are all, even Kitty, capital walkers."[14]

The youth Fowell Buxton was deliberately pursuing his objective. And Hannah, though innocently unaware of his intentions, was at least no longer distracted by an infant

---

[13] His paintings can be seen in the National Gallery, London, and in the Metropolitan Museum of Art, New York. He died at Norwich in 1821.

[14] *Gurneys of Earlham*, I, 116.

niece. Fortune smiled on them that they were, in the first blush of their youth, happily advancing in intimacy, forming a thousand ties of sweet haphazard memory: the scent of damp thyme, the rush of falling water; pleasant fatigue on a warm hillside; a "jolly ride home, just we three, in a farmer's cart."

Hannah had no time to develop a private life of her own. She was captured from the beginning by a stronger personality, and woven up as one of the strands in the web of his life.

But Elizabeth herself at this time felt quite submerged in being Mrs. Joseph Fry, and willingly so, save for the ache of unused capacities that she could not define. There were "other duties."

But meanwhile, there was the month of March advancing relentlessly upon her, and she struggled to obtain strength for the "day of expected trial." She tried to place her confidence in the Power that alone could help. She reasoned with herself, in her customary note of realistic resignation to the inevitable. "Suffer we must in this world: and the less we kick against the pricks, the happier for us."

It was rather a comfort that Joe's boisterousness was subdued by his anxiety for her. A pleasing melancholy was a substitute in him for the deep-seated seriousness that lay dormant in even the liveliest Gurney. Elizabeth sometimes missed that note of seriousness in his free-and-easy, jovial, good-humored nature. It was why a person like young Fowell Buxton could arrive at a bound at a much deeper intimacy with the family at Earlham than Joe Fry had been able to establish in several years of acquaintance and two of close relationship. Joe Fry was a nice fellow; but Fowell Buxton talked their own language.

So Elizabeth records with satisfaction: "My Joseph appears low and not very comfortable but that is preferable to me to seeing him in an exhilarated state of mind, as he is more lovable to me when under a little discouragement. I feel lowish myself this morning."

4

Her second child, Rachel, was born on March 25, and on April 12 she wrote: "My heart abounded with joy and gratitude when my dear little girl was born perfect and lovely. Words are not equal to express my feelings, for I was most mercifully dealt with. My soul was so quiet and so much supported." [15]

She was, however, very ill after it, and not until June does she write, "I am now once more entering upon my usual occupations." But even then, "my nerves are in an irritable state, I am soon overcome and overdone."

Her sister Rachel was again with her through her time of trial and recovery, this time accompanied by Priscilla, and Kitty also came on later from Bath, where she was sharing lodgings with Mary Anne Galton, and "stayed for a short time with Betsy at Mildred's Court." [16] It was during this London visit that Kitty attended a Church of England service that gave her great religious help, and set her on the path that led her finally to membership in the Church of England. "I never can forget the enjoyment and encouragement of that evening, and the delight of the whole church service on that occasion. It was what I wanted. But there it ended for a long time."

Meanwhile, England's breathing space was over. The diplomatic wrangling that had been going on ever since the Peace of Amiens finally ended in severance of diplomatic relations on May 12, and England made declaration of war on May 18. Nelson sailed from Portsmouth on the twentieth to take command of the fleet, and on May 22 Napoleon

[15] *Memoir*, I, 131.
[16] *Gurneys of Earlham*, I, 121.

outraged all international codes up to that time by capturing and interning all English travelers in France and Holland, and laying an embargo on all English vessels in ports under his control. "This detention of harmless visitors was unprecedented, and aroused universal reprobation. They were not well treated, and besides were harassed by being moved from place to place." [17]

The unexpectedness of this internment and its tedious duration make it, up to the present date, the worst in history. Mothers were separated from little children whom they had left behind in England, young people parted on the eve of marriage, heads of businesses cut off from their offices, boys prevented from return to college; and all were held in the misery of exile and hope deferred for nearly ten years. It was a gesture of no military value. It was one of pure spite. And it destroyed generosity. The miseries of St. Helena were its retribution.

The year 1803 was an exciting one in which to begin to practise the art of banking, and young Sam Gurney took to it like a duck to water. He this spring became an inmate of his sister's house at Mildred's Court in order to learn the banking business from his brother-in-law, Joseph Fry. No arrangement could have been happier. The tie between Elizabeth and Sam had always been a warm and living one. She had been the one of his older sisters to whom he had taken his childish troubles, the one to whom his reticent and sturdy disposition had granted confidence. It was to her that he had run in the dark night when wakened by a bad dream. Before she had children of her own, her maternal feelings had been aroused and exercised by this particularly masculine younger brother, six years her junior, whose escapades with the farm horses, and increasing excellence at manly sports, appealed to some secret streak of daring in Elizabeth herself. Now, at seventeen years

[17] John Ashton, *Dawn of the XIXth Century in England*, 174.

old, a handsome boy with a fine presence, it was delightful to have him as an inmate of her household, and he added to the happiness of the domestic circle.

"He took to business and liked it," wrote his niece Katherine long after. "In the counting-house, as well as in domestic life, he was liked and beloved by the whole establishment. When at work, he was thoroughly industrious, and though no one more enjoyed to break off from it for a drive into the country with my father, or to get up a game of cricket in the fields at Plashet, yet in the evening, on returning to town, he would cheerfully go down after supper into the counting-house, and call over the books for an hour or two. He was popular everywhere, and the family were seldom invited to any friend's house without being requested to bring Samuel Gurney with them."

And Priscilla, writing to Hannah from St. Mildred's Court in February 1803, says, "I think I never saw Sam in so sweet a mind as he is in now. It is quite delightful to be with him. His present situation seems completely to suit his taste, and he shines in it more than he has ever done before. His partiality for Mildred's Court and Joseph and Betsy seems likely to increase, and he seems more attached to them than ever. He has quite gained the affection of all the Frys by his sweet and attentive behaviour to them" (courtier-like manners have, after all, their uses), "and I often wonder whether he will be a plain Friend or not. As far as we can foresee things there appears to be some probability of it. Joseph and Betsy have a great influence over him in that respect. . . . It is difficult, I think, to be here long without feeling the influence of Friends, and Betsy is so very nearly connected with us that it is now and then painful not to be able to feel as she does."

It was not very long before gentle Priscilla did "feel as she does." But Sam maintained to the end his middle way. It was the next brother, Joseph John, now studying at Ox-

SAMUEL GURNEY

Drawn by George Gillett Whitney from an engraving of a miniature

ford,[18] who became the distinguished Quaker among the men of the Gurney family.

Remote in thought from the French wars, Betsy traveled peacefully to Earlham with her husband and babies for the usual summer visit, in the latter part of July. But they had hardly been there a week (during which Betsy's chief concern had been to see Joseph giving way to his love of music, and playing the piano, an instrument which the Fry influence had kept out of Mildred's Court) when the war was brought forcibly to her attention. On July 27: "I was quite sorry to see a letter from my brother William that expressed he was so fully occupied that my Joseph thought it best to determine to go to London in a few days. This vexed me much, more particularly," says Betsy, plaintively, "as Joseph did not appear the least to mind leaving me, but even seemed to wish to go. I felt rather low and delicate."[19]

How far Joseph's wish to go was influenced by his irritation on the subject of music and how far by his sense of the urgency of the situation in London it is difficult to judge. But it was the latter that finally took him away. On the thirtieth Betsy records, "I went to Norwich this morning with my husband, and when there we received a letter from William expressing a desire for Joseph's immediate return. The account rather vexed me; and also the gloomy appearance about the French coming cast a gloom over the party." But that evening at Earlham, French or no French, they had a heart-warming, jolly time. John came over from Lynn, where he was now in charge of the branch bank, and Sam was already present, so there was a complete reunion. "It was truly pleasant, all twelve of us and the two children being here together." Joseph and Betsy set aside their difference on the subject of music (though Betsy knew that

---

[18] With a private tutor. As a Dissenter, he was debarred from attending the University.
[19] *Memoir*, I, 132.

she was right) and their farewells next day left Betsy, at any rate, comforted. "Took leave of my dear Joseph. My love for him is only known to a superior to mortals."

5

Joseph Fry was much more aware than his wife of the danger of French invasion. Napoleon had now a large army encamped at Boulogne, which he boastfully called the Army of England. He was preparing a flotilla of flat-bottomed boats in which to transport this army across the Channel when the moment arrived to hurl it at England's shores. How seaworthy flat-bottomed boats might prove in the choppy and uncertain waters was another question. But the menace was visible and unmistakable, terror and anger swept over England, and four hundred thousand volunteers offered themselves for national defense.

When Joseph Fry reached London he found that preparations had been made for flooding the marshes of the River Lee and breaking down the bridges on the Essex road. It was arranged that the King should be ready to flee from London to Chelmsford, the Queen and the treasure to Worcester, at the first news of the landing. Beacons made of barrels of tar were set on all the church towers along the south coast, and huge beacons, each of eight wagonloads of wood and faggots with four or five tar barrels, were built on strategic hilltops, where in fire by night or smoke by day they would send unmistakable signal over miles of country. England had felt nothing like it since the threat of the Armada. Napoleon himself, the invincible, the man of legend, was at Boulogne, and was reputed to have said, "Let us be masters of the Channel for six hours and we are masters of the world." Week after week the state of strain continued. The fleet defended the Channel, but the fleet could not be everywhere. Napoleon, having distracted its attention by means of his ally, the Spanish fleet, might get out from Boulogne and attack England on some other side. Why not the east coast?

By autumn the panic had spread to the east coast. John Gurney ordered that four carriages should be kept constantly ready at Earlham to start at a moment's notice for the Isle of Ely, in case of a landing on the Norfolk shore. Priscilla wrote to Elizabeth in November: "My father is going to Lynn this afternoon. From Lynn he will continue his journey to Liverpool, and, I suppose, will not return for a fortnight. I think we shall be in a very unprotected state if the French should land whilst my father is away, without a single man, or even boy, to take care of us. We had quite a serious conference about it yesterday morning: thee would have been entertained to have heard the various plans that were proposed. It is, however, now finally settled that as soon as ever we hear the news of their arrival, we six [the six sisters], Danny, and Nurse, and, if we can manage it, Molly and Anne,[20] are immediately to set off in the coach-and-four for Ely, where we are to take up our abode, as my father thinks it is a very safe place, being so completely surrounded by marshes. I hope, as soon as ever you hear of the French being landed in Norfolk, that you will imagine us setting off post-haste for Ely.[21] Mrs. Freeman[22] is to stay to take care of the house, as it will be necessary for somebody to be here. My father intends to write down directions for every individual of the family, so that there may be no confusion or bustle whenever the moment of danger arrives, if it ever does arrive."[23]

One sees that this sort of excitement was not altogether unpleasant, and one can only hope that Mrs. Freeman was contented with the part assigned her.

But after Betsy had rejoined her husband in London in

---

[20] Servants.
[21] A distance of about forty miles.
[22] The housekeeper.
[23] *Gurneys of Earlham*, I, 130.

August, and while Napoleon still felt a very, very long way away from Norfolk, the Gurneys had gone off nonchalantly for a seaside holiday at Cromer, and Richenda's account of it in a letter to Betsy is a reminder of the immense detachment possible in days when war itself was conducted with apparent leisure. The telegraph that gives every moment the news of the instant seems itself to speed up events. Two of the best minds of the period, Jane Austen and Charles Lamb, consistently ignored the war, and no one thought the worse of them. So, while Napoleon's flotilla tried to practise frightfulness on the edge of the Channel, many a wealthy English family disported itself serenely on remote seacoasts and gave its whole mind to innocent and peaceful pleasures.

But Elizabeth did not envy them at Cromer. She, too, was enjoying herself. Like Florence Nightingale later, she did not wish people to be ill, but she did like to nurse. By her own illnesses she had learned various of the little arts that make a sick person comfortable. She had practised them on Joseph's sick headaches and on the alarming illnesses of baby Katherine. And now she eagerly devoted herself to a more serious task. Her mother-in-law was gravely ill, and William had come in a panic to entreat her help at Plashet and to ask her "to go for Dr. Willan, which I did; and . . . went with Dr. Willan to Plashet to see my mother. I was quite sorry to find her so ill, and felt real love for her." From this day until the death of Mrs. Fry in March, Elizabeth's time was divided between the two houses. "I have been so much occupied in attending my mother in going backwards and forwards to Plashet that I have had little time for writing my journal." It seems a little odd that William's wife Eliza, who was in residence at Plashet, could not take charge of the emergency. She had no children and all of her time free, whereas Elizabeth was in control of a complicated household, with one baby of two years and another of six months, and a thousand and one daily demands on her time and judgment. Yet William himself judged Elizabeth the more capable of the two, the woman to whom he naturally turned for help in things which were a woman's business. And Joseph may well have been proud at the spontaneous tribute to his own wife, even though it cost him the sacrifice of her company. It is particularly striking evidence of Elizabeth's power to inspire confidence in view of the fact that she and William never hit it off very well. His medical ideas were particularly repugnant to her, and she had many a trying moment at Plashet. "Animal magnetism has been a very uppermost and also worrying subject to me, and when it is going on as it has been lately at Plashet, my mind cannot be at rest about it. I have so much natural dislike to it."

Joe Fry had entertained her in the early days at Earlham by talk about animal magnetism, and the Frys in general were very much bitten by it. It appeared to be a mixture of faith healing, "magnetic" healing, and mild hypnotism. Volta, with his electrical experiments, and Mesmer with his trances, had set going various surprising ideas which flowered among non-scientific minds into curious superstitions. Religious people who have squeezed their religion dry of all elements of imagination are the most prone to fall a victim to semi-magic cults. And William Fry in particular found a peculiar release up this channel. Savery's journal gives the fullest account, as he heard of it in July 1798. "Drank tea at W. Fry's Mildred Court, with Anna Savory, William Fry's Junr and Senr, with their wives, and Thos Fry. Never before heard so much ab. animal magnetism and the power of sympathy. The Whole family Except Ellis and Thos are great Proficients and have performd Surprising Cures. Wm Fry Junr can tell by the power of sympathy what part of the Body of a person disordered is most affected or has the most pain — this has been several times prov'd. Fevers are not a Disorder but the effect of a Disorder. All this Intelligence was Extraordinary to me, yet Cannot doubt in the least the Veracity of the friends."

Perhaps, after three years of near acquaintance and observation of William's animal magnetism, Elizabeth was inclined, if not to doubt the veracity of the Friends, at least to feel impatient with their perseverance in self-deception. The correct description of the nature of fever did not counteract the injury to health of trying to treat it by "sympathy." And Elizabeth was all for common-sense, simple remedies, and close attention to the orders of a good doctor. She could not prevent William from entering the sickroom and practising his magnetic arts upon his suffering mother. But it was a trial to her patience. Neither was it the only one. Eliza would fuss about, out of turn, trying to nurse, and the querulous invalid would sometimes, with the perversity of the sick, make unreasonable choice of her more familiar, though more ineffective ministrations. Elizabeth at last finds time to let off steam in her diary, a safety valve that always calmed her down. "I have, like myself, felt moments of a sort of jealousy at her preferring Eliza's nursing to mine; however, think it has generally been a uniting time amongst us all, more particularly Eliza and me. I never remember feeling so much for her as I have lately. I felt for her trials, though I cannot exactly say what they all are, but she, like others, is tryed, and I have really sympathised with her." Above all, Betsy is emphatic: "In the first place I have felt a good deal for my poor mother."

Elizabeth Fry always suckled her own children and did not, as her mother had done, employ a wet nurse. During the first few months of her trips to Plashet she had to take her nursing baby with her; and in addition she was pregnant with her third child. Yet her spirits remained resilient, except when she recorded "my darling babe seriously unwell."

It is a side light on the medical practice of the time to find an account in the *Morning Herald*, February 18, 1804, of the illness of the King with "water in the chest of the body," to counteract which they "scarified his legs." Strange to say, the next day they needed four doctors instead of two. But the King recovered. On March 28, the *Herald* proclaims him "restored to all his domestic comforts."

But Mrs. Fry had then been almost a fortnight in her grave.

6

By March, Napoleon and his flotilla had become a national joke. Preparations for flight subsided. The war receded to a comfortable distance. It had never come near enough to Elizabeth to engage much of her attention, and she instinctively resisted the idle contemplation of an evil which she could do nothing to prevent. Her genius was practical, and demanded always the concrete and the immediate. She must serve God and humanity in the persons of suffering individuals. Eyes to the blind, feet to the lame. She saw, as she went about her daily ways, the pageant of poverty in the London streets, and when once she had her domestic situation under control, she set to work to undertake those "other duties." Often, after business hours of a fine light evening, she and her husband would go to a poor district to follow up some person who had aroused her sympathy. It was an activity not without danger, in the narrow and dingy streets, in those days of footpads. And Joe Fry, too, wore his unpopular Quaker coat. But to that kind of danger, Fry was equal, and as to Betsy, she was unconscious of it. She trembled at rebuking a servant, she was terrified at speaking in public, but she never in her life was afraid of a robber. But though risky and unsavory side streets must be traversed to reach their sordid destinations, the main part of their trip was usually delightful. The river was still the great highway. "We went and returned by water."

Some of their adventures were disconcerting. There was the woman who had begged so touchingly of Betsy, and whom, when with difficulty they ran her to earth, they found living "almost like a gentlewoman" and who brazenly asked them for thirty pounds to pay her debts. Worse was the woman who had had a baby in her arms — a pathetic, sick baby, with the whooping cough — and who turned out to be a baby farmer, and fled them to escape the clutches of the law. It was not like the simple, straightforward poor of the Earlham countryside or the slums of Norwich. But there were deserving cases. And sometimes, in looking up a deceiver, they discovered by chance a case of desperate need. Then Betsy was filled with intense happiness. She felt — it was incredible, but it was true — that she was actually and literally being used by God to do a little bit of his concrete will on earth; she, Betsy Gurney, was the servant of the Great Master, the tool in the hand of the divine Artificer. At such moments she truly lived.

Another thing in which she delighted was to go to the Workhouse to read and talk to the children. When first appointed a Visitor to the Islington Workhouse by the Friends of Gracechurch Street Meeting, she felt all her usual overwhelming diffidence. But when she screwed up her courage to go, and took the children things for their tea, and something to read to them, and was really among them, and felt the impact of their forlorn childish need, she forgot all her shyness. It was so easy that she felt it could not come from God, it could only be from her own heart and understanding. None the less, it was very encouraging. Their response was so eager and so genuine. Her natural clearness of mind flowed forth in her speech. It was like the days of her Imps come again.

In the bright hours of daylight, as she found time, she would go on many such errands alone. "I went to see a poor woman (it is always a cross to me leaving my child) but going over the bridge I enjoy. The air, sky and water look so sweetly."

It was old London Bridge upon which her feet delayed with pleasure at air, sky, and water. Wordsworth had paused upon a bridge a little higher up the river, not many months before, and had recorded the opinion, "Earth hath not anything to show more fair."

Elizabeth Fry never met either Wordsworth or Charles Lamb in the flesh, though she narrowly missed it. The Priscilla Lloyd who was such a close friend of the Gurney sisters was a sister of the James Lloyd who was Elizabeth's first suitor, and of Charles Lloyd, the friend of Lamb and Coleridge. Charles Lamb had visited at Bingley Hall, Birmingham, the Lloyd home, and was acquainted with Priscilla. And Priscilla Lloyd married the poet Wordsworth's brother, the Christopher Wordsworth who was Master of Trinity.

Had the Fry household been of the sort to attract such people as Lamb and Wordsworth, they might easily have become acquainted, with so many possible points of contact. Charles Lamb was especially accessible, living in London, eager for friends, and most sympathetic toward things Quaker. But such people were unlikely to gravitate toward the Fry orbit. The Opies were the only ones of that world who still remained faithful to Betsy, and even they found it heavy going. Oil and water would not mix. The Frys and their friends made it difficult for people of the world. *They* would not practise courtier-like manners; and they were embarrassed when their bluntness was met by chilly politeness. Even Joseph complained, rather sullenly, that Betsy's "gay" friends did not treat him well.

Betsy resigned herself, willingly and sweetly, to the necessities of her situation. "We ought to make it an object in conversation and in conduct to oblige those we are with, and rather to make the pleasure of others our object than our own. I am clear it is a great virtue to be able constantly to yield in little things." [24]

Her sisters — though their manners were always perfect — never tried to amalgamate with the Fry circle. Even Priscilla, the most Quakerly of them all, and who adored Betsy, wrote to Hannah in 1807: "Thee knows *how* dull Mildred Court can be, so I need not describe it to thee. The children have been my only comfort. Little Rachel, Johnny and I have been drinking tea together, and they have made me quite cheerful and happy. Now Johnny is playing by my side; he is most sweet. I wish he could spend an hour or two with thee, thee would so much enjoy it."

And Louisa writes in 1804: "We have had a regular Mildred Court day, poor people coming one after another till twelve o'clock, and then no quiet. And each day I have been here we have had the Frys, or my uncle, or some one else at dinner. Dear Betsy gets through her bustles by letting them pass without teasing herself about them; she does feel them, but knows they must be borne."

Her sisters, however, had their ways of escape. They would drive off in a glass coach to St. James's Park, and walk about there admiring the flowers and the fashions, and forget which gate they came in by and wander about in gales of laughter and dismay "for nearly two hours, almost despairing of ever again reaching home," until at last they spied their coach and joyfully reëntered it.

Or of an evening they would go out into the world. "I went with Gatty [25] to Willis's Rooms, where we had a most

---

[24] *Memoir*, I, 137.   [25] Cousin Agatha Barclay.

pleasant evening. The room I think is the most elegant I ever saw, and the company was no little amusement to us. The music was capital. Braham sang to perfection; but of all the singers I ever heard or people I ever saw, I never, I think, was so struck by any one as by Grassini, the new actress. She is most fascinating, and as soon as you see her, you feel her effect. Every movement and every look has something in it perfectly different from any I ever saw in any one before. She has a beautiful and fine figure and a handsome face, but it is more the finished grace of all she does that makes her so conspicuous. I do wish you could have heard her singing. I can only say how delighted I was with it. It is wholly different from the high, clear notes of Mrs. Billington, but she has a depth of something like hoarseness of voice, with an expression that is most interesting." [26]

How the tales of their adventures enlivened Mildred's Court and made currents of merriment stir in that sometimes too serious air. If Charles Lamb had come in then, he would have found himself in his element. How he would have defended Braham's singing against all comers! "The little Jew has bewitched me! I follow him like as boys follow Tom the Piper. He cured me of melancholy. I was insensible to music till he gave me a sixth sense." [27] And he and Betsy, at a quieter moment, could have compared notes on *No Cross, No Crown*, that most capital book, good thoughts in good language, which Betsy also was reading in the summer of 1804 to fortify her soul. But though their spirits sometimes wandered in the same places, Lamb never entered Mildred's Court.

Betsy's third child and first son, little Johnny, — John Gurney Fry, — was born in July. As usual, Betsy's confinement, acutely dreaded beforehand, was followed by weeks of

---

[26] Grassini also fascinated Napoleon. See Ludwig, etc.
[27] Lucas, I, 393.

illness — "sickness, faintness and nervous irritability." This time she was taken to Bath for a cure before going on to Earlham, and Louisa returned with her from there for a further visit at Mildred's Court. Betsy was still the only married sister, and had a powerful claim upon her sisters' comparative leisure.

Louisa writes to her on the first day of the New Year, 1805, after return to Earlham: "I have often thought of thee lately, and imagined thee in thy different offices; and amongst the many other pleasures of having been with thee is that of knowing exactly how thy time goes. I often seem to see thee in thy pink acorn gown attending to all thy flock in the dining-room, drawing-room, and — as I imagine — in the parlour, alternately running after thy servants, children and poor. In short, I never felt before the kind of home interest in all of you in St. Mildred's Court which I feel now."

Louisa was to learn the joys of domesticity before long from her love for that very Sam Hoare who had kissed her when she was twelve years old and who had waited patiently for her ever since. But though Louisa was the next one to be married, Hannah was the next to be engaged.

7

Fowell Buxton was now in his twentieth year, an undergraduate at Dublin University, with two more years of study between him and his degree. But his future appeared secure, he was heir to considerable estates in Ireland, and the sisters were united with him in feeling that his affair with Hannah should be put on a definite footing.

Rachel's letters to Elizabeth give the clearest possible picture of the final courtship and "the sunshine that prevailed on every countenance when they came in. . . . Anna [Buxton] cried for joy." A dance had been previously arranged that day, and "as it happened, it turned out very pleasantly. Several gentlemen, Mr. Pitchford, Ives, a Mr. Turner and Miss Day dined here. We had a quiet and pleasant company, and in the evening a remarkably pleasant dance, in which though I know it cannot quite excite thy sympathy, it will be a satisfaction to thee to know that neither Fowell nor Hannah nor the girls seemed to be in the least thrown off their centre; while as a divert from the cares of the morning" (that is, the anxiety as to whether Hannah and Fowell would return from their walk "engaged" or not), "it was of use to the whole party."

Pitchford had proposed to Rachel immediately on Enfield's defection, but she had refused him. His friendship with the family had been, however, gradually restored. John Gurney was himself entirely free from religious prejudice, and valued Pitchford's company.

A regular epidemic of engagements took place in the Gurney family during the period in which England was thrilling to the victory of Trafalgar and sorrowing for the death of Nelson. Sam Hoare, whose prosperous banking business had put him in a position to marry years before, at last obtained the promise of headstrong Louisa. And John Gurney the younger, recovering from an unhappy love affair, fell violently in love with his beautiful first cousin, Elizabeth Gurney of Keswick Hall,[28] daughter of John Gurney's elder brother Richard. The marriage of first cousins was much frowned upon, and there was a perfect uproar of opposition from both families, but young John Gurney, with all his father's obstinacy, carried his point. After all, John Gurney had provoked the affair by thought-

---

[28] Near Norwich, the paternal home of the Gurneys, "a charming place, with woods above the river," purchased by John Gurney's grandfather, Joseph Gurney, in 1747. It has nothing to do with Keswick in the Lake District.

lessly inviting them both on a prolonged family tour: three chariots and a whiskey; and Hoare and Buxton along to display the privileges of betrothal.

Long engagements were never the Gurney way, with the single exception of Hannah's to Fowell Buxton, who had to finish college. Louisa's wedding was set for the end of December. By December 6, Joseph Fry and Elizabeth and their children had arrived at Earlham, including the little William Storrs Fry, who had been born in June, with Richenda this time as the attendant aunt. Elizabeth had presented her father with four grandchildren, and the only grandchildren up to date. He considered her as amply and abundantly doing her work in the world, and rejoiced to see her sitting on the couch, pale and rather thin, but happy, to watch the festivities of her sister's wedding.

Fowell Buxton, away at Dublin University, was the only member of the family absent. But how thoroughly they thought of him as a member of the family, how much of a brother to them all he had become, is shown by the letters, warm, intimate, and entirely free, that he constantly received from his future sisters, from each of them in turn. None of the other brothers- or sisters-in-law ever attained the footing of Fowell Buxton.

Elizabeth was at this time the one who knew him least. But in later years she was, except for Priscilla (and, of course, his wife), the one who knew him best; and to her he became a friend and brother second only to Sam.

Louisa was married at the Friends' Meetinghouse at Tasborough, near Norwich. All eleven Gurneys were present. The whole day was without a cloud. Sam Hoare had been studying his Louisa for nine years; it would have been odd if he had not known how to make her happy.

"*December 31st. 1806.* Louisa and Sam returned yesterday from Cromer, where they have been spending nearly a week in retirement, so that they have now the effect of married people who have begun their career together. Louisa looks sweetly and Sam truly happy." [29]

Elizabeth was delighted at having a sister come to settle so near her as Hampstead,[30] and one of the first letters Louisa wrote as a married woman describes a visit from her. The letter, dated January 25, 1807, is written to Hannah, and is full of good advice from a married woman to a little sister about to enter the state of matrimony. However, confessions creep in. Like Betsy before her, she feels the difficulty of adjusting to her husband's family, even though, in her case, they are the kindest and best-known of cousins, and she has her own house to herself. But she is getting used to "acting as Sam's wife before them all," and Catherine is with her to settle her in. "My first full company-day at home" was the day of Betsy's visit. "It was Sam's day out, so I determined to enjoy dear Betsy and all her darling and noisy flock. They arrived in a hack about one. . . . Fowell walked in with Dan [31] at his side a little before three, and soon after that we dined, the children in the drawing-room and we in the dining-room; I quite 'mistress,' anxious about my dinner and the nice entertainment of all my dear guests. It was so very strange to me to feel myself in this capacity with all of them. We chatted pleasantly in the afternoon, and after an early tea, Betsy, Catherine and brats left us three to a truly snug and happy evening. But first," she hastens to add, a little conscience-smitten about that word "brats," "I must tell you how very sweet the darling children were, and what a treat it was to me to have them routing about the house. They all seemed thoroughly to enjoy the novelty, and were quite happy with their exalted ideas of 'Aunt Hoare' and her house, which

---

[29] Rachel to Fowell Buxton.
[30] Sam Hoare took a house for his bride not far from his old home at Hampstead Heath.
[31] Daniel Gurney, youngest of the Earlham eleven.

little Rachel said was almost as fine as the King's house. . . . About eight dear Sam came in, looking most sweet and cheerful, rejoicing to be at home and delighted to see Fowell. We all sat round the fire, talking, laughing and easy and happy. . . . Indeed, Hannah, I do think thee has got a delightful husband, I did think what two prizes they were when I saw him and Sam walk off arm-in-arm this morning, both looking so very agreeable, handsome and delightful." That reminds her of "one more hint about marrying," and she is off on another couple of pages of wise advice, ending up with a warning about mad dogs and the necessity of making one's menfolk go out in boots, "for they generally bite men's legs."

8

On May 7 Joseph Fry and Elizabeth were back at Earlham for the wedding of Fowell Buxton and Hannah. Buxton's hopes of inheritance had fallen through, his prospects were at the moment very uncertain, but he went forward with his wedding immediately on taking his degree. His self-confidence was fortified by University honors, and by the final tribute of having been asked to sit in the British House of Commons as Member for Dublin University. He declined it, since he had a living to earn for Hannah (Members were not then paid), but it turned his attention to the possibility of a political career, later to be so ably fulfilled. On that joyous day in May, however, nothing was further from his thoughts than the crowning honor of a monument in Westminster Abbey.

Buxton's mother was a Quaker, a sister of Uncle Richard Gurney's wife, but his father, long since dead, had been a Churchman, and the children had all been brought up in that communion. Perhaps that is why his was the first Gurney wedding with bridesmaids. "The house was overrun with bridesmaids in muslin cloaks and chip hats. . . . At dinner were my father's fifteen children and four grandchildren. Afterwards the whole party dispersed in different parts of the house. Hannah sat with Elizabeth in her room."

Fowell Buxton was six foot four in height, and was affectionately called by his brothers-in-law, "the Elephant." Before the year was over he was offered by his uncle, Sampson Hanbury, a promising position in the firm of Truman and Hanbury, London brewers, with the prospect of a partnership after three years' probation. So he and Hannah also moved to London, and Betsy had another sister within reach of an afternoon visit.

It may be remembered that Mrs. Micawber had this firm in mind when she confided to Mr. Copperfield that she had long felt the Brewing business to be particularly adapted to Mr. Micawber. "Look at Barclay and Perkins! Look at Truman, Hanbury and Buxton! It is on that extensive footing that Mr. Micawber, I know from my own knowledge of him, is calculated to shine; and the profits, I am told, are e-Nor-mous!"

Buxton certainly found them so.

John Gurney the younger had married Cousin Elizabeth very quietly in January, blessed by the friendly attentions of his home sisters and a long and warm letter from Betsy, though the two fathers ostentatiously went for a walk during the ceremony to mark their official disapproval.

Three weddings within so short a time were rather overcoming for those left behind. Rachel writes, without pretense, "I daresay, dearest Fowell and Hannah, you do not wonder that, in certain moods the past should rise up mournfully before me. The sight of you all happily married brings some sad regrets, but happily their acuteness is very much gone . . . my murmurings are hushed and the storm becomes a calm."

Like Charles Lamb, she entered silence as a kind of temple of the spirit, and in it found healing and religious peace. "I have often thought the benefits of true silence are far too little sought after, even by those religiously disposed; and this I do not say as a Quaker, but as one who has some little experience of the necessity of having the human nature brought into subjection before God. . . . It is 'in the stillness of all flesh' that we must approach the Father of Spirits."

The melancholy of an emptying house began to fall upon Earlham Hall. Four were now married; Sam was in London, Daniel away at school; and the remaining sisters were often visiting the married homes. Buxton, like all the men who married Gurneys, assuaged his bride's homesickness by spending the last weeks of the honeymoon at Earlham; but when they finally drove away with Priscilla to be their first guest, the house and grounds were taken with a dreadful quiet. "After you drove off on Tuesday evening," writes Rachel, "my father and Joseph and I walked through the garden and along the path towards the violet-grove, all deeply impressed by parting with you. At last my father burst into tears, which, you may be sure, affected us not a little. Upon recovering himself he opened his heart to us in the sweetest manner about you. . . . Indeed, though the way in which he spoke of all his children drew tears from me, it has left a peaceful impression on my mind. After this intimate disburdening of our feelings we became more comfortable, and on our arrival by the river-side, found some boys fishing, whom we brought in for a feast of strawberries." But a final touch of forlornness comes next morning. "We three were the only Gurneys at Meeting."

At Mildred's Court, however, everything was cheerful bustle and increasing life. Betsy had been warmly concerned, though at a distance, with the love affairs of Louisa, John, and Hannah. But she had one going on under her own wing and eye in which her feelings were of necessity more deeply involved. Her dearest Sam had become acquainted, while under her roof, with a most charming and suitable girl, Elizabeth Sheppard, who lived with her parents at Ham House in Essex, close to Plashet. Mrs. Sheppard was a Gurney, a cousin of the Earlham group, and Betsy had undoubtedly, in encouraging free intercourse between Ham House, Plashet, and Mildred's Court, been indulging in a little innocent matchmaking. Samuel Gurney was not twenty-one years old, remarkably handsome, with a fine bearing, and already showing promise of that genius for finance that was to make him one of the richest men of his time. His father had recently started him in business with the firm of Richardson and Overend, bill brokers in Lombard Street, in close connection with the Norwich Bank. His ambition was finding scope for action. But before Elizabeth Sheppard's shy and gentle beauty his self-confidence vanished. He was "almost afraid to look at or be near her . . . exceedingly in love." At last he wrote to his father to apply for him in due form; they were engaged in November, and married in April 1808 at Barking Meetinghouse, London.

Betsy was almost prevented from being at the wedding by the ill-health following the birth in February of her fifth child. But on April ninth she records triumphantly: "Poorly all night, so much so that my attending dear Sam's wedding appeared almost out of the question, but to the surprise of all that knew my state of body I attended this wedding. I did feel deeply for dear Sam and Eliz."

This fifth baby was another daughter, Richenda. A nursery governess had now been added to the Mildred's Court household. "I felt a good deal about Mary Ann Davies coming to teach the children and live here, fearing for the peace of our nursery establishment." But Joseph is certain that it will be for the best. It will help Betsy to keep well, and give her more time for other things. "My dear Joseph's truly sweet and amiable state is a great comfort to me."

And now May is here again. It seems only yesterday that Hannah was being married. But another call and of a different kind summons the family together to Earlham among the scents of spring. Last year the Hall was overrun with bridesmaids in roses and chip hats, and a wedding chaise drove gayly down the avenue. But now it is a hearse that advances slowly under the flowering limes. And of the group that waits it by the doorway all are weeping. Ah, Betsy may sometimes feel "in a valley mentally and bodily"; may record that she feels as if she had "hardly any sense of any good thing or hardly a good desire, and also tryed with nervous feelings"; but these things pass. Health returns. She has five lively children as her recompense at home. But John's cousin wife, the beautiful Elizabeth, has died of her first child.

Did John think that it was a judgment on him? At any rate, he was never the same man after. Body and mind declined, and he died seven years later at the age of thirty-four.

With the falling of the leaves that year, Father Fry also put off his worn-out body and brought to a suitable finish his honest and unremarkable life. Avoiding the tricks of animal magnetism, he came to Mildred's Court and put himself unreservedly into the capable hands of his daughter-in-law. Five weeks of nursing fed their mutual affection. In a moment of consciousness before the end he murmured to her gratefully that he was "comfortable, comfortable, comfortable." And it drew from her tears of pleasure. She had long forgotten the rough words and ways that used to vex and pain her. "I loved him very dearly, and his memory is sweet to me."[82]

[82] *Memoir*, I, 153.

VIII

THE LADY OF THE MANOR

1

THE death of William Storrs Fry made a very great change in Elizabeth's life. Her husband inherited the house and estate of Plashet, in the parish of East Ham, near Epping Forest, and for the next twenty years Elizabeth was the mistress of a home as ample and as beautiful as Earlham Hall.

But before she could give her attention to preparing for removal and the organization of a new household, another case of sickness claimed her skill. Sister Hannah fell ill. Fowell Buxton had two sisters-in-law in London, one of whom as yet had no children, and he had an unmarried sister of his own not far off. But in his extremity neither he nor Hannah hesitated to call on Betsy. And Betsy did not hesitate to respond. None of them knew, until too late, that the illness was scarlet fever. "Being the only sister at liberty I have nursed her. This I consider a great privilege to be able to do: though I have felt it a very serious thing, with a young babe, and the mother of so many little lambs, to enter so catching a disorder." She is half afraid of a reckless selfishness in this matter; it would be very wrong to risk the children's health "to gratify inclination, which leads me to enjoy nursing those I love so dearly." But "indeed, I had hardly an option, as I was in the first instance brought into it not knowing what the complaint was; and in the second, there was no one else that I thought proper to take my place, as dear Louisa was prevented."[1]

Fortunately, neither Hannah's young baby nor Elizabeth's caught the disorder that time, and, though probation periods were not understood, neither did any other of Elizabeth's "little lambs" — perhaps partly owing to the advanced hygiene taught and practised by Dr. Sims. Elizabeth takes up the thread of her unoccupied life, and begins to make plans for Plashet, going down there with Joseph and seeing about rearrangements, engaging servants and all the rest. She is so obviously "at liberty" that it is only natural that Aunt Hankin, falling ill toward Christmas time, should demand her help. Betsy takes it as a matter of course. "Since I last wrote I have been much occupied in attending poor Aunt Hankin who is very ill."

And what, one wonders, this time prevented dear Louisa?

Curiously enough, by January, Elizabeth herself was ill and exhausted, so much so that she thought of death and wistfully begged Providence "that I might live long enough to do a little more good here." But by the middle of February she was conscious of a double reason for living. "I think I feel my present situation almost like a fresh tie to the world. These dear babes do attach me very much here. I think the trying times I mostly have after my confinements are evidently for my good and prevent my *resting* in the enjoyments of increasing family as I might otherwise do." September is a long way off, one can be philosophical; and meanwhile one hopes one is not getting *too* dependent on Dr. Sims, "his having been an instrument of help and comfort in many tryed moments." But in almost the next entry her innocent heart and warm temperament are feeling

[1] *Memoir*, I, 154.

"love without bound" for a traveling Friend, John Wigham, "a nice old man in the lower line of life, but indeed there appears something better than himself to live in him and sanctify him." And oh, the delights, the unspeakable delights, of Plashet in the spring! To roam into Epping Forest with the children, and dig up violets and primroses and carry them back to plant under her own trees; to feed the fish in the ornamental fish ponds; to watch the birds building and brooding and rearing their young; to renew the pleasures of her childhood, and more than that, for here was a new freedom, and the proud joy of authority. She was mistress of these wide acres. Joe of course was master, and she deferred to him winningly. But Joe was a banker, and had to go up to the city every day. The management of the house, gardens, and farm more and more fell to Elizabeth.

It was a life after her own heart, especially as she saw already many things to do in the village beyond. Joseph too was intensely happy. Peace flowed like a river. "My beloved Joseph sweetly tendered under a sense of good. I felt him a sweet companion, and that we may be inabled to go hand in hand helping one another and not drawing one another back."

But in the meantime there was the May visit to Earlham (how glad she was afterwards that not even spring at Plashet had prevented that!) and then there was Yearly Meeting, and Mildred's Court must offer its usual hospitality; and that was hardly over before there was an urgent message from her dear brother Sam, who could trust no one but herself to see his precious Elizabeth through her first confinement. In this case at least, though it was a "privilege," Betsy could not feel herself to be gratifying inclination. Only by the most urgent appeals to her unseen Helper did she feel able to go through with it. She knew too much; and her own time was too near. Nerves, imagination, and sympathy were strained to the utmost. She could only record it as "a trial . . . which at one time I felt no strength to encounter; but power and courage were given me sufficient for the day."[2]

What astonishing cruelty young husbands can perpetrate on their sisters when thinking only of the welfare of their wives. However, that was hardly over when sister Fry broke a blood vessel, and was dangerously ill. William, panic-stricken, threw animal magnetism to the winds and called for Elizabeth; and Elizabeth came, and nursed, and admired Eliza's patience!

But afterward, somehow, Betsy did not feel at all well. She moved about her duties at Plashet, or sat out on its pleasant lawns, low-spirited and languid, and reproached herself for "nervous complaints." She must simply endeavor to bear them patiently; she thought she knew herself what was best to take for them. August was better; August was lovely. And then came September, and the harvest moon, and blackberries thick on the hedges; it is the thirteenth. "Time runs on apace. I desire my imagination may not dwell on that which is before it."[3]

Her sixth child, Joseph, was born at Plashet on September the twentieth.

2

She was at Tunbridge Wells, recuperating, when a budget of news arrived from Earlham. Brother Daniel, now in the bank at Lynn, had been sick of the scarlet fever, and dear old Nurse, taking care of him, had taken the contagion and died of it. Priscilla was now lying ill with scarlet fever at Earlham Hall, and Father was seriously ill after an operation. While they were considering how urgent this news might be, further word arrived that John Gurney was dying.

[2] *Memoir*, I, 159.   [3] *Ibid.*, I, 160.

Then, without further delay, they undertook one of those miserable journeys, so wretched to endure, so forlorn in retrospect; hounded on by suspense, yet unable to hurry; the only hope before them that of seeing once more the beloved in the dear familiar shape of human life.

In spite of Betsy's delicate state, they made the journey from London in one day,[4] and reached Earlham Hall at midnight. It was not without compunction that Betsy, stepping out under the dark shapes of the sighing trees and seeing pale and tear-stained faces in the shifting light of lanterns, realized that she was carrying her newborn son into a house where fever was. But her father, at this moment, had the first claim. Someone took her child and her wraps, Joe's hand was supporting her, Rachel's arm was round her. They went at once up the staircase to her father's room. So "I once more saw him who has been so inexpressibly dear to me through life, since I knew what love was. He was asleep, but death was strongly marked on his sweet, and to me, beautiful face."

In that sleep he gently died, at dawn, the twenty-eighth of October, 1809.

The funeral was at the Gildencroft, the green and quiet Quaker burying ground in the heart of the city of Norwich. The family were all present, including Dan and Priscilla, who had just risen up from beds of sickness: "Catherine composed throughout, but Richenda sobbing audibly. It was truly affecting to see Dan in the Meeting-house, scarcely able to support himself, leaning on the coffin with one arm and holding up his sobbing sister Priscilla with the other. I cannot express how touching Mr. Joseph Gurney's simple address was."[5] In the silence that followed, a silence that

---

[4] They did spend one night in London, at Mildred's Court, after coming there from Tunbridge Wells.

[5] Account of an eyewitness, quoted by Hare, in *Gurneys of Earlham*, I, 206.

might, in the Quaker ritual, equally suitably remain unbroken or be broken by any man or woman who felt "led" to do so, a remarkable thing happened. A sudden uprush of sweetness and love took place in Elizabeth's heart, a certainty of God and of life beyond the grave, with all its accompanying joy. Without effort, as spontaneously as a child, she opened her lips to give that feeling an inevitable utterance. Her sweet, clear voice was heard, saying a text in the form of a prayer: "Great and marvellous are thy works, Lord God Almighty, just and true are all thy ways, thou king of saints: be pleased to receive our thanksgiving!" [6] That was all. But the effect was electric. To her husband, her brothers, her sisters, her friends, and afterwards to herself, it marked an epoch.

Ever since the visit of William Savery to Norwich, Elizabeth had looked forward with dread to this sort of possibility. Now it had come; and it brought with it a great, an extraordinary, release. She felt "a quiet, calm and *invigorated* state, mental and bodyly, as my portion afterwards."

The reactions of her family were various, and she was made aware of most of them. Uncle Joseph was, of course, most deeply pleased. Her sisters were mainly sympathetic and encouraging. Even Catherine (who had recently joined the Church of England and marked it by wearing mourning in solitary correctness at her father's funeral) felt that it had been suitable. If you could not have the dignity and poetry of the Church burial service, why, it was better to have something than nothing at all. Brothers Joseph and Samuel were cordial supporters. To each, Betsy was a favorite sister; and both were also markedly Quaker in their outlook, particularly Joseph, who was already an able speaker himself and was warm to welcome Betsy into that service. But John, who had, up to his bereavement, been much more of the

[6] *Memoir*, I, 165.

"swell," the society man of the family, who had been in great social demand, and who had, more than anyone, used all his influence, all his arts, to prevent Betsy from giving up dancing, had a strong masculine prejudice (most unquakerlike) against any public speaking by women. He made his discouragement felt. Daniel was too young to do so; but he recorded in later life that it was the funerals more than anything — the "public exhibition" of the family, with both men and women speaking — that had driven him away from the Society of Friends. However, no one could avoid giving Betsy "great love and kindness." And above all, she had her husband's full and frank approval. "My husband has been a true helpmate and sweet counsellor."

None the less, on the human side, grief would surge back. Whatever one might believe of heaven, the earth was sadly changed. One was too painfully conscious of "not-returning Time." "Now to have father, mother and nurse all taken from us, and to be ourselves occupying the situations they then held, and to have children coming on, who are in the same way to succeed us" — such reflections bring home to one the relentless march of the generations. And Earlham, dear as it is, and often as they may gather there, will never be the same again. It has lost its heart.

3

November is not England's loveliest month, but at Plashet that year it held for Elizabeth an immense peace. The smell of burning leaves, the dim aisles of the denuded forest, the purple, misty distances, brought her health of body and mind after a strenuous season of pain. Walking with renewed vigor about the quiet lanes, meeting now a countryman in white smock frock, or an old crone in a red cloak, or a scattering of children, with bobs and curtseys, she felt no more the old nostalgia for her childhood at Earlham. This richer, softer country was truly home, was truly hers. She felt herself again taking root, and hoped that this time it might be forever. She wanted nothing better than this.

It would have been hard to say whether she or Joseph or the children were the happiest to leave their London house behind. The children were exuberant; but Joseph was far from in a low spot. Even the ride or drive in daily to the city was an enjoyment to him. And no one knew what it meant to Elizabeth to come out of her front door in the morning and smell again wet grass instead of coffee, to watch the arrowy play of other birds than sparrows, and to feel around her the wide peace of the country. She loved the settled and the permanent. She liked to feel that "the poor" here dwelled year after year in the same little cottages, were born and married and died, and could be truly and intimately known. They were "her poor." And she set to work at once, now that winter was coming on, to find out their needs and supply them. Delightful task! Sweet privilege of riches!

The Vicar, Mr. Angelzaark, and his devoted wife were overjoyed to find the new mistress of Plashet in this temper. You never knew with Quakers whether they would co-operate at all with affairs outside their sect or not. The former owners of Plashet had stuck very firmly inside a narrow Quaker orbit. But Mr. Angelzaark found that the heirs were very different. Mr. Fry was bluff, good-natured, and generous. Mrs. Fry was not only easy of approach, but behind her beautiful manners lurked an actual eagerness to meet him more than halfway, to draw on his information, to seek his advice, to share in his labors for the betterment of the parish. Mrs. Angelzaark acted as guide to many a needy home. A warm friendship sprang up between them.

It was to Mrs. Angelzaark, many years later, that Elizabeth Fry made one of the most intimate confidences of her life. She showed her one day the text in the Bible that spoke the closest to her: "Lord, I believe: help thou mine unbelief!"

As winter mud and snow made progress difficult about the lanes, and hunger tightened the belt in overcrowded cottages where children were numerous and reserves were few, Mrs. Fry started a soup kitchen in one of her large barns, where all who cared to come with some home vessel could be supplied for the asking.

Such lavish, indiscriminate charity encouraged vagrants, as Harriet Martineau was later to point out: but a generation struggling inadequately with unemployment relief could only answer that even vagrants must be fed. And it is cheaper to feed them gratis than to let them steal.

Elizabeth Fry was never, like Harriet Martineau, a theorist. But if she had a theory of the social order it was that if all who had money did their duty for the benefit of their immediate neighborhood and any others of their fellow creatures who aroused their interest, then misery would soon cease to exist.

Before she died, she did hear vaguely of some people called Socialists, and uttered a few sentences in their condemnation. As far as she could make out, their chief peculiarity was that they did not believe in God.

By the time the short English winter passed and the slow spring began, the Plashet family felt themselves entering on a happy routine of life that might go on indefinitely, pleasantly varied by the changing seasons. The projects which each formed for the future were suggested by their surroundings, and made possible because of them. Joseph Fry bethought himself of his old well-loved sports of hunting and fishing, as well as the improvement of the estate; the children had schemes connected with farm, garden, and animals; and Elizabeth had plans on foot far more lively in her interest than dull, though necessary, soup. But she, too, loved the garden. She loved to plant, and pull up weeds, and neaten and beautify. Some of the best memories that her children had of her in later life centred around their joint gardening in the spacious grounds of Plashet, when they fluffed and fussed around her with their little trowels and forks, and had their own individual gardens to attend to, as well as importantly helping her with hers.

There were other jolly hours with her for her children to remember, in the village, visiting the poor. Each child was allowed to have something to give, and to give it at his or her own impulse and will, being only required afterwards to render a good reason for it. Irish Row was particularly fascinating, a little colony of Irish about half a mile from Plashet, where wit and warmth of heart and happy-go-lucky tempers, and pigs and chickens actually in the house with you, gave a charm to dirt and poverty, shed somehow a fairy-tale atmosphere about the Fry children, who had never had a fairy tale. "Oh, Mother, do let's go to Irish Row!" And Elizabeth liked it almost as well as the children. It made her laugh to be offered an overturned bucket for a seat with ceremonious, eager politeness, and to be in the midst of a great fluster of chickens that her hostess was trying to scurry out of the apartment. How the children laughed, simply roaring until tears ran out of their little eyes. And the Irish children would join in, just because laughter was so easily contagious, and the ragged mother would laugh in the midst of her exasperation with the stupid chickens. And there would be a gale of cheerful noise and a feeling of sunshine even if the skies were gray. One would leave one's gifts, all warmed, all mellowed and sweetened by good will, and go home in a glow.

Or, if the Irish were in sorrow, how intense was their grief! Madam Fry would share with the priest the task of comfort, around the rough coffin with the paper cross upon the dead. Quakers had discarded symbols only to endeavor to come closer to that which the symbol stood for. "There are differences of administration, but the same spirit." And she would help them to defray the expense of the funeral, not closely inquiring as to whether she was paying for a Mass.

For her guidance in educating her children she had written in her journal: "Children should be deeply impressed with the belief that the first and great object of their education is to follow Christ and indeed to be true Christians; and those things on which we, the Society of Friends, differ from the world in general, should not, I think, be impressed upon them by only saying, as is often done, 'because Friends do it,' but singly and simply as things that the Christian life appears to us to require, and that therefore they must be done. They should also early be taught that all have not seen exactly the same, but that there may be many equally belonging to the church of Christ who may in other respects be as much stricter than ourselves as we are than they in these matters."

Holding these views, it was natural that she not only should coöperate warmly with Mr. Angelzaark, but should enlist his help in her own projects. The first and most important of these was of course a school.[7]

She found a large, disused room not far from her house that served every purpose as a schoolroom in days when even Christ's Hospital, with its high standard of scholarship, taught all its 600 scholars in one large hall.[8] A competent schoolmistress was engaged, trained in the Lancasterian method, and by the vicar's help some seventy children were soon enrolled, each one of whom was ere long able to read aloud in the evening to its astounded parents out of real books, and write, if necessary, all the family letters. Books themselves being very scarce, Mrs. Fry was quick to give a whole Bible to proficient readers. And there is no better or more compact library.

[7] *Memoir*, I, 155.
[8] Lamb's Essay on "Recollections of Christ's Hospital."

The matter of the education of the poor was much under discussion in the early nineteenth century. Some argued for a scheme of national education, and some maintained that book learning would only unfit the laborer, and especially his wife, for their tasks, and give them ideas above their station. "It is undoubtedly to be desired that everyone should be able to read," said the poet Wordsworth, in 1828, "and perhaps (for that is far from being equally apparent) to write." But he makes the point that one of the best and happiest men he knows is quite illiterate. "I cannot but think that there is too much indiscriminate gratuitous instruction in this country." His final argument is clinching. "Can it, in a *general* view, be good that an infant should learn much which its *parents do not know?* Will not the child arrogate a superiority unfavourable to love and obedience?" [9]

As for a system of national education, fundamental principles apart, it would obviously be impracticable in a country like England. "In Switzerland, or Sweden, or Norway, or France, or Spain — or anywhere but Great Britain — it would be comparatively easy.[10] . . . My dear Wrangham, begin your education at the top of society; let the head go in the right course and the tail will follow." [11]

But Mrs. Joseph Fry of Plashet House did not care a pin about heads and tails, about implications and far-reaching

[9] Letter to Hugh James Rose.
[10] Germany was far ahead. Lady Lyttleton visited Leipsig in 1814 and "went to the Burgerschule. Great, clean, orderly establishment for 700 citizens' children, girls and boys. Each pays but about a guinea and a half a year, and learns reading, writing, accounts, geography, Latin, and general knowledge on subjects of natural history. We attended a lesson given to a room full of girls on natural history. Pretty girls of all ages answering very unshyly and not particularly well. . . . Heard of a fine school for 700 poor children here, and six or seven other great schools, so that 7000 children receive instruction daily in this town." (*Correspondence of Lady Lyttleton*)
[11] Letter to Francis Wrangham.

effects, about unfitting the laborer for his station or setting the child above the parent. She knew that reading and writing were tools for the soul, keys to regions of the spirit. And she set out to give them, and other benefits of schooling, to every child that she could reach. She did not think in national terms but in personal ones. Here were John Smith's five children, and the head gardener's two, and the coachman's seven, and the ten little rowdies of Judy O'Grady, and so on, in a sum of human units, as she grew to know her countryside, family by family. The school flourished exceedingly, and outlived her, being finally absorbed in the scheme for National Education.

Health was an equal concern with her. As we know, she loved to nurse. She could not actually nurse her sick cottagers, but she could advise and oversee, could provide remedies and comforts, could get good Dr. Sims or Dr. Willan to prescribe; and above all, she could vaccinate. She kept her neighborhood clear of smallpox.[12]

Her reputation flew about the countryside. When the gypsies came on their annual round and camped in a green lane near Plashet, and a desperate older brother sought her help for a sick child, she took them also under her wing. Each year she would go down to their camp with comforts for the frail or ill, and advice to the mothers on the care of babies. Her clear courtesy and friendly dignity appealed to them. She became "*our* Madam." They liked to see her Quaker dress kneeling in the green grass among their caravan, her fair face, framed in its dainty muslin cap, bending over one of their dark-skinned children, while her cool hands at once diagnosed and comforted. And the bold, hardy people had a charm for her. Something adventurous in herself responded to them.

But what opportunity for adventure was there for the wife of a wealthy banker? Except, of course, the adventure of

[12] *Memoir*, I, 191.

childbirth, which was excitement enough for most women.

The recurrent minor chord of the penalty she paid for maternity is a necessary part of the theme of her life. Body, mind, and soul were profoundly affected by it; and its very completeness, in dread, in anguish, in exhaustion, and in joy, makes her the more a whole woman.

4

But all the activities of the lady of Plashet remained secondary to a profounder activity in Elizabeth herself. On the day of her father's funeral she had taken a definite step into a new career. She believed that she had found her life work. It had been for years in the bottom of her thoughts that she might have to do the sort of thing that William Savery and Deborah Darby did (only, of course, in a smaller and humbler way). No other avenue of service appeared to her so valuable and important as this. But timidity had seemed to place an insurmountable barrier in the way. The removal of her fears seemed like a miracle. "What has appeared almost impossible to flesh and blood has been made not only possible but easy." Yet "it is very awful to be thus publicly exposed."

She was acutely sensitive to her husband's opinion, and would probably have been unable to make headway against it. But she could record, in October 1810, "my beloved Joseph a true helpmeet and sympathizer with me. I think the late public service I have been called into has very closely united us, and I believe proved a stimulant. What a comfort!"

In February 1811 her seventh child, Elizabeth, was born, and in March she was recorded on the meeting books as an approved minister. Priscilla was with her, and she was very happy. The "recording" seemed to her one of the important events of her life. It did not appoint her to preach, or require her to preach, anywhere or at any time, but it expressed approval of her speaking and a hope that her gift would continue to be exercised.

Priscilla was recorded by the Norwich Meeting a few months later. And the same distinction was conferred on Joseph John Gurney.

The practice of "recording ministers" has been now entirely dropped by the Society of Friends in England. There are no "Quaker ministers" of this generation to be found there. The reasons for discontinuing the practice were that it was almost universally misunderstood by other churches; and it led to a certain cleavage, a slight approach to "priesthood" and "laity," within the spiritual democracy of the Quaker body. The Quaker ideal is very different from this. It demands a universal responsibility, an alertness in every mind to the possibility of being on this occasion, if never before or after, the channel for Truth.

Such were some of the meetings of George Fox's period, into which Robert Barclay, Elizabeth Fry's great-great-grandfather,[13] entered as a stranger and said, "When I came into the silent assemblies of God's people, I found a Power among them which touched my heart."

A very lively, fresh, spontaneous sort of preaching can arise here and there, through different individuals, out of the Quaker method. And Elizabeth Fry, now thirty-one years old, not all her girlish grace entirely lost, although with a matronly dignity beginning to show itself, with her singer's voice, and her slightly different way of putting things, made an immediate appeal. It gave, too, the right kind of example to all other young women. There were many mothers whose domestic cares made them quite indifferent to the needs of the meeting, and whose spirits were becoming stifled under piles of cookery and baby linen. "Come away from these things for an hour," said Elizabeth's

[13] On her mother's side.

example, "are not we also citizens of the Kingdom of Heaven?"

For Elizabeth herself, it was more than an escape. Laying aside her troublesome accounts, and the bothersome questions of little Rachel's pert manners, and whether Baby's gums needed lancing or not, she pressed toward the veil of the Unseen. Another world, a world more real than this, seemed to lie beyond it. She almost, for the moments of her speaking, shared its life. Some air, some influence, passed through to her. "I have renewed evidence that there yet remains a God, hearing prayer." She acted on that evidence, and it increased. To become, even in the smallest degree, the messenger of God was an overwhelming experience. It deepened in her daily the sense of God's reality that she had so often felt slipping from her. And it seemed to lead her into that larger life of which she had dreamed.

But one of the drawbacks which Elizabeth soon found in being a recorded minister was that, being expected to sit on the "facing benches" or "minister's gallery," she could there from a point of vantage observe — and helplessly observe — the atrocious behavior of her children!

5

Katherine was now ten, Rachel eight, John seven, William five (there was something very sweet about William!), Richenda three, Joseph two, and of course little Elizabeth almost nothing. I suppose five little wrigglers came to meeting; and meeting lasted two hours. No wonder an agitated mother sometimes "broke up meeting prematurely . . . my dear children behaved so badly."

Well did she know that her more exalted station caused people to point the finger at her and say that "folk should practice what they preach," and "physician heal thyself," and other well-worn words. But when her children grew beyond babyhood, there was no denying that she found them very hard to manage. And her being a "minister" had nothing whatever to do with it. The children had been just as bad before. Had she but known it, sister Louisa's letter to sister Hannah could have witnessed for her that years before she undertook any public work her children had been noisy little brats.

Because of course it was not only in meeting. They were there, after all, comparatively quiet. It was at all kinds of times, and especially if one wanted them to behave particularly well. At Earlham, for instance, under the critical eyes of their maiden aunts, how they had romped and routed about, and quarreled and shouted! Betsy's journal at Earlham, in June 1808, had said: "The children not being more orderly has tryed me. I hardly know exactly how to act towards them but I do desire best direction and I have both hope and, I hope, a little faith concerning them that it will be well with them eventually." In the privacy of home she often found them "naughty and trying." [14] It was dreadfully discouraging. "I feel at times deeply pressed down on account of my beloved children. Their volatile minds try me, but," says her staunch mother-heart, "I have a secret hope concerning them that all will end well." [15]

Criticism of her children by other people, however, was politely suppressed (except for the most delicate of hints, perhaps, from dear Kitty or dear Aunt Jane) until Elizabeth began to demonstrate an ability to speak in meeting and an accompanying concern to visit, occasionally, other meetings. And then indeed there was an uproar. What! A mother leave her family? "But, Elizabeth, consider! Look at the results on your children!"

Elizabeth Fry was not away from home on any visiting or at other meetings until the summer of 1810, when she makes an apologetic reference to it in August. On

---

[14] *Memoir*, I, 182. [15] *Ibid.*, I, 182.

September 1 she was at Earlham on a "religious visit" to Norwich, Ipswich, and Colchester, and was home again by the tenth, "my little ones appearing to have prospered in my absence." [16] But in April she had been on quite an extensive business trip with her husband through the West of England; and in December she had taken three of her children into Gloucestershire to visit William and Eliza Fry (who were now living at Hill House, Rodborough, for Eliza's health), and left the major part of her family at home. Yet it is entirely her absences from home "in the ministry" that are picked upon as evidences of neglect.

Elizabeth's journal for February 4, 1811, reads: "Two things weigh on my mind and trouble me. One is hearing from dear Eliza the view John takes of my having to speak to others in ministry and that Norfolk journey, and the other the view I believe others take of my children — indeed it is an awful thing to have to *preach* when practice is so imperfect. I desire to examine where I can mend towards my beloved little ones, but it is not in my power to *turn* them or alter their motives, but I must in humility endeavour to do my best."

In August 1811 she was away for a little more than a week accompanying an American Friend, Henry Hull,[17] on some visits. And on August 20 she records that sisters Chenda and Louisa deal with her. "Dear Chenda thought the children ought to be under more subjection." (Dear Chenda is not married yet.) "Louisa thought I devoted that time to Friends that I should devote to them."

In September, Joseph John Gurney, now master of Earlham, invited her to the inauguration of the Norwich branch of the Bible Society, where the Bishop of Norwich and other attending clergy were astonished — but charmed — to have

---

[16] *Memoir*, I, 179.

[17] Her unmarried sister-in-law, Elizabeth Fry, was often her companion on these visits, applying for an "accompanying minute" so frequently as to vex E. F., who liked a variety of companions. And there was the confusion of identical names.

a lady take vocal part in the proceedings. Betsy stayed on until the end of September for a great family gathering, and during her visit "believed it best to tell Rachel and also told Priscilla my idea of attending the Suffolk Quarterly Meeting. They of course did not like it, but dear P. cast me very low by saying her faith was at times tried by my so often leaving my family. This was a home stroke."

No one had ever felt their faith tried by Betsy's leaving her family to nurse scarlet fever or broken blood vessels or a dying mother-in-law. But Betsy never uses this defense. She only clings fast to her conviction that she has duties outside her home as well as in, and that she must herself somehow find the right balance between them. After all, she reminds herself when very hurt, life is short, and what do people's opinions of one matter in so short a span? Yet she does mind, too. She minds always, very, very much. But she keeps on her course.

After all, no one knows better than she that she is not always good for her children. Perhaps "I indulge them too much when young, I mean very little, and perhaps their nurses do so too."

Occasional absences seem rather to readjust their relationships, and soothe irritated nerves on both sides. It is not, alas, as if she were a really good educator of youngsters so willful, so determined, and so dear. After the heart-searching occasioned especially by her dear, her loyal Priscilla, she says, in October 1811, "My beloved children cause me much uneasiness. I fear they suffer much from my not having the knack of managing them. I often feel very low and much try'd by it. I think neither my husband nor myself have the right art with them."

Yet her letters to her children are the only readable letters she ever wrote.[18]

On that West of England journey with her husband,

---

[18] Except one or two that she wrote to officials on the subject of prison reform.

which included a visit to William and Eliza, she wrote home to her children from Cowley Bridge, April 1810: "I suppose my sweet little flock will be glad to hear of the adventures of their papa, mamma, Sarah,[19] and baby, and therefore I mean to make as good a story as I can of what has happened to us, in our journey from Mildred's Court [20] to Cowley Bridge. In the first place, we admired the grand houses, and saw the Queen's Palace, and before we had gone much further we passed near one belonging to the King; but much as I should have liked it, we neither saw King nor Queen. Of the first day's journey I do not remember much, except that I often thought of you who were left at home. There were some beautiful deer feeding in a park, that I think you would have liked very much to see. I almost longed for my little gardeners with our trowels etc. to get some of the many primroses and violets there were in the hedges.[21] In some places almost like a carpet of green, blue and yellow, and the further we have gone the more we have seen.

"On Sixth day (Friday) night we slept at Andover, and I felt rather low. I hope, my dear children, you will each try to give me the pleasure, when I come home, of hearing you have been going on as I should like.

"On our second day's journey we went up and down a great many hills till we arrived at Dorchester, where we met dear Anna Buxton and went with her to a Friend's house at Bridport, who had fourteen children, and one nearly the age of each of you; and they quite enjoyed to hear of you.

"To-day we arrived here to dinner, and I hope I find your dear aunt not worse than when we parted from her. The place is very beautiful, hills, vales and water.

[19] The accompanying female attendant.

[20] They drove in from Plashet to Mildred's Court, spent one night there, and from thence started their main journey.

[21] There were only fifteen million people in all England in those days, and it was quite all right to dig up a few wild flowers for one's own garden.

"My love to Harriet and Mary Ann, and kind remembrance to all the servants. Yours in tender love. . . ."[22]

And when any of them were ill, what a nurse she was, as one of her nieces gratefully recorded, with "her soft hands, her sweet voice, her delicious company."

Deplore as she may her shortcomings as a mother, the fact remains that hers was the largest and the most vigorous family of the Earlham stock.

6

So the river of her life deepened and widened, and she thought that she saw clearly the course it was taking and was to take. It was an abundant life, full of opportunities and of variety.

The mere hospitality of a house like Plashet was no trifle. There were house parties ("eighteen in addition to our own family slept here last night"), garden parties, dinners. Every Sunday, either Fowell Buxton and Hannah, or Sam Hoare and Louisa, would drive over from Hampstead; or brother Sam and his Elizabeth would stroll over from Ham House; or all of them at once, with their increasing children, in a family gathering that suggested the old days at Earlham — with a difference. Priscilla was often a guest of one or the other. And though there were gray times, as when "I believe that five of my dear children have the hooping-cough," there was on the whole that atmosphere of sunny peace which indicates in the beginning of the middle years that the pattern of life is now set, and set pleasantly.

Yet there were moments when Elizabeth would oddly record, "I long . . . not to be a drone"; or, with stranger discouragement, "I fear that my life is slipping away to little purpose."

[22] *Memoir*, I, 174.

On September 12, 1812, her eighth child, Hannah, was born.

7

In October 1812 began Napoleon's retreat from Moscow. The reverberation of that terrible march made itself felt in England in unsettled finances. There was a run on several of the private banks, and the Fry Bank itself was in danger. When the first warnings of trouble reach the seeming security of Plashet, Elizabeth takes note of the fact that she is far from indifferent to fortune. "I could desire . . . that if right for us, we may be able through life to live in the open liberal way we do now, endeavouring to make all around us comfortable, and that we may be able to continue generous friends to the poor. I fear to be much limited would be very difficult to me." [23]

On October 18 her shock vibrates in a bald entry: "It appears that without help the banking-house must stop payment." But on November 2 "brothers John and Sam and Hudson and J. Overend met at M. Court to look into the real state of our affairs which proved very satisfactory, all things being in such nice order and the state of the business in general so good that there appear'd no doubt Gurneys would do what was needful for us and according to human probability we should be safely carried through."

It was a time of mental strain, just when she was in any case feeling low and unwell after her confinement. And to have to close Plashet for the winter and move in to Mildred's Court was a very unwelcome plan. "I am almost surprised at myself, the tears have often risen; very few, I believe none know, how sweet the quiet and the beauties of the country have been to me; it takes hold of some of my tender feelings." [24]

[23] *Memoir*, I, 214.   [24] *Ibid.*, I, 220.

But her destiny required her to be in London that winter. And the unheard horn of the future was at her ear when the grayness of London around the house in Mildred's Court made her say to herself that compared with Plashet it was like a prison.

IX

STEPHEN GRELLET

1

IN the winter of 1812–1813 there came to London a Frenchman, who was also an American Quaker, called Stephen Grellet. Like William Savery before him, he was "travelling in the ministry." He had been in the British Isles since June 1811, and, though more evangelical, he resembled Savery in charm of address and in a passion for peace, which he never hesitated to express even in time of war. As he passed from one Friends' Meeting to another, he took every opportunity of visiting the French prisoners, some of whom had been fairly recently captured, and some of whom had been in durance since long before the abortive Treaty of Amiens.

"Baneful indeed is the scourge of war," he wrote in his journal in 1812. "With deep anguish of spirit I have visited this portion of my fellow-men. . . . Some of them have been prisoners for nine years, and many, I find, have been brought up tenderly, even in affluence, having been conscripts that were forcibly taken from their homes, bands of whom I saw in France, fifty or more chained together, dragged as sheep to the slaughter. . . . Some of them are contented in their present bonds, under the consideration that were they liberated and sent back to France, they would soon be driven again into the army and placed in a condition worse than the present."[1] He exhorted them to liberate their spirits from sin, by faith in Christ, even if their bodies should remain many years more in captivity; but arriving in Birmingham in the heart of the munition industry he called together a large meeting of munition makers and used the sufferings of the prisoners, among other examples, to point remarks already sharp and burning in their quality. "The crowd in the house was so great and those out of doors so numerous that I feared for the consequences."[2] But that did not make him hesitate "to proclaim what the Christian religion is, it leads to love and peace; the cause of war was unfolded, its awful and dreadful consequences, misery, wasting and destruction." Everyone in the early nineteenth century had at least a conscience. Grellet's words were temporarily painful. There was no riot. "The meeting concluded in stillness."

He had told the French prisoners that later he intended to take his message to France, and so he did, and was several times arrested and more than once in danger of death. But that is another story.

His position in England was doubly peculiar as a Frenchman who was also an American, for the War of 1812 had broken out, and England was at war with both countries. There were at least two Acts of Parliament that could have been invoked against him, the Alien Act of 1793 for the supervision and, if necessary, removal of aliens, and the Seditious Meetings Bill of 1795. But the war fever of 1793, which immediately followed the first declaration of war after the French Revolution, was not so hot in 1812.

Grellet went on his illuminated way unmolested, both ignorant of his risks and indifferent to them. And of course

[1] Benjamin Seebohm, *Memoirs of the Life of Stephen Grellet*, I, 211.
[2] *Ibid.*, I, 209.

the majority of his meetings were of a more "gospel" turn, closely resembling the preaching of John Wesley, and politically inoffensive. But he was a man of intense, even passionate sympathies. His journal, like Savery's, is full of information about social conditions. Born in wealthy and cultivated circles, and never having known the need of money (first by birth and next by his own ability), he none the less knew and felt the wrongs and sorrows of the poor. Many traveling Friends would pass through a country with their eyes exclusively fixed on their own and others' spiritual condition. But not Grellet. He notes that in the Yorkshire and Lancashire dales, in the autumn of 1812, wheat is at twenty-two shillings a bushel and oats at twelve shillings, reducing the poor to a diet of potatoes and chaff. "They knit woolen stockings; men, women and children, walking in the fields or highways, keep on knitting as fast as they can."[3]

Grellet reached London in midwinter. "Felt deeply for the sufferings of a large portion of the laboring class in this city, believed it to be my duty to have religious meetings among them; great numbers are out of employment, in consequence of the stagnation of business caused by the desolating war; general scarcity of bread throughout this country."[4] The importation of wheat, oats, and so on, had been forbidden, in a mistaken effort to maintain the prosperity of agriculture by keeping up the price of home-grown grain.

But no longer are Quakers being rolled in the mud for it. A new generation has come to maturity, with a new point of view, a wider sense of responsibility. "Friends [that is, Quakers] generally active and liberal. One of them has sent to London from his own purse the enormous amount of 17,000 pounds sterling, besides what he has bestowed in his own neighborhood."[5]

It is quite touching to learn that some of the rich were

[3] Seebohm, I, 204.   [4] *Ibid.*, I, 215.   [5] *Ibid.*, I, 215.

trying, in self-sacrificing stupidity, to help, by reducing their own consumption of bread and eating rice and other cereals instead.

Stephen Grellet felt that "rich and poor, but especially the last, including not only those at large and in the various poor-houses but also their inmates of prisons and places where many are confined because of their various vices, rested heavily upon me." [6]

With the consent of London Friends, who were by this time entirely under his remarkable spell, he called a meeting in the Meetinghouse, St. Martin's Lane (as most convenient for his purpose), for thieves, pickpockets, and prostitutes. Since such people were night-hawks, the meeting was set for seven P.M., January 19, 1813. Strange to say, a large number of these dregs of the population turned up. Grellet was greatly moved to see that they were mostly young people. "I wept bitterly over them." That indeed was what they had not expected. "The lofty heads, the proud looks were brought down. I have seldom known such brokenness and so general as it was that evening." [7]

The Chief Police Magistrate, much impressed, kindly offered to collect *all* the scum of London for Mr. Grellet. But Mr. Grellet declined, and asked only for a permit to visit the prisons.

So in due course he came to Newgate, "which occupied some days, having religious opportunities in the many separate apartments where the miserable inmates are confined. Several were under sentence of death. . . ." [8] And at last he had been everywhere except to the women's quarter.

"The visit to that part of Newgate which is occupied by the women prisoners had very nearly been frustrated. The jailer endeavoured to prevent my going there, representing them as so unruly and desperate a set that they would surely do me some mischief; he had endeavoured in vain to reduce

[6] Seebohm, I, 214.   [7] *Ibid.*, I, 220.   [8] *Ibid.*, I, 221.

them to order, and said he could not be responsible for what they might do to me, concluding that the very least I might expect was to have my clothes torn off." [9] Grellet, however, was certain, as usual, where his duty lay, and obtained his end. He visited not only the women's yard, but the "sick ones upstairs." He had seen much misery in his time, but what he saw there was so beyond the limits of humanity that it seemed to him amazing that the very jailers could bear to leave it as it was.

"On going up, I was astonished beyond description at the mass of woe and misery I beheld. I found many very sick, lying on the bare floor or on some old straw, having very scanty covering over them, though it was quite cold; and there were several children born in the prison among them, almost naked." [10]

This was January of a cold winter. "On leaving that abode of wretchedness and misery, I went to Mildred's Court, to my much valued friend Elizabeth J. Fry,[11] to whom I described, out of the fulness of my heart, what I had just beheld, stating also that something must be done immediately for these poor suffering children. The appeal was not in vain. She immediately sent for several pieces of flannel, and had speedily collected a number of our young women Friends, who went to work with such diligence that on the very next day she repaired to the prison with a bundle of made-up garments for the naked children. What she then saw of the wretchedness of the prison induced her . . ." Ah, to what?

So simply, directly, and humanly was Elizabeth Fry

---

[9] Seebohm, I, 222.   [10] *Ibid.*, I, 224.

[11] Stephen Grellet always inserts her husband's initial into her name, to distinguish her from her two sisters-in-law, (Miss) Elizabeth Fry, and (Mrs.) Elizabeth Fry, William's wife. A young English Quaker called William Forster accompanied Grellet to the prison and also on his visit to Mildred's Court. He there met Anna Buxton, whom he married two years later. See *Memoirs of William Forster*, by Benjamin Seebohm.

called to that which others have chosen to regard as her life work.

2

Yet that visit of Stephen Grellet to Elizabeth Fry was, unknown to him, the last link in a very strange chain. There is often something psychic in the affairs of the Quakers. Elizabeth herself — neither mystic nor psychic — never knew what elaborate forces had apparently been set to work to bring her to flower. Or, to put it more modestly, at least what a curious set of coincidences had finally opened to her her path of service.

Far back in the year 1795, when Elizabeth had been a girl of fifteen, learning her lessons and playing pranks at Earlham, Étienne de Grellet du Mabillier, a young émigré from the French Revolution, had landed in New York with his brother. Their father was the son and heir of wealthy porcelain manufacturers in Limoges, had been ennobled by Louis XVI and made comptroller of the Mint. When the Revolution took place, the Grellets had found themselves naturally on the side of the aristocrats, and Étienne, then sixteen, had served in the reserves of the army which hoped to restore the King.

Now he and his brother sought their fortunes in a new world. Their estates were lost, and their father and mother in prison in France, likely any day to be brought to the guillotine.[12]

The young Grellets — who now dropped the rest of their name — had money enough to last for some time, with care, and soon left New York for a cheaper and quieter place. They picked on Newtown, Long Island, and, according to their father's maxim of always seeking the best company, shortly called upon the principal gentleman of the place,

---

[12] They were released the day after the death of Robespierre.

one Colonel Corsa, whose wife was a Franklin. Stephen's good looks had been marred by smallpox, but his graceful manners and interesting story won him the immediate friendship of the kindly Americans, and they were proud that their daughter's French was equal to the occasion. The two Grellets soon became intimates of the Corsa household, and worked hard at their English.

Naturally a youth like Stephen Grellet, brought up as an aristocrat, who had lived through the French Revolution and was now becoming a citizen of the new American republic, was bound to be thinking a great deal about theories of government. In this connection he made some inquiries about William Penn, and the intelligent Miss Corsa lent him the only book of Penn's in the house, a volume called *No Cross, No Crown*. Perhaps she had not read it herself. At any rate, a little work with the dictionary made clear to young Grellet that this book was not a political or social treatise, and he set it aside.

But it had touched something in his sensitive subconscious, and a few weeks afterwards, when walking in the fields alone, he had the first of those psychic experiences of which he was to have many. He was in a state of vague reverie, not religious (as he carefully explains), when "I was suddenly arrested by what seemed to be an awful voice proclaiming the words, 'Eternity, Eternity, Eternity.' . . . My whole man shook and it brought me, like Saul, to the ground."[13]

He returned home, took up *No Cross, No Crown*, in earnest, and struggled through it with a dictionary, twice. And thereafter began something of the same labor with an English Bible. Being a Catholic, he had not one in French.

In this curiously prepared state, "my brother and myself, being one day at Colonel Corsa's, heard that a Meeting of Divine Worship was appointed to be held the next day in the

[13] Seebohm, I, 20.

Friends' Meeting House by two English women on a religious visit to this land, to which we were invited. The Friends were Deborah Darby and Rebecca Young."

In the meeting, it was chiefly the silence which affected him, he was "so gathered in the temple of my heart before God," and could understand little of what was said. But he and his brother were invited to dine at Colonel Corsa's with D. D. and R. Y. After dinner, there was serious conversation, which the young Frenchman found it almost impossible to follow. "I could hardly understand a word of what was said, but as D. D. began to address my brother and myself it seemed as if the Lord opened my outward ear and my heart. . . . She seemed like one reading the pages of my heart, with clearness describing how it had been, and how it was with me. . . . No strength to withstand the Divine visitation was left in me. . . . I was like one introduced into a new world . . . my heart glowed with love to all . . . to be remembered as long as I have the use of my mental faculties." [14]

So Deborah Darby, of Colebrook Dale, was made the instrument of Stephen Grellet's "conversion."

Like Elizabeth Gurney with William Savery later, Grellet had many other conversations with her, taking trouble to go to places where she was to be found, and always finding that first great impression confirmed, that here was one who knew what it was to feel the Real Presence of Christ, and who could put him in touch with God Himself.

In the fall of 1796, Stephen Grellet became a Quaker. Speaking, and "travelling in the ministry," followed. His extraordinary psychic powers — which he interpreted as sensitiveness to the direct and immediate leadings of the Spirit of God — caused him often to speak with piercing exactitude to the condition of a person in the meeting who was completely a stranger to him. A murderer, for instance;

[14] *Ibid.*, I, 21.

or the President's wife. In 1809, at Washington, "D. Madison, the President's wife, and her sister, who were at meeting, appeared tender, and invited me to go and see them; they were formerly members of our Society."

These leadings also impelled him to go to the right place and person at the right time, as when he was "sent" to help with the yellow-fever epidemic in Philadelphia; "sent" suddenly home, in the midst of a preaching journey, to his wife and family, whom he found (without having had any outward communication from them) seriously ill; "sent" to England; "sent" to Newgate; and "sent" to Elizabeth Fry.

These people — Savery, Deborah Darby, Grellet — never had a dull moment. Their lives were filled with interest and surprise. They were forever engaged in purposeful activity of which they did not even require to know the result, satisfied with the mere doing. Life had in it nothing that they could fear (Grellet was able to experience an ecstasy of divine companionship in the torments of yellow fever) and death was shorn of power. In their "obedience" lay a peculiar magic.

If Deborah Darby had not dug herself out of her comfortable home on the borders of Wales and taken the long voyage across the sea in pursuit of an idea, what would have been the use of her later saying to young Elizabeth Gurney that she would one day be eyes to the blind, feet to the lame, speech to the dumb? But she went, and touched Grellet. And Savery went, and touched Elizabeth; and Deborah Darby touched Elizabeth, and now Grellet, many years later, touched Elizabeth in his turn. The pattern was woven, the circle was completed. And practical Elizabeth Fry, who could not experience the mysterious, definite leading from within, was given, exactly when she needed it, the right impetus, from people who came from far away to give it.

On February 15, 1813, Elizabeth remarks in her diary, with unwonted satisfaction, that she has lately been engaging in "laudable persuits, more particularly seeing after the prisoners in Newgate, with Anna Buxton."

X

INTRODUCTION TO NEWGATE

1

THE outside of Newgate Prison was familiar to every Londoner as one of the most beautiful buildings in the city. Old Newgate had been burned by rioters[1] in 1780 (nine years before the burning of the Bastille), and the new prison, erected on the same site and on much the same interior plan, had been designed by the architect George Dance, who also did All Hallows Church and St. Luke's Hospital. Dance was an able artist, but he was always bothered by windows. Newgate had no windows, and therefore became his architectural masterpiece. The walls rose sheer up to the cornice in plain rusticated blocks of masonry, relieved by deep shadowed niches containing cheerful eighteenth-century figures — Liberty, with her French cap, and Plenty with her cornucopia. Nothing could be less prison-like than that façade until one noticed over the doorways a pleasing design composed of leg irons, fetters, and chains.

Newgate, in fact, looked inwards, upon her own narrow and ill-drained courts, and John Howard, making a careful inspection of the prison soon after it was finished, commented briefly and sufficiently, "All I will say is that with-

[1] The Gordon Riots. A new prison had been intended, and Dance had begun the plans in 1770. The new building was finished in 1782.

out more than ordinary care the prisoners in it will be in great danger of the gaol-fever." [2]

The plan of the prison was not complicated by sanitary considerations, or care for ventilation. Indeed, the window tax had caused several windows originally in the design to be blocked up. And the unsullied beauty of the outer wall prevented any through draughts. The building was arranged in three quadrangles, the middle and main one for the men felons, the small one on the left for debtors, and the one on the right for women. The ground plan of Newgate shows six rooms, or wards, surrounding the women's yard, and allotted to their use. The chapel, "plain but neat," was in the exact centre of the main building. Under it were the punishment cells for refractory prisoners. Two rooms upstairs, one for men and one for women, were used as an infirmary — that is, as a separate place of confinement for the sick, but without additional conveniences. Men jailers attended to both sexes.

Those under sentence of death, whether men or women, whether sick or well, were confined in the condemned cells. When Howard made his survey "some of the condemned had been long sick and languishing in their cells."

This part of the prison, the block of condemned cells, had been left over from Old Newgate, having successfully resisted the fire. They were peculiarly forbidding, measuring nine feet by six, "with a vaulted roof near nine feet to the crown," and a small window double-grated. The stone walls round each cell were lined with planks, studded with broad-headed nails. "I was told by those who attended them that criminals who had affected an air of boldness during their trial, and appeared quite unconcerned at the pronouncing sentence upon them were struck with horror, and shed tears, when brought to these darksome solitary abodes." [3]

[2] John Howard, *The State of the Prisons in England and Wales*, 213.
[3] *Ibid*, 214.

The ordinary prisoners, unclassified as to age or crime, but usually known as "transports" and "fines," were all together, locked up into several large rooms at night, and allowed the use of both rooms and yard during the day. Beer was on sale at the tap in the prison, and provisions could be bought from the jailers. Poor prisoners who depended on the prison rations fared badly.

Religion was not neglected. One Carlile, a political prisoner condemned to Newgate in 1825 for atheism and blasphemy, asserts, "I dare be sworn that there was not one [felon] but would have felt himself offended had we questioned his belief in a God." Attendance at chapel in the ordinary way was not compulsory, and the noise of non-attenders in the yard disturbed the services. Howard remarks that there was "a pew for the keeper, whose presence may set a good example and be otherwise useful." But there was usually an almost hundred per cent attendance at the Condemned Sermon, a curious piece of psychological brutality that took place on the Sunday before every batch of executions.

"Here is a short description of one at which we were present," writes our prisoner. "Three unfortunate men were ordered for execution. On the Sunday morning they were placed in the condemned pew, which is an oval-shaped, sable-coloured box, with a coffin on a table in the middle. The pew is large enough to contain thirty individuals. It is in the centre of the chapel. Here the condemned are the gazing-blocks of the other prisoners and of those who paid a shilling for admission to the gallery." One of the three, a man of good position condemned for forgery, entreated to be spared this final humiliation. But he was told it was a necessary part of his punishment. "The Chaplain preached on 'Be not deceived, God is not mocked etc.' . . . told them they would in all probability never hear another sermon . . ." and went on at great length with scolding "to wretches already worn to the bone with misery. Next morning at half-past seven the clergyman's voice was heard in the vaulting passages, 'I am the resurrection and the life.' ... Christianity appears more hateful to me every time I reflect on this circumstance."

This rebellious and articulate gentleman continues, with the passion of experience, "I do not believe that there ever yet was an individual possessed of sufficient fortitude to bear a long imprisonment with patience. The prisoner from the moment he enters his dungeon seems to have severed the last link connecting him with human nature. His preconceived horror of a prison falls far short of that which overwhelms him when he has been a few days a prisoner. All the courtesies of civilised society are laid aside, and human nature, deprived of the decent mantle of politeness, stalks before him in naked, horrible deformity. . . . When I first came here even the sick men, through a whole winter, had heavy irons about their legs."

Of course this gentleman and his friends could not enter the women's part of the prison. He could only look over at them and be shocked. It is to Stephen Grellet that we owe the most vivid account of the women's quarters.

"They occupied two long rooms, where they slept in three tiers, some on the floor and two tiers of hammocks over one another. . . . When I first entered the foulness of the air was almost insupportable; and everything that is base and depraved was so strongly depicted on the faces of the women who stood crowded before me with looks of effrontery, boldness and wantonness of expression that for a while my soul was greatly dismayed."

Many of the prisoners, both men and women, were under sentence of transportation, and were only detained at Newgate until the sailing of the next available transport to Australia. But even those under short sentences were uncertain of the length of their sojourn, since at the expiration of the term set by the judge they had to pay a fee to the jailer before they could be released, and they were often detained for want of the money.

This general uncertainty added to the intense depression and acute nervous irritability that were the prevailing atmosphere of the prison. There was no kindness, there was no humor, no order, even of meals, and no occupation. The only diversions were gambling, fighting, and drunkenness, the first two being either means to or results of the last and chief. Happiest those who were dead drunk. "Sir," said a nineteenth-century gentleman in a letter to the *London Chronicle*, "of all the seats of woe on this side hell, few, I suppose, exceed or equal Newgate."

So it was a vast surprise to the keeper and turnkeys on a biting January morning in 1813 to have two ladies descend from a hackney coach laden with bundles, and enter the prison of their own accord.

"Traversing sundry vaulted passages (which being lighted with gas have a very gloomy appearance),"[4] they came, by turning to the right from the keeper's house, to the women's yard, at the extreme southern end of the building.

2

If Elizabeth Fry's first impression of Newgate, as seen from without, was one of orderly beauty, and her second impression, on entering, was one of gloom and bad smells, her third, and most overwhelming, was pandemonium. The sounds which echoed down the vaulted passages and grew louder as they approached were hardly human. And when Elizabeth and her companion, following their guide, passed the barred gateway of the women's yard, they were forced to stand and look. The women, seeing visitors, pressed to the bars, stretching out greedy hands, whining,

[4] Gas was adopted for lighting the streets of London in 1810.

ELIZABETH FRY ENTERING NEWGATE PRISON
Painted by Mrs. E. M. Ward

begging for pence to spend in drink at the tap of the prison. Those in front were fought with by those behind, hands snatched them back by the hair, pinched them, punched them in the ribs with fists and elbows. Elizabeth's wide eyes missed nothing. She had seen drunken Irish, gypsies in the extremes of poverty, the squalor of the London slums, but she had never seen before a mass of women, by the hundreds, reduced to the level of wild beasts.

The men prisoners in Newgate themselves were shocked at the depravity they observed in the women. One of them describes going to the partition that divided the women's piece of yard from the men's. "We looked over, and the scene was even more disgusting than in the other yards. Their manners, gestures, language alike indicative of vice and ignorance. One of them had blackened her face and was dancing for the amusement of her companions. Oh, my happier, more enlightened countrywomen, while you are subscribing your thousands and tens of thousands for the propagation of Christianity, little do you think what misery exists in your own land and among your own sex."

Elizabeth gazed, and went on. Her errand was to the "infirmary" upstairs. And there she found all that Grellet had described. Here was the very bottom of misery's hell; here indeed dwelt Misery her very self. And eagerly Elizabeth set to work to rout her, hand to hand. It was just the kind of concrete attack on evil that she loved. After an hour or two of work, she and Anna Buxton had every baby snugly clothed, every mother a little comforted, and all the sick given at least the relief of thick, clean straw between them and the bare boards.

The turnkeys, who brought what the ladies paid for, were not ashamed. "You see, lady, straw an't 'allowed' here free, nor in most prisons it an't. Prisoners gets it as pays for it. If we gave it, we 'd have to pay for it ourselves and it would soon mount up, ye see."

Beds? Well, that showed how unreasonable ladies were. As the higher authorities later said to Carlile and his fellows, "If beds were to be allowed to every prisoner where are they to be put in a prison like Newgate?"

Elizabeth perceived that there was more to be done here, even for the immediate emergency, than could be done in one visit. Many of the women themselves needed clothing, none had adequate covering against the cold. And her medical eye detected that soup was more needed than medicine. She had made three visits before she mentioned Newgate in her diary at all, casually saying that she had been twice before.

On the last visit, when, their task completed as far as it could be, the ladies said farewell, they commended the poor wretches to the care and the mercy of God. And the weeping women tried to pray with them. It was four years before Elizabeth Fry returned to Newgate.

She took up again the broken threads of occupations disturbed by the urgency of Grellet's call. Her journal at this time is full of the complications of housekeeping at Mildred's Court with a double household, caused by allowing the clerks and their servants to remain who had taken over the house as a sort of dormitory when Joseph Fry removed with his family to Plashet. Another frequent source of discussion with her book is her speaking in meeting and traveling in the ministry, its dangers, trials, and duties, and the fussiness and tactlessness of the elders. And she fills pages with foggy scriptural language, common to many diarists of the period, which probably had a hypnotic, soothing effect on the spirit without exercising the mind.

3

In April the Frys returned to Plashet, leaving Mildred's Court again in possession of the clerks. It was very joyfully that they resumed their country life. The children raced wildly about the lawns, dug vigorously in their gardens, got out their ponies and rode about the countryside as their mother and their critical aunts had done when young. And as long as they were not rebelling against lessons or meeting, their mother as well as their father rejoiced at and encouraged their spirits and their activity. It was sometimes discouraging to visit dear Louisa at Hampstead and see how orderly and obedient her children were. For Louisa had grown into a regular expert in juvenile education and was even writing a book about it. But Elizabeth, while admiring her sister's ability and the wonderful results, could not help secretly hoping (and almost believing) that her children would turn out as well "in the end."

She would not have the tutors or governesses whip them. "Much grieved, nay shocked, so as not to have yet got over it, by an apparent accident when at the cottage [5] to overhear sad screams from poor Johnny and to find that he had been whip'd or was whiping in a manner truly unmerciful which I stop'd, but it has left a painful remembrance." After all, she had not herself been fond of lessons; and Joe Fry was himself not very fond of meeting. He had already been dealt with by the elders about it. It made Elizabeth feel "rather fussed."

In September, the month of apples, "I begin to think another child is on the way. This has also laid me low from my fearful mind, but I look upon it as one of the services of my life to bear children. The prospect of more children is sweet at times, very sweet, but my weak nature sadly flinches at suffering."

Financial difficulties are by no means over. Joseph Fry drives home from the city with tired lines in his jovial face; and though able to enjoy a game of cricket with his boys in

[5] Plashet Cottage was the residence of Joseph Fry's unmarried sister Elizabeth.

the fine, light evenings, he sinks into unwonted gravity when their bedtime leaves him alone with his wife. She has always found his moods of depression especially endearing. And as for him, he not only draws upon her womanly comfort but on her clear, cool, Gurney mind. He talks things over with her very frankly.

But how the large sweep of her temperament does hate a pettifogging economy. "To cut down expenses?" Well, she is willing, she longs to; but how? She confesses herself "burdened by temporal concerns, but I hope to get through; a feeling as if our expenses exceeded what they ought is at times painful . . . being thought much richer than we really are."

Winter comes on with singular severity, full of delights for the children in skating and snowballs, — they are thankful not to be mewed up at Mildred's Court! — but Elizabeth is worried about the poor, the weather is so sharp; and the soup that is being made for them in the barn is not quite up to the quality of former years.[6] Neither has she unlimited stores of warm things and blankets to give away. She thinks of the poor creatures in Newgate that she helped last winter. But her hands are tied in all directions. There is so much to do and she cannot do it. Domestic duties and financial limitations hamper her on every side. She can only escape, now and then, by visiting meetings. And her thirty-fourth birthday draws near. "Thus my time slips away."

Her ninth child, Louisa, was born in June. Rachel was again with her, the faithful Rachel, "a tenderly beloved friend, a most watchful and valuable nurse, and a most loving sister." Perhaps it was the sight of the sort of queenship that happy marriage and abundant maternity give a woman,

---

[6] Mrs. Fry was much wounded at seeing one woman pour out some of her share of soup to the pigs. But perhaps she took this too seriously. Even pigs have to be fed.

but "some old wounds in her mind were opened, which brought her into a very low state and made me feel more in parting from her."

Elizabeth at this time had to administer a household of "nine children, governess, tutor, 8 indoor servants beside many outdoor." But in December she innocently notes, "I have been much engaged in attending our dear Sam and Elizabeth's little Catherine, who has been dangerously ill."

What hope is there for the remote claims of prisoners, however wretched, to press themselves upon a life so full?

4

It was the drastic cutting of financial retrenchment that finally freed Elizabeth Fry for the work that she even yet did not realize as peculiarly hers.

The Battle of Waterloo, in June 1815, ended the French wars in a great blaze of glory, but did not stabilize finance. On the contrary, the disbanded armies, flooding back into the country, still further disturbed social conditions at a time when the abnormal demands of war for munitions and manufactured goods had stopped overnight.

The problem was proportionately as great then as in our own time. Sir John Fortescue, the distinguished military historian, writing in the *Times* of July 30, 1932, said, "Between 1804 and 1814 the proportion of men under arms, afloat and ashore, to the total population of Great Britain, was exactly the same as in the last war, one in fourteen."

It may be inquired why Fry's Bank was negotiating with difficulty when Gurneys' remained unimpeachably sound, and Overend, Gurney and Company, bill brokers, were making money hand over fist. A full answer is impossible, but the easiest one — that Joseph Fry was a poor man of business — is almost certainly incorrect.

Difficulty was more common at this time than security.

There is, after all, an element of luck in all finance. More than one hint can be found that William Fry had been unlucky or ill-judged in some of the speculations in which he had involved the firm. And we have Sam Gurney's own powerful word for it that he respected Joseph Fry's ability, and regarded the sound training he had received from him as the foundation of his own fortunes.

Drastic retrenchment became necessary to a great many people whose interests were involved in investments abroad or manufactures at home, and Joseph pointed out to Elizabeth that they could not much longer continue to support their large household. There was even some talk of giving up Plashet, but neither of them could bear to do that if any other way could be found. While they sought for some reasonable plan that would not harm their children's present and future prospects, life and death kept on their disregarding way; and parents who possessed nine children and were expecting a tenth learned how little they could spare even one. Little Betsy, their delicate child, died in November 1815, after a week's illness. She was then between four and five years old.

As hymns and droll stories mixed in the lively chatter of her feverish state, and the mother's practised eye discerned, with growing alarm, increasing signs of danger, Elizabeth prayed passionately that her little one might be spared suffering — at least spared suffering. And God heard that prayer. On the last day, after a sleepless night, with the child in their room, Joseph Fry stayed home from the city and sat with his wife hour by hour, holding her up with his loyal devotion, his own dumb sorrow, as they helplessly watched the little ebbing life. The doctor could do no more. "Her breath grew more and more seldom and gentle till she ceased to breathe." [r]

Then Elizabeth learned, to the dregs, the meaning of

[r] Cresswell, 64.

anguish. The rain of tears is evident upon her journal "for losing so sweet, so kind a child . . . but surely not a real evil." Is there not a Heavenly Father who has shown "His unutterable loving kindness to my tenderly-beloved little one, who had so sweet and easy a life and so tranquil a death?

"Liable to the frailty of childhood, at times she would differ with the little ones, and rather loved her own way; but she was very easy to lead, though not one to be driven. She had most tender affections, a good understanding for her years, a remarkably staid and solid mind. Her love very strong to her father and me, and her little attentions great; and remarkable in her kindness to servants, poor people, and animals."[8]

The mother tries to regard it as the best way of all ways, the Will of God. But every morning there is a fresh stab of human agony "to awake and find my much and so tenderly-beloved little girl so totally fled from my view. . . .

"My much-loved husband and I have drunk this cup together, in close sympathy and unity of feeling. It has at times been very bitter to us both . . . but we have in measure been each other's joy and helper."[9]

With spring life blooms again. In April 1816 "my sweet little boy was born about 8 o'clock on the 8th" — tenth child and fourth son, Samuel Gurney. This boy was always called "Gurney," to distinguish him from his uncle.

But little Betsy's vacancy was never filled in her mother's heart. After the finality of this loss it was easier to endure the comparative triviality of money worries.

At Earlham in June, Elizabeth writes in her journal, "It is often the prayer of my heart that we may get through our difficulties and trials without others in any way suffering through us." Later: "My husband left me on 7th day under a heavy cloud, business going on so very seriously.

[8] *Ibid.*, 62, 64.   [9] *Ibid.*, 64.

My brother William coming here to consult my brothers. What will be the result I know not, and I desire to leave it. As for our own poverty or our children's, though I enter into and feel its great seriousness, and poor dear Wm. and Eliza's, yet this is with me a very secondary consideration."

Plans were at last made which, as they affected her household, seemed to Elizabeth painfully drastic. Her two older girls were to go to Northrepps, near Lynn, where Rachel was keeping house for brother Daniel. And the two older boys were to remain at Earlham until Christmas, and then to go to boarding school.

Why these arrangements were made, and how Elizabeth felt about them, is fully recorded in her journal written at Earlham, August 22, 1816. "I have been to Northrepps to settle my beloved girls with their aunt Rachel and Uncle Dan. I can hardly express what I feel in thus giving them up at so critical an age. Owing to our loss of property I cannot keep them at home and have them attended to as may be required at their age, either as to their heads or hearts. I should say, give up almost any show or indulgence to have them under my wing, but this cannot be in justice and honor because we are obliged to keep up appearances for the sake of business, and situated as we are almost every optional expense appears a breach of honesty. . . .

"This should be esteem'd a providential opening for us — a truly valuable and tender sister, one who loves good and follows it — a dear brother just out of a serious illness with his heart opened towards good and towards me and mine in our adversity, and these offering to take them, feed them, clothe them and educate them for nothing. . . . I see no way but to fall in with it."

The two children next in age, Richenda and Joseph, were to be similarly cared for by Sam and Elizabeth at Ham House, and join the merry schoolroom party of their little cousins. That left only four-year-old Hannah, two-year-old Louisa, and bran-new little Gurney to keep Elizabeth company at Plashet. But it was some time before Elizabeth realized that this was freedom. At first it only felt like aching loneliness.

PLASHET. *Ninth month. 1816. Evening.*

MY DEAREST GIRLS,

After drinking tea alone in your father's little dressing-room, and taking a solitary walk, and sitting in the rustic portico at the end of the green walk, I am come to write to you, as I cannot have your company. Only think! This evening I have neither husband nor child to speak to, little Hannah being gone to tea at the cottage. I found it even pleasant to go and stand by poor old Isaac the horse, and the cows and sheep in the field, that I might see some living thing to enliven poor Plashet. The grounds look sweetly, but the cherry tree by the dining-room window is cut down, which I think quite a loss. The poor little school-children, when I see them, look very smiling at me, and I suppose fancy that they will soon see you home. Poor Jones's little boy is still living; such an object of skin and bone I have hardly ever seen. I fear she is greatly distressed.

Our house looks charmingly, as far I think as a house can — so clean, neat and lively — but it wants its inhabitants very much.

Your most nearly attached mother,
E. F.[10]

And in her very next letter she is making plans for their return in the spring, if things go well. "I mean that you shall have a certain department to fill in the house among the children and the poor, as well as your own studies and enjoyments; I think there was not often a brighter opening for two girls . . . your little room is almost a temptation to me to take it for a sitting-room for myself, it is so pretty and so snug; it is newly furnished and looks very pleasant indeed. . . . And I shall be glad to have the day come when I can introduce you into prisons and hospitals."[11]

---

[10] *Memoir*, I, 273.   [11] *Ibid.*, I, 274.

What would not Florence Nightingale have given for a mother with such ideas!

Yet Betsy could not resist writing out for her sons a set of "Rules for a Boy at Boarding School" in which she showed only too clearly that she had not the right art with them.

XI

NEWGATE IN EARNEST

1

SOMETIME before Christmas they settled in with their diminished household at Mildred's Court for the winter. Elizabeth Fry's detractors have accused her of getting rid of her children in order to get on with her public work. Nothing, it is apparent, could be farther from the truth.

Elizabeth Fry up to the close of 1816 had no public work (except her visiting of meetings), nor did she look forward to having any. And though the claims of the bestialized women in Newgate had never left her mind, and reasserted themselves strongly as winter drew on, she saw her opportunity, as always, in terms of an immediate task, and not in the large general terms of a career.

She went down to Newgate after Christmas, not because she had decided to take up prison reform, but because she had thought of something that she could do.

This is the difference between her and the men who were at this time becoming concerned about social evils, including prisons. These gentlemen, including her brothers-in-law, Sam Hoare and Fowell Buxton, could see the magnitude of the evils; could inquire into the causes; could perceive that legislation was necessary, new methods and new prisons; and they helped to form, in 1816, the Society for the Reformation of Prison Discipline, with many noble lords on its committee.

The philanthropic nineteenth century was coming into its own, and theories of the perfect social order were bandied to and fro. But in all the mass of evil under survey, it was hard to tell where to start. The farseeing theorist gentlemen sometimes overlooked the small beginning. Elizabeth respectfully supposed that prison reform, and social reform in general, was indeed a matter for Parliament. But her quiet opinions, backed by fact and observation, had their influence. No doubt the increase of crime, the horrors of prison and transportation, the rights and wrongs of the death penalty, were frequent subjects of conversation on those Sundays at Plashet. Both Sam Hoare and Fowell Buxton individually and separately invited Elizabeth to pay visits to various prisons in London with them during the years 1814, '15, and '16; and on one occasion she records with horror that she took two of her children, and discovered afterwards that there had been scarlet fever in the prison — an object lesson which was not lost on her. She had also become acquainted with Peter Bedford, a famous Quaker who had been stirred up by Grellet to an interest in the vagrant boys of London, shared as well by Hoare and Buxton. Elizabeth sympathized in all their theories and efforts. She listened especially to Buxton's well-marshaled arguments; she had great hopes of his going into Parliament and doing much there — as he did in 1818 — and she got as good a bird's-eye glimpse of the prison problems, and their magnitude, as her brothers. But her view was different.

"Men I think are cleverer than women and yet I think the judgment of women equal to that of men in most if not all cases," she had secretly confided to her diary in 1803. And she had probably seen little reason to change her opinion.

The month of January, 1817, afforded an interesting contrast between the cleverness of a farseeing man and the judgment of a near-seeing woman as exercised within the walls of Newgate. Fowell Buxton wrote from his house in Hampstead to his wife Hannah, January 5, 1817: "I went to Newgate with Charles and Peter Bedford. I was in some degree interested by the boys, forty-four little wretches, some of them under sentence of death, though the certainty that none of them will be executed rather took off from the awfulness of their situation. I saw, however, four other poor creatures who are to be executed on Tuesday next. I did not speak to them — in fact it was hardly possible, but the sight was enough. I felt no further inclination to examine the prison. It had made me long much that my life may not pass quite uselessly, but that, in some shape or other, I may assist in checking and diminishing crime and its consequent misery."[1]

Elizabeth, going to Newgate about the same time, and knowing no more of Buxton's visit than he knew of hers, had equally no further inclination to examine the prison. She went to make a human contact with the prisoners.

2

On a cold January day in 1817, in the gloomy vestibule outside the women's yard at Newgate, two turnkeys might have been seen arguing with a lady. The row inside the yard was as great as usual. Even while they talked, a woman rushed wildly out of a doorway and, with shrieks of furious laughter, snatched off the caps and headgear of every woman that she could reach. "And she would n't stop at doing that to you, ma'am. Tear off your things — scratch and claw you — that's what they'd do, ma'am." The turnkeys felt that delicacy forbade telling all that

[1] Charles Buxton, *Memoirs of Sir Thomas Fowell Buxton, Bart.*, 64.

could be done by these harridans to a lady that ventured alone into their midst. They themselves knew better than to go in alone. They always went in two together; the Governor himself went in guarded. But the lady was obstinate. She had in her hand a powerful permit from the prison Governor. She smiled, and gave the men a little money. But she talked to them with an unconscious authority, as she would have talked to her gardeners at home. "I am going in — and alone. I thank you for your kind intentions, but you are not to come with me," was the purport of her speech. At least, then, she must leave her watch behind. They could see the glittering chain on the quiet richness of her Quaker dress. But the unreasonable lady would not even do that! "Oh, no, I thank you. My watch goes with me everywhere. I am not afraid! Open the gate for me, please!"

Reluctant, sullen, and very much alarmed as to results, the turnkeys pressed open the gate against the begging, scuffling crowd, and Elizabeth Fry went in. The gate clanged and locked behind her. There was an instantaneous silence of sheer astonishment. Then every woman in the yard surged forward. Curiosity can be as dangerous as violence in a rough crowd. The lady was surrounded, the turnkeys could only see the tip of her white cap. But no one was snatching. Now was seen one benefit of Quaker dress. It was not provocative. There were no feathers, no flying, fancy scarves to tempt a mischievous finger or an unsatisfied cupidity. And the Quaker dress was an outward and visible mark of religion. All these wicked women, as the Newgate prisoner had said, respected religion and believed in God. Yet Elizabeth was in great danger. If she should now show fear, or say or do the wrong thing — But she had never been less afraid in her life. Look, what is she doing now? She has picked up a filthy little child and it can be seen fingering her bright chain. She lifts her hand for attention, and she is attended to.

"Friends, many of you are mothers. I too am a mother. I am distressed for your children. Is there not something we can do for these innocent little ones? Do you want them to grow up to become real prisoners themselves? Are they to learn to be thieves and worse? . . ."

Ah, she has touched the spot. She has pierced their armor to the very heart. What, save our children? Sobs and tears answered her appeal. They gave her a chair, and brought their children to show her. What tales they told in their inarticulate way, of wickedness, remorse, injustice, and despair! She remained with them for hours. She tried to cheer them up by mention of a mysterious person called Christ (some of them asked who he was) and by telling them a curious story about a man who owned a vineyard and hired laborers by the hour, and paid the people who came in at the eleventh hour as much as the people who came in at the first. But chiefly she was showing them how to do something that had been in former days the chief sign of their humanity and that had been crushed out of them by harsh bondage — she was making plans with them. And when at last she bade them farewell, and the barred gate opened for her civil egress, she left behind her an inhabitant very strange to Newgate, one usually as much abandoned at its doors as at the very gate of Hell, that revivifying spirit of human vitality called Hope.

3

What, then, was Elizabeth Fry's remarkable project? It was very simple. Hardly anyone could disagree with it. It required no Act of Parliament, nor any great outlay of money. In short, it was nothing more nor less than to start a school, in Newgate, for the children of prisoners and for juvenile criminals.

This idea appeared to her as so natural, so modest in its scope, that she did not think it necessary to invoke the aid of the noblemen's committee or of her stately brothers-in-law. By the genius of her common sense and practical simplicity, she took the shortest way to her end.

But it was much more than the shortest way. By invoking the aid of the women themselves, she put herself more than a hundred years in advance of the most advanced thinkers of her time. She set going in that instant the most genuine "reform" that any have been able to approach. It was a renaissance of soul.

On her next visit Mrs. Fry was welcomed as already a familiar friend. Remnants of lost manners returned to the women in response to her serene courtesy. They proudly presented to her the schoolmistress they had chosen from among themselves, a young woman called Mary Connor, recently committed for stealing a watch, but in other respects well qualified to instruct the young. Mrs. Fry praised their progress, and talked over with them in detail the necessary rules that would have to be established for the school. She could not go forward without the assurance of their complete coöperation. Armed with this assurance and with consequent definite suggestions and regulations, she then approached the authorities. They met her at the Governor's house — the two Sheriffs of London, the Ordinary,[2] and the Governor of Newgate himself. It was one of the occasions when it was an advantage to be regarded as "richer than we really are." Only a lady of wealth and standing could have commanded the ear of these important men. As it was, they gave her every attention, but displayed, with all politeness, the usual official attitude. Her plan was a very nice plan, it did both her heart and her mind credit,

[2] The Ordinary of Newgate was the Chaplain.

but, alas! Mrs. Fry did not know Newgate as they did. These bad women were incorrigible, irretrievable. It simply would not work. Mrs. Fry still pressed for an experimental trial, and the badgered gentlemen promised her to look into it and to see her again. But at the second interview they expressed their regret that the experiment was impossible; after a thorough examination of the prison they were assured that there was not a single room that could be spared for it.

With an astuteness worthy of her brother Sam and with that other quality common to them both that had been known in their childhood as obstinacy, Mrs. Fry persuaded the gentlemen to commit themselves to the statement that the absence of a room was now their only objection. She then politely withdrew, and went down to her allies, the women prisoners.

To state her problem to them was to solve it. They felt they had space to spare. When Grellet had seen them, they had been crowded into two rooms and part of a yard. They now — owing to the pressure of Buxton's committee — had six rooms and a cell or two, and the whole yard. One of the smaller rooms was found to be, by common consent, unneeded for any other purpose, and Mrs. Fry therefore appropriated it as a schoolroom. "Upon this she returned to the Sheriffs who told her she might take it if she liked and try her benevolent, but almost hopeless, experiment." [8]

The very next day was appointed for the start. Mrs. Fry was as impatient to begin as the prisoners themselves. No Gurney could ever see the virtue of delay.

She left the women full of business, occupied — happily and virtuously occupied — in tidying and preparing their children and themselves for the great chance. The next day she returned accompanied by a friend, Mary Sanderson,

[8] Fowell Buxton's account, written in 1818.

laden with old schoolbooks, installed Mary Connor as teacher, and formally opened the school.

So casually and simply Elizabeth Fry began a work which within a few months had grown to a dimension which carried her name all over the country, within three years was to place her in correspondence, as prison adviser, with most of the crowned heads of Europe, and which since her death has given her a niche among the great women of history.

She opens her neglected journal at Mildred's Court, February 24th, 1817, and makes a hurried entry. "I have lately been much occupied in forming a school in Newgate for the children of the poor prisoners, as well as the young criminals, which has brought much peace and satisfaction with it; but my mind has been deeply affected in attending a poor woman who was executed this morning. I visited her twice. This event has brought me into much feeling, attended by some distressingly nervous sensations in the night. . . . This poor creature murdered her baby; and how inexpressibly awful to have her life taken away! The whole affair has been truly afflicting to me; to see what poor mortals may be driven to, through sin and transgression, and how hard the heart becomes, even to the most tender affections. How should we watch and pray, that we fall not by little and little, and become hardened and commit greater sins." [4]

4

It is characteristic of Elizabeth Fry that she does not give much space in her journal to her practical activities. She writes either because "my mind is full and wants relief" or because she wants to induce in herself a particular state of mind. If we depended upon her journal, we should know almost nothing of what she did in Newgate. As it is, the

[4] *Memoir*, I, 279.

starting of the Newgate School cannot be dated to a day. But her brother-in-law, Fowell Buxton, wrote a very full account of her prison work,[5] and many other contemporaries provide side lights upon it.

By the report of Mary Sanderson to Fowell Buxton, we know that, even the very first day of the starting of the school, another and larger problem presented itself. And at the very time when Elizabeth Fry was pouring out her heart in her diary regarding the execution of a poor murderess, her days were engaged with a very revolutionary activity in which she was making good headway.

Thirty pupils, mostly children of seven and under, were enrolled in the school; and the "narrowness of the room" would hold no more. But the door was besieged with girls in their teens and women in their twenties, and older, beseeching, with tears, to be allowed in and taught. It was heart-breaking work to dash their hopes and to deny a desire so right and so reformatory. Elizabeth comforted herself and them by promising that the denial, forced from want of space, should be only temporary.

She would try to do something for them, if they would be patient and help her to plan. In her daily visits to the school, with various of her friends, she passed through the appalling life of the yard, and saw it from many angles. There was no question now of danger; she was known by all, respected by all, and loved by many. But she saw and heard and was aware of all kinds of filth, drunkenness, and degradation. She knew that, under the care of men jailers, the utmost abuses were rife. She knew that men prisoners were let into the women's quarters at night. She knew things "too bad to tell," so that she never dared take any "young person" into that place. She was not dulled by habit or frightened away by horror. And she neither

[5] Sir T. Fowell Buxton, *Sketch of the Origin and Results of the Ladies' Prison Association*. 1818.

despised nor despaired. Her eyes and ears, her heart and mind, were wide open; and the question that she asked herself and them was, "What can be done?"

The more intelligent ones told her the very first day what they needed — employment. And what they wanted to be taught — to read and to sew. The enforced idleness, the dreadful ennui of prison, was worse to them than its other miseries. It was itself a direct incentive to vicious behavior, as a relief from intolerable monotony.

But if Elizabeth Fry was to start, as she first called it, "a school" for the women, there were various difficulties to be faced. They wished to sew; and how understandable, how right. But sew what? Clothes for their children and for themselves. And after that, what?

None of them had thought beyond that. But Elizabeth mentally proceeded to the conclusion that they should sew things to sell. And being herself of the merchant class, she realized that she must answer the questions: Sell to whom? And by what means? Also, money would be needed to buy the initial materials. And where was the money to come from?

She consulted Fowell Buxton and Sam Hoare, and to her distress they threw cold water on the whole idea. Quite, quite impossible. All materials given out to prisoners for such work would be stolen. The women, even if they did a little work at first, would soon be tired of it. Countrywomen, accustomed to labor, might be more persevering, but most of these Newgate prisoners were the very scum of the city, prostitutes and thieves from their youth up, whose every friend, every connection, every influence, was and had been of the lowest and most criminal description. Old habits and violent passions would soon assert themselves against a temporary desire for betterment or novelty. Elizabeth Fry and her friends would only waste their time and money, and get their feelings hurt, by attempting such an extraordinary experiment. Why, what authority could they invoke against creatures who had already set at defiance the law of the land? What punishment could they appeal to, in order to subdue beings already under penalty?

No punishment at all, said the unreasonable Elizabeth. It was no use even Buxton's talking to her in his large, noble, and emphatic way about female felons. She persisted in regarding them as women.

If Buxton and his committee could not help her, she decided to have a committee of her own. Several of her friends had already become actively interested in the Newgate school. She got together ten of them, all Quakers but her friend Mrs. Angelzaark, the wife of the clergyman at Plashet, and explained to them her scheme. The ten ladies united under her leadership and formed the Ladies' Association for the Improvement of the Female Prisoners in Newgate; usually briefly called the Ladies' Newgate Committee. They bound themselves to take turns in going daily to Newgate to oversee and instruct the women, to provide funds for the necessary work materials until the city should relieve them, to arrange for the sale of the work, and to pay the salary of a matron who should be on the spot night and day.

Elizabeth Fry always had her plans fully shaped before she approached the entrenched conservatism of authority. Then objection after objection could be met because foreseen and provided against. But now that further step was necessary, and she dreaded it: "My mind and time have been much taken up by Newgate and its concerns. I have been encouraged about our school, but I find my weak nature and proneness to be so much affected by the opinions of man brings me into some peculiar trials and temptations: in the first place our Newgate visiting could no longer be kept secret, which I endeavoured that it should be, and therefore I am exposed to praise that I do not the least deserve; also to some unpleasant humiliations — for in trying to obtain helpers I must be subject to their various opinions; and also, being obliged to confer at times with strangers and men in authority is to me a very unpleasant necessity."

Her husband came to her rescue. He knew, and he only, that beneath the stately air, the slower movement of the handsome matron of thirty-seven, there beat still a heart that was subject to girlish tremors. When it became evident that the development of affairs in Newgate would require further sanctions and coöperations from the Governor and Sheriffs, Mr. Fry invited the daunting officials to meet his wife in the wealthy atmosphere of his own house and under the dignity of his protection.

Not that Joseph Fry was a dignified man in the sense in which the Gurneys and Fowell Buxton were dignified. They were natural princes. But Fry was a man of consequence. His farmerish figure was well known in the city, and it meant money. It meant credit, and honesty and success. Fry's Bank, backed by Gurneys', was to weather the storm for many years to come. And in those days it gave a wife "countenance" to have her husband show openly that he favored her activities.

So it was beneath the roof of Mildred's Court, where she had once thought herself reduced to being merely "a careworn wife and mother," that Elizabeth Fry really entered into her full career.

Mr. Cotton, the Ordinary, and Mr. Newman, the Governor, came together; and Mr. Bridges, the Sheriff, came alone. They listened, they argued, they discouraged; and they consented. They had, in fact, handicapped themselves by the admission of the school. That had been, it turned out, the little end of the wedge so justly dreaded by conservatives. Mrs. Fry's new proposals were but driving the wedge a little farther in. Yet within a fortnight it had split the rotten timbers of prison administration clean asunder.

On the following Sunday, at Mrs. Fry's suggestion, the

two Sheriffs, with Mr. Cotton and Governor Newman, met the ladies at Newgate. "Upwards of seventy women (prisoners) were collected together."[6] Mrs. Fry then addressed the women, reminding them that only by their coöperation could the desires they had expressed to her be fulfilled, and that if they were to be taught and employed as she hoped, it would be necessary for them to agree to keep to certain rules, in order that everything might be organized for the good of the whole. She told them that the ladies who proposed to come to their help and teach them and provide them with work did not come with any authoritative pretensions; that it was not intended that they should command and the prisoners obey, but that all should act in unity and by agreement; "that not a rule should be made or a monitor appointed without their full and unanimous concurrence; that for this purpose each of the rules should be read and put to the vote; and she invited those who might feel any disinclination to any particular" to express their opinion freely. She then read the rules, which she had talked over with the women beforehand in many visits, and each rule was voted on separately by a show of hands. They were all unanimously adopted. The Governor then made a brief speech of confirmation, reminding the prisoners that this innovation was an experiment, and only their good conduct would justify its continuance. He then turned to Mrs. Fry and her committee with a shrug and a gesture — "Well, ladies, you see your materials!"

One of the ladies replied — and closed the proceedings — by reading the parable of the prodigal son.

5

The rules were chiefly propositions in relation to organization. A matron was to be appointed for general superintendence. The women were to be provided with materials

[6] Fowell Buxton's account, 1818.

and instruction in needlework, knitting, or any other suitable employment. They were to be divided into classes or small groups, of not more than twelve, with a monitor over each;^r the monitor to be chosen by the women themselves from those among them who could read and who showed themselves capable of responsibility. A yard keeper was to be elected by the women to inform them when their friends came, and to go with them to the grating; and to see that they did not spend any time there except with their friends. This was an aid to the enforcement of the rule that begging, drinking, and other bad habits should be given up.

At nine in the morning and at six in the evening the women were all to assemble in the workroom for a short Bible reading by one of the visitors, and to have the work for the day distributed and collected. The monitors were to keep a check on the work of their groups, and the matron was to double-check this by "an exact account" of all the work done by the women, and of their conduct. The monitors were to see that their charges came to work with clean hands and faces, and behaved quietly while at work. Any monitor found unsuitable was to be deposed, and the next most suitable member of the group elected in her place.

No penalties were attached to these rules. Any infringement was to be "reported to the matron," but the ladies had of course no power to punish, and the matron was at the beginning their employee. Later, Elizabeth Fry instituted a system of rewards for good behavior, but never any punishments, other than the losing of the rewards.

Governor Newman, who, shrug as he might, was by this time entirely under Elizabeth Fry's peculiar, grave fascination, sent down the carpenters and had the prison laundry cleaned, whitewashed, and fitted up as a workroom. There Elizabeth Fry started what she still called a "school," and in this laundry she certainly had Imps indeed.

^r The Lancasterian method.

It may be inquired why laundries were so available for schoolrooms in the late eighteenth and early nineteenth centuries. As far as Newgate is concerned, the handing over of the laundry in so complete a way is probably a reflection on defective prison hygiene, as well as a reminder that little laundry came under the heading of prison supplies when there was no bedding or table linen to be washed, and where prisoners wore their own clothes. But at Earlham Hall, the standard of cleanliness was as high as the period could boast, and the amount of laundry to be done considerable. It is probable, however, that Earlham followed the custom of other large country houses of the time, as described by the Gurneys' neighbor and client, Parson Woodforde of Weston, near Norwich, who takes it for granted that all gentlefolk have a great washing-week once in five. Such a custom would leave the laundry openly at leisure between times for three or four weeks at a stretch.

In the superfluous laundry at Newgate, then, those of the women prisoners gathered who wished to, were divided into groups, elected their monitors, and proceeded to learn. It is another queer parallel between this, the most famous effort of her life, and that other first school at Earlham which had no fame at all, that the number of scholars in each was about seventy.

One third of the women in Newgate were unable to read at all; another third could only read "a little." Mrs. Fry believed then, as she believed and wrote ten years later in her little book on prisons, that "they ought to be taught to read, write and cipher, as well as to make a ready and profitable use of the needle."[8]

Within a month of the start of the experiment, the Lord Mayor of London, the Sheriffs, and several of the Aldermen came down to Newgate by invitation to see how it was getting

[8] Elizabeth Fry, *Observations on the Visiting, Superintendence and Government of Female Prisoners*, 1827, p. 46.

on. "Many of those," says Buxton, "knew Newgate, had visited it a few months before and had not forgotten the painful impressions made by a scene exhibiting perhaps the very utmost limits of misery and guilt. They now saw what, without exaggeration, may be called a transformation. . . . They saw no more an assemblage of abandoned and shameless creatures, half naked and half drunk, rather demanding than requesting charity. . . . This 'hell upon earth' exhibited the appearance of an industrious manufactory or a well-regulated family. The magistrates immediately adopted the whole plan as a part of the system of Newgate, empowered the ladies to punish the refractory by a short confinement, undertook part of the expense of the matron," and of course said very flattering and enthusiastic things to Mrs. Fry and her helpers.

On February 21, 1818, the Grand Jury of the City of London drew up the following memorandum: "They cannot conclude their report without expressing in an especial manner the peculiar gratification they experience in observing the important service rendered by Mrs. Fry and her friends, and the habits of religion, order, industry and cleanliness which her humane, benevolent and praiseworthy exertions have introduced among the female prisoners; and that if the principles which govern her regulations were adopted towards the males, as well as the females, it would be the means of converting a prison into a school of reform; and instead of sending criminals back into the world hardened in vice and depravity, they would be restored to it repentant, and probably become useful members of society."

6

The first sewing work which the women of Newgate did, after the needs of their own clothing, was patchwork. Thousands of scraps of material in various colors and textures were freely given by Quaker merchants in the drapery trade, led by the Francis Eveleigh who had married Anna Savory and from whom Elizabeth Fry had purchased the flannel for her first layette. This was good work on which to learn to sew, it was gay and cheerful in the prison, it was inexpensive to provide, and it found a ready market. There was, for some reason or other, a demand for patchwork in the remote colony of New South Wales.

Perhaps to those far-off exiles in so strange and different a world, where the stars themselves were foreign, a patchwork quilt looked more homelike than anything else they could think of; and underneath its folds, thrown across their grass hammock or their bed of fern, among the incessant cicadas, they could dream themselves back into the English cottage bedroom of their childhood, with the thatched roof, the quiet night, Carter's Wain [9] out of the window, and the scent of hay.

Mrs. Fry visited Dixon and Company of Fenchurch Street, who handled most of this trade, and they at once gave a ready guarantee to purchase — no doubt at something under the market price — all that the prisoners could supply. Knitted goods, especially stockings, were later added.

The money earned by the prisoners was mostly saved up for them against the day of either their transportation or their release. But Mrs. Fry knew well the value of the immediate and the tangible. To prisoners, as to children, a bird in the hand was worth two in the bush. Some remuneration for their work even while in prison, she urged, would be a powerful stimulus to industry. Let them be able especially to buy tea and sugar! In 1820 she could state, "There is now a little shop in Newgate for harmless articles of food and other useful articles for the prisoners to buy."

---

[9] The common English name for Ursa Major, called in the United States the Great Dipper. The four stars are the wain or wagon, and the three stars, the horses.

It was before the day of trade-unions. But Elizabeth Fry, daughter, sister, and wife of able businessmen, was not blind to the economic problem presented by paying prisoners for their work in a period of excess unemployed free labor. In her book on prisons she warns against competing with local manufactures and undercutting local rates; she is convinced that "the benefit which society derives from the employment of criminals greatly outweighs the inconvenience which can possibly arise to the mass of our laboring population from the small proportion of work done in our prisons." [10]

In directing the products of the Newgate prisoners to New South Wales, she was trying to avoid competition and at the same time sending the prison manufactures to a very logical destination. For New South Wales was chiefly a convict settlement; and who had a better right than felons to supply the needs of felons?

So rapidly were the essentials of this reform accomplished that by April 12, 1817, Elizabeth Fry could write: "I have found in my late attention to Newgate a peace and prosperity in the undertaking that I seldom, if ever, remember to have felt before. A way has been opened for us beyond all expectations to bring into order the poor prisoners; those who are in power are so very willing to help us — in short the time appears to be come to work among them. Already, from being wild beasts, they appear harmless and kind." [11]

A gentleman visitor to the prison gave a vivid account of the new order: "I obtained permission to see Mrs. Fry, and was taken to the entrance of the women's wards. On my approach, no loud or angry voices indicated that I was about to enter a place which had long been known as 'Hell above ground.' The courtyard into which I was admitted, instead of being peopled with beings scarcely human . . . presented

---

[10] *Observations on the Visiting, Superintendence and Government of Female Prisoners*, p. 49.

[11] *Memoir*, I, 289.

a scene where stillness and propriety reigned. I was conducted by a decently dressed person, the newly-appointed yards-woman, to the door of a ward, where, at the head of a long table, sat a lady belonging to the Society of Friends. She was reading aloud to about sixteen women prisoners, who were engaged in needlework around it. Each wore a clean-looking blue apron and bib, with a ticket having a number on it suspended from her neck by a red tape. . . . Instead of a scowl or ill-suppressed laugh, their countenances wore an air of self-respect and gravity, a sort of consciousness of their improved character and the altered position in which they were placed. I afterwards visited the other wards, which were counterparts of the first." [12]

Mrs. Fry found herself in command of ample funds for her work. Her husband had always been a generous provider, for her private, household, and charitable concerns alike, but now that his resources were limited, and she hesitated to ask him for money, her cousin Hudson Gurney, her uncle Robert Barclay, and above all her wealthy brothers, came to her aid. Even the Sheriffs, in their new enthusiasm, subscribed eighty pounds.

The work was going smoothly, and could safely be left for a while. And the stagnant air of the prison was becoming warm. Spring was abroad. The flower sellers of London were hawking primroses at the street corners. Joseph and Elizabeth Fry were filled with nostalgia for Plashet and for their children. It did not seem reasonable to return to the country until after Yearly Meeting. Mildred's Court must dispense its customary hospitality, in spite of the Frys' depleted purse; and Elizabeth was left by it, and by the criticisms freely offered by Friends as to the unwisdom of her public duties, in "some lowness and discouragement." But there were joys to come.

"We have been daily watching with some anxiety for a

[12] *Ibid.*, I, 296.

letter to say when we were to expect you . . . indeed we long to have you all once more around us. We are a little like children at school, counting the days till the holidays," writes the eager mother. And, Plashet open and ready in the first days of June, with the dog-roses the children all come home. Elizabeth's life swings back into its domestic orbit, and with more difficulties, because there are fewer servants and no governess. It is easier far to run a prison than to run a family. *"June 28th,* I am alone at home with my nine children, a great and very precious charge; at times they appear too much for me, at others I greatly enjoy them; I desire that the anxiety for their welfare and to have them in order, should not prevent my enjoying thankfully the blessing of being surrounded by so sweet a flock."

In September, Joseph John Gurney married Jane Birkbeck, and there was a family gathering at Earlham for the wedding, including Richenda and her handsome clergyman, Francis Cunningham, whom she had married in 1816. Richenda had a church wedding, and was given away by her cousin, Hudson Gurney. A bad example for her young nieces. And yet how warm a friend, how much a member of the family, the Reverend Francis Cunningham has become.

When Church of England clergymen are such thoroughly nice people, and become the beloved uncles of one's children, how difficult it is to bring up rebellious young Quakers in their neighborhood! For a year past Katherine and Rachel Fry had been within visiting distance of the Cunninghams, as well as living under the non-Quaker influences of Dan and Rachel. Now that Elizabeth has them again under her wing, she feels the change.

In November the Frys are back at Mildred's Court, and Mrs. Fry is once more in the thick of affairs at Newgate. "A remarkable blessing still appears to accompany my prison concerns; perhaps the greatest apparent blessing on my deeds that ever attended me . . . but my beloved children do not appear sufficiently under the influence of religion. I am ready to say, oh! that I could prosper at home in my labors as I appear to do abroad. Others appear to fear for me that I am too much divided."

But that division preserved the balance of her life. It kept her incurably and triumphantly the amateur. She never became your professional reformer. Ably executive as she was, her husband and her children preserved her softness. To the end of her life, people felt her fascination before they felt her ability. And at any tug of duties, the public duty gave way to the personal. It was a kind of preservative of her gentleness and her spontaneity that in the first flush of her success at Newgate in 1817 she had to return to Mildred's Court at regular intervals to give suck to her nursing child.

And now, in the winter of 1817 to 1818, home troubles steadied her against the storm of publicity that was beginning to beat upon her. What a comfort it was, after all, that her two naughty little daughters, unquakerly as they might feel, were proud and glad to help her with the mass of correspondence which now poured in from every side. Katherine and Rachel were seventeen and fifteen respectively, and very efficient little secretaries they proved. No doubt business hints as to method were forthcoming from Joseph Fry, and perhaps, in an overwhelming emergency, the loan of a clerk. Letters came from people of importance all over the British Isles and even from the Continent, asking "how."

Newgate was suddenly on the map of Europe.

XII

REMEDIES FOR CRIME

1

The month of February seemed peculiarly marked in the stars of Elizabeth Fry. It was in February that she met Savery, in February first went down to Newgate for Grellet, and in February started her school there. So in February one year after the starting of her school she received the signal distinction of being called to give evidence before a Committee of the House of Commons on the Prisons of the Metropolis. She was the first woman other than a queen to be called into the councils of the government in an official manner to advise on matters of public concern.

George III was still on the throne. The only paid occupation open to an educated woman was that of governessing. The suffrage was still limited to the higher taxpayers among men, and the dream of ever granting it to women had hardly dawned in the boldest minds. Yet the early nineteenth century is remarkable for the notable influence of women in the government. Elizabeth Fry, Caroline Norton, Harriet Martineau, and Florence Nightingale left their mark indelibly on the course of English law. The beautiful Caroline Norton,[1] who fought for and won the legal right

[1] Meredith's original for *Diana of the Crossways*.

of a mother to share in the company and education of her children after her separation from a brutal husband, was the only one who used her beauty and charm as instruments. The other women were as impersonal as men. The reforms they worked for were not inspired by personal wrongs. Their weapons were intelligence and information, clarity of mind and a firm purpose.

Elizabeth Fry was the most timid as she was the first in time of this group. Yet she took the Parliamentary summons in a spirit of great simplicity. She was nervous, she dreaded it, but when the time really came she found, as before, that timidity subsided, and poise and self-confidence took its place. She had no fear of being caught out. She knew what she had done, and what she wanted to do, and she knew what ought to be done in the remoter future. She had moved from the particular to the general. And she perceived that this meeting with representatives of the House of Commons was an opportunity.

How much did she know of past efforts in this direction? It is very difficult to say. John Howard, her immediate predecessor in prison reform, died in 1790, when Elizabeth was ten years old. He left behind him a book as large as a dictionary, a sort of encyclopædia of prisons. He had given evidence before the bar of the House of Commons in 1774, and some of his reforms had already been incorporated into law, though not enforced.

There is no mention of the name of John Howard in Mrs. Fry's journals or of his book among her lists of reading. But Howard's light was not hidden under a bushel. Men like Buxton and Hoare must have discussed him and his work. Certainly there is a close parallel in some respects between the recommendations of Elizabeth Fry and those of John Howard. There is also a very sharp divergence.

Howard was a great advocate of separate cells for each prisoner, both day and night. He believed in the value of silence, solitude, and meditation as softeners of the heart and agencies of reform. He practised them with disastrous effects on his only son. He left them as a terrible legacy to the boys of Christ's Hospital whose solitary punishment dungeons, instigated by him, were responsible for more than one case of hysteria and insanity. And we see Howard's system of solitary confinement as one of the most dreaded and dehumanizing agencies in the run of British prisons to-day.

But one great difference is immediately apparent, and may account for Mrs. Fry's indifference to Howard's book. Howard was almost entirely concerned with men, and Mrs. Fry was quite wholly concerned with women.

On the twenty-seventh of February, then, 1818, Mrs. Fry was driven down to Westminster. Quaker dress again had its advantages. "What to wear" presented no problem. The current fashions of the *beau monde* were extravagant, hugely puffed-out sleeves, befeathered bonnets, and tortured hair, designed apparently to show the frivolous nature of woman and her absurd subservience to the whims of man. Quaker dress was restful, unprovocative, neutral. When Amelia Opie abandoned fashions and went Quaker a few years later, Maria Edgeworth wrote that Amelia was all-over Quakerized, to the great benefit of her appearance. "It is indeed a pretty dress."

Elizabeth Fry was just approaching her thirty-eighth birthday. A pen portrait of her has been left us by a Scotchwoman who met her that year for the first time. "She is about forty, tall — thin — sedate, with physiognomy gentle but very observant. . . . Her voice and manners are delightful, free and unembarrassed. . . . Really, I never before felt anything like inspiration or enchantment."[2]

The type of Quaker cap which she wore was one which

[2] Description by Dr. Stewart's niece, in Rev. Thomas Timpson's *Memoirs of Elizabeth Fry*, 85.

David, the French artist, who saw its counterpart on Mrs. Opie, frivolously said was like a Phrygian helmet and had *un air classique.*

So Mrs. Fry entered the House of Commons feeling, on the whole, like herself, and was received by the august committee in a large room warmed by a good coal fire. There she sat, with her free and gracious manners, in the simple dignity of her Quaker dress, and answered the gentlemen's questions and ventured to give her own opinions. Her training in speaking in the meetings of the Quakers stood her in good stead. Her answers and remarks were neither flurried nor wordy; and none could have been clearer. She wanted the ear of the government on two important points: women warders for women prisoners; and, better still, an entirely separate prison for women. The College of Physicians, immediately behind Newgate, was shortly to be sold. And she had her eye upon it as a possible women's prison.

The experiment in Newgate, or, as Mrs. Fry called it, "our institution," had now been going for ten months. "Our rules have certainly been occasionally broken, but very seldom. . . . I think I may say we have full power amongst them [the women] for one of them said it was more terrible to be brought up before me than before the judge, though we use nothing but kindness. I have never punished a woman during the whole time, or even proposed a punishment to them; and yet I think it is impossible, in a well-regulated house, to have rules more strictly attended to.

"They knit from about sixty to a hundred pair of stockings and socks every month; they spin a little." But something regrettable had already occurred in regard to the work. The output could not be limited to New South Wales, and competition and exploitation had not been successfully avoided. "They have made twenty thousand articles of wearing apparel," said Mrs. Fry, presenting the facts, "the generality of which is supplied by the slop-shops which pay very little. The earnings of work, we think, average about eighteen pence per week for each person."[3] Dickens, in *David Copperfield*, uses the word "slop-shop" for "dealers in secondhand clothes." Probably the prisoners' work was mending and renovating, as well as making cheap coarse garments for the poor.

The economic factors of demand and supply, of profiteers and middlemen, have been too much for the inexperienced organization. Mrs. Fry does not put a gloss on the facts; she calls a spade a spade. But one is conscious of an undercurrent of reasoning that says it is better to be occupied in work that is useful and interesting than to have nothing to do, or to be set to the cruel and stupid labor of the tread wheel and the crank. It is better to be underpaid than to be paid nothing. And the labor and rate of wage of less than a hundred prisoners cannot make much difference to the unemployment situation or the underpayment of labor in general. None the less, she is not willing to be a party to such a scheme for long.

"My idea with regard to the employment of women is that it should be a regular thing, undertaken by Government; considering (though I perhaps am not the person to speak of that) that there are so many to provide for; there is the Army and the Navy, and so many things required for them; why should not Government make use of the prisoners?"[4]

But she makes it clear that of course Government must pay them a fair rate, and allow them the immediate use of part of their earnings.

"Do you think that any reformation can be accomplished without employment?" asked the gentlemen. Perhaps they expected some pious reference to the reforming power of religious conversion, but Mrs. Fry's answer is uncompromising. "I should believe it impossible. We may instruct as we will, but if we allow them their time and they have

[3] *Memoir*, I, 317.   [4] *Ibid.*, I, 324.

nothing to do, they naturally must return to their evil practises."

Another advantage of profitable employment in prison is that it carries on outside the prison. It provides a discharged prisoner with a possible means of livelihood. Mrs. Fry gives an instance of "a poor woman for whom we have obtained a pardon. . . . We taught her to knit in the prison. She is now living respectably out of it, and in part gains her livelihood by knitting."

Classification of prisoners is absolutely necessary, to keep criminals apart from first offenders, and small crimes from ones of greater wickedness; but above all to segregate the prostitutes. The crowding of all prisoners together, night and day, is very bad, especially at night.

A gentleman whom we might have met yesterday inquires, "What is the average space allowed to each woman to lie upon, taking the average number in the prison?" But Elizabeth Fry is no John Howard, with a measuring tape in her pocket. "I cannot be accurate, not having measured."

She has something more important to say, and presses on while the idea is hot. "If I may be allowed to state it, I should prefer a prison where women were allowed to work together in companies, under proper superintendence; to have their meals together under proper superintendence, and their recreation also. But I would always have them separated in the night. I believe it would conduce to the health both of body and mind."

Solitary confinement? Never. Or almost never. At least "only in very atrocious cases." And then not for long. But, gentlemen, this is what she has really on her mind. "If there were a prison fitted up for us, which we might visit as inspectors, if employment were found for our women, little or no communication allowed with the city, and room given to class them," with women officers and wardens only, except for the doctor and chaplain, and all well-fed and clothed — then "if there were a thousand of the most unruly women, they would be in excellent order in one week; of that I have not the least doubt." And, what is more, "many of those, now the most profligate and worst of characters, would turn out valuable members of society."

The gentlemen were impressed. After she had left them, they wondered how much of the reform in Newgate was due to admirable ideas, applicable anywhere and enforceable by that vaguely benevolent entity, Government, and how much was due to the unique personal quality of Mrs. Fry. They drew up a cautious minute: —

"The benevolent exertions of Mrs. Fry and her friends in the female department of the Prison have indeed, by the establishment of a school, by providing work and encouraging industrious habits, produced the most gratifying change. But much must be ascribed to unremitting personal attention and influence."[5]

Meanwhile, Mrs. Fry is terribly afraid lest all the newspaper publicity, and letters of admiration and requests for advice, and being consulted by Sheriffs and Members of Parliament, will make her unduly puffed up. "I fear I make the most of myself and carry myself rather as if I was somebody amongst them." But then with these uppish gentlemen it is only too clear that "a degree of this sort of conduct appears almost necessary."

2

The Government had not a very open ear about building reformed prisons. Death or transportation was its favorite remedy for crime. There had been plenty of room for superfluous undesirables in some of the American colonies. American independence had closed that opening, but there

[5] *Memoir*, I, 317–24.

was still plenty of room in Australia. Convicts disliked it even more, because it was farther off from home.

In 1787 the first cargo of criminals was sent out to New South Wales, and since then boatloads had been deposited there at fairly regular intervals. One would have thought that all the criminals in England would have been got rid of long ago; yet on the contrary there were more convictions every year. This human refuse was shipped off to a place famous for its flowers. When Captain Cook in 1770 anchored off the coast in the *Endeavour,* and took possession of New South Wales in the name of the British Crown, he was touched almost to a streak of poetry. "The great quantity of plants which Mr. Banks and Dr. Solander collected in this place induced me to give it the name of Botany Bay."

That name had now, unfortunately, acquired another connotation. None of the world's waters bore so frequently a load of human misery as the broad, shallow waters of that bay, once a paradise of nature.

Colonists and settlers obtained convicts as laborers from the authorities. Their state was little better than slavery. On the complaint of their masters, against which there was no appeal, men were sentenced to a flogging by the magistrates for offenses ranging from insubordination and rudeness to negligence in grooming a horse. Many instances were even on record of wives who had followed their convict husbands out to the colony and taken up land and had their husbands assigned to them as laborers (a situation which might well lead to freedom and peace), and then, either corrupted by their new powers and greed of gain or in a spirit of revenge for former cruelties, ordered their own husbands to be flogged. Women convicts as well as men were absorbed in this system of slavery, with the usual results of cruelty and degradation.

But Australia was a long way off, and the home government remained comfortably blind and deaf. Its responsibility ceased with getting these wretches out of England. This indifference began at the dock; or, perhaps it would be truer to say, had begun already in the prison. Says Howard, "The 'Censor' had one hundred and thirty-seven convicts for our settlements; many of whom being sickly objects and in want of clothes and bedding, I was persuaded would die in the passage."

Mrs. Fry first came in contact with the convict ships when some of her own Newgate prisoners fell due for transportation. She found, one day, the jailers in a great state of nerves. They explained that there was always a riot in the prison the night before a transport. The women all went mad, got drunk, tore things up, broke and set fire to all they could, and fought all comers. Only by main force, and by putting irons on them, which in itself was a dangerous and difficult proceeding (the turnkeys were sensitive to being scratched and spit at), could they be loaded into the wagons which were to take them down to the ship. Anyone familiar with Hogarth's picture of the Execution at Tyburn knows what those open wagons were like, and can readily imagine how, when filled with chained women, they were pursued and surrounded by a yelling, jeering, cat-calling, mud-flinging mob all the way to the docks.

Elizabeth obtained all the facts, and then went to the Governor and asked to be given control of the situation. But she stipulated that there should be no ironing of prisoners, and no open wagons. They must be taken in closed hackney coaches. The Governor, now her loyal and admiring friend, consented, though with dubious warnings.

The night before the transport, Elizabeth stayed with her women until late, reading to them in her marvelous voice, comforting them, making plans for the voyage and for their future, and above all promising to go with them on the morrow all the way to the ship. Instead of a night of riot and wickedness, it was a night of sad farewells. The women who were to remain took up a collection for those who were to go, and generously pressed it on them. Friendship and pity had come to dwell in Newgate, along with self-respect. The next day, Mrs. Fry and some of the ladies came early to the prison. The poor transports got soberly into the closed hackney coaches, trusting in the protection of their friends, and drove quietly away. As one turnkey said to another, watching the procession leaving the gate of the prison, it was like a funeral.

The convict ship *Maria,* to which they were taken, remained six weeks in the river, and Mrs. Fry paid it frequent visits, driving in from Plashet during the summer of 1818. Before it left, she had established her sway over the stranger convicts brought from other prisons, had got the hundred or more women divided up into classes of twelve with their monitors, had numbers for them, — they valued the numbers, as it simplified the keeping of their own seats at table and their own small possessions, — and had provided them all with materials for the making of patchwork on the voyage. She had also established a school in the after part of the ship for the fourteen children on board, one of the prisoners to act as schoolmistress. Indeed, she saw them well started in industrious and orderly habits before the heart-wrenching day of final farewell.

When, after reading to them for the last time on deck, — sailors in neighboring vessels climbing up the rigging to see that strange sight on a convict ship, — she, with another lady, took the little boat for the shore, one of the prisoners leaned over the side of the vessel and said "very distinctly, yet with evident emotion," "Our prayers will follow you, and a convict's prayers will be heard."[6]

From that time onward, Mrs. Fry visited and organized every convict ship that carried women prisoners to the colonies until her final illness in 1843. A total of 106 ships

[6] Timpson, 138.

and 12,000 convicts came under her hands.[7] The whole system of transportation was doomed by the rising tide of public opinion after the Parliamentary report of 1837, but it lingered on by inertia for many more years.

One of Mrs. Fry's earliest experiences was to see twelve women arrive on board a transport handcuffed, having so made their journey. Eleven others from a distance had iron bands around their legs and arms, and were all chained together. If one got down from the coach, all must. Another woman had a fetter round her ankle, which, being in the beginning too small, had become deeply embedded in the swollen flesh. The agony caused by the process of its removal was so great that the victim fainted away. Facts like these had only to be represented in high places by Mrs. Fry to obtain prompt redress. Any ironing of women prisoners on their transit from prison to convict ship was presently made illegal. Another government regulation that she obtained related to mothers and children. Women convicts were to be allowed to take with them all their children under seven; and the mother of a nursing baby might not be embarked until her child was weaned.

The Ladies' Committee — now enlarged into the British Society of Ladies, with the Duchess of Gloucester as patroness — soon had their activities down to a system. They knew what to do on board a transport, and what to ask for, and they had a set of gifts ready for each prisoner, to be marked with her own number for the voyage, and to be inalienably her own. This circumstance was in itself unutterably cheering to people long denied all possessions and all rights. These gifts were listed: "one Bible, one Hessian apron, one black stuff ditto, one black cotton cap, one large Hessian bag (to keep her clothes in); one small bag containing one piece of tape, one ounce of pins, one hundred needles, four balls of white sewing cotton, one ditto black, one ditto blue, one

[7] Timpson, 118.

ditto red, two balls of black worsted, twenty-four hanks of colored thread, one of cloth with eight darning-needles, one small bodkin fastened on it; two stay-laces, one thimble, one pair of scissors, one pair of spectacles when required, two pounds of patchwork pieces, one comb, one small ditto, knife and fork, and a ball of string."[8]

The outbound ships touched at Rio de Janeiro, and industrious convicts were often able to sell their patchwork quilts there at a guinea each. But if not, they could readily sell them immediately on arrival at Sydney, and so obtain ready money and, more, a possibility of future employment. Under such comparatively cheerful influences, it is not surprising that "some captains of the convict ships, on their return to England, have reported well of the health, attention to cleanliness and improved appearance of the women during the voyage."

Sometimes a traveling missionary or clergyman would be granted a free passage in return for taking over the superintendence of the convicts. Sometimes the ship's surgeon was made the responsible party. In every case, the prisoners were no longer crowded together all the time below decks, in stuffiness and seasickness, but had many of their group activities on the airy spaces of the open deck.

Captain Livesey, writing from Sydney in December 1834, gives a detailed account of the voyage of his transport. In this case a Baptist missionary, Mr. John Saunders, and his wife had been given free passage in return for their care of the convicts. "His kind attention to the unfortunate criminals has been unceasing. . . . Some of them who, when they came into the ship, could neither read nor write, have left her well capable of doing both. His wife, a most amiable young woman, was also very kind and attentive to them. The whole of them will have to acknowledge that the *George Hibbert* has been to them a comfortable home."

[8] *Ibid.*, 116–17.

The *Hibbert* had on board 150 women, 41 children, and 9 passengers.

In 1842, the *Rajah* carried a clergyman who was returning to his duties, and who assembled the free passengers, the crew, and his own especial charges, the prisoners, on deck in "the evening of each passing day" for a vesper service, with singing. A woman warder from the Penitentiary had also obtained passage in return for care, and she wrote a journal letter on board. "It was, as you will imagine from our latitude, excessively hot, but an awning was fixed up, and gave the deck much the appearance of a church. Seats were temporarily made of planks and tubs, so that all the women were accommodated in an orderly manner; while apart, but in equal order, were arranged all the sailors.

"The women for the first time put on the cool white jackets and checked aprons provided for them, and I cannot tell you how picturesque and neat they looked . . . it was equalled only by their breathless attention during the service. The congregation so interesting, the circumstance of more than 200 persons assembled in such order on the deck of a ship to worship God . . . alone on the ocean . . . produced such feelings as I believe none of us ever before experienced." [9]

As early as 1826, Mrs. Fry could remark, "We visited the two female convict ships now in the river, and their order, cleanliness and general appearance delighted me, and made me really struck with the wonderful change wrought since we first undertook them."

Libraries were provided from the very beginning by the ladies on every transport. As one of the matrons wrote, "The library was of great use, as it was only on condition of good conduct that they were allowed to have a book. . . . At three o'clock we dined, and then they were left at liberty to amuse themselves; and it was very pleasant to see

[9] Timpson, 131.

here and there a group seated listening to one of their companions reading aloud." [10]

The books selected included travel, biography, history, serious poetry, and religious works, but all "novels, plays and other improper books" were carefully excluded.

3

Meanwhile there was Government's other great remedy, death.

Fowell Buxton, in 1819, seconding in the House of Commons the motion of Sir James Mackintosh for a committee to amend the Criminal Laws, said, "There are persons living at whose birth the Criminal Code contained less than sixty capital offences, and who have seen that number quadrupled — who have seen an act pass making offences capital by the dozen and by the score; and what is worse bundling up together offences trivial and atrocious." [11]

The idea that by the liberal killing off of criminals one could stamp out crime was far older than the nineteenth century. Henry VIII hanged 72,000 persons for robbery alone; and Sir Thomas More wondered that "while so many thieves were daily hanged, so many still remained in the country, robbing in all places." Queen Elizabeth hanged more than 500 criminals a year, yet complained bitterly of the lawlessness of the people. As Buxton said in the House of Commons in 1821, "We have gone on long enough taking it for granted that capital punishment does restrain crime, and the time is now arrived in which we may fairly ask, does it do so? . . . Kill your father or a rabbit in a warren, the penalty is the same. . . . Meet a gypsy on the highroad, keep company with him or kill him, the penalty by law is the same." [12] With over two hundred capital crimes on its

[10] *Ibid.*, 133.
[11] *Memoirs of Sir Thomas Fowell Buxton*, 87.
[12] *Ibid.*, 116.

statutes, Government's intentions were energetic. But practice could not keep pace with theory. Judges and juries would fall short of the letter-of-the-law ideal. In Buxton's famous speech on capital punishment, he told Parliament that he held in his hand 1200 cases of juries who had committed perjury sooner than bring in a verdict of guilty for a small offense which carried the death penalty. Reprieve was another loophole of escape. Howard, in his passion for facts, collected a number of statistics between the years 1750 and 1772 of the number actually executed in any given year. The total condemned during that period at, for instance, the Norwich Assizes was 434; but the number executed 117.

The figures became even more disproportionate as time advanced, and especially after forgery became a capital offense in 1807. In the year 1824, 1066 persons were sentenced to death in the whole of England, and forty executed; in 1825, 1036 were condemned, and fifty executed.

Up to 1811, it was a capital offense to steal linen from bleaching grounds, until the linen bleachers themselves came to Parliament and begged that the penalty might be mitigated. Yet the bloodthirsty will of the lawmakers was demonstrated in the same year by a bill making machine breaking in the factories — hitherto punished savagely enough by fourteen years' transportation — into a capital offense. That bill passed into law over the passionate protest of Lord Byron, whose plea for the starving operatives afforded his only contribution to debate in the House of Lords.

In September 1801, a single session at the Old Bailey rendered the following sentences: "Sentence of death was passed upon Thomas Fitzroy . . . for breaking and entering the dwelling-house of James Harris in the daytime and stealing a cotton counterpane. Wm. Cooper for stealing a linen cloth, the property of George Singleton, in his dwelling-house. J. Davies for a burglary. Richard Emms for breaking into the dwelling-house of Mary Humphreys in the daytime and stealing a pair of stockings. Magnis Kerner for a burglary and stealing six silver spoons. Robert Pearce for returning from transportation. Richard Alcorn for stealing a horse. John Goldfried for stealing a blue coat. Joseph Huff for stealing a lamb, and John Pass for stealing two lambs."[13] In those days, one might indeed as well be hung for a sheep as a lamb. "Crowds witnessed the executions, which took place in front of Newgate." Death was by strangulation, and the victim's friends, and even the executioner, would hang upon his legs to shorten his sufferings. As a young woman criminal said to Mrs. Fry, hardening herself to endure, "Well, if the worst comes to the worst, I shall but have to dance for an hour."

Very early in her Newgate career Mrs. Fry found herself in great demand by women about to die. And her opinion of capital punishment was formed then. We have heard of the first woman, the murderer of her child. Another was one Elizabeth Fricker, executed for robbing, or being accessory to robbing, a dwelling house. Mrs. Fry's journal for March 4, 1817, reads: "I have just returned from a most melancholy visit to Newgate, where I have been at the request of Elizabeth Fricker, previous to her execution to-morrow morning at eight o'clock. I found her much hurried, distressed and tormented in mind. Her hands cold, and covered with something like the perspiration preceding death, and in an universal tremor. The women who were with her said she had been so outrageous before our going that they thought a man must be sent for to manage her. However, after a serious time with her, her troubled soul became calmed. But is it for man thus to take the prerogative of the Almighty into his own hands? Is it not his place rather to endeavour to reform such, or to restrain them from the

[13] Ashton, 446.

commission of further evil? At least to afford poor erring fellow-mortals, whatever may be their offences, an opportunity of proving their repentance by amendment of life. Besides this poor young woman, there are also six men to be hanged, one of whom has a wife near her confinement, also condemned,[14] and seven young children. Since the awful report came down, he has become quite mad, from horror of mind. A strait waistcoat could not keep him within bounds: he had just bitten the turnkey. I saw the man come out with his hand bleeding as I passed the cell. I hear that another, who had been tolerably educated and brought-up, was doing all he could to harden himself, through unbelief, trying to convince himself that religious truths were idle tales. . . . He sent to beg for a bottle of wine, no doubt in the hope of drowning his misery and the fears that would arise, by a degree of intoxication."[15]

In the case of Elizabeth Fricker, the man convicted with her declared, the night before his execution, that she was innocent, and that "a boy concealed had let him into the house." But Elizabeth Fricker was executed none the less. And so was the pregnant woman forger, when she had recovered from her confinement, thus leaving eight orphans on the hands of the State. This woman, Mrs. Woodman, was a great worry to one of Elizabeth Fry's helpers, who tried to read to her in vain. "So unnatural is her situation that one can hardly tell how to meet her case. She seems afraid to love her baby."[16]

Cases of this sort were like personal sorrows to Elizabeth Fry. They haunted her in the night. And as she gained more weight in the world, she used it to obtain pardons and reprieves wherever excuse seemed to offer. She boasted gently to the Parliamentary Committee about "Lord Sidmouth having been very kind to us whenever we have applied

[14] Both for forgery.   [15] *Memoir*, I, 287.   [16] *Ibid.*, I, 303.

for the mitigation of punishment since our Committee has been formed."

But in that she made a mistake. Sidmouth was made of very different stuff from her other new friend, Admiral Sir Byam Martin, Comptroller of the Navy, who helped put into effect her reforms of the convict ships, and whose loyal confidence, once gained, was gained for life.

Henry Addington, Viscount Sidmouth, was a petty and narrow-minded man, the tool of the Conservative interest, a notorious anti-reformer. His first rise in Parliament, under the wing of Pitt, caused a catchword to be coined about him: "As London is to Paddington, so Pitt is to Addington." McCarthy says of him, "Neither Lord Liverpool nor Lord Sidmouth had ever given any evidence, we will not say of statesmanship, but even of parliamentary aptitude." Yet this pompous nonentity, as touchy of his dignity as a raw police sergeant, was Prime Minister of England (as the pawn of Pitt) during the first years of Elizabeth's marriage, and in 1818 was Home Secretary. As Home Secretary, he was the final appeal in matters of life and death, and the first appeal Elizabeth made to him after her unwise words to the Parliamentary Committee was promptly refused.

The case in point was a particularly glaring one. A young woman, Harriet Skelton, had been arbitrarily chosen for execution out of a number condemned for forgery, and the whole women's side at Newgate felt the shock. Harriet was not a criminal type. Her charm, her quiet demeanor and good behavior, her superior refinement, and the fact that her only crime had been to pass a forged note at the imperative instance of the man she loved — perhaps not even knowing it was forged — had made all the women certain that she would be one of the greater number reprieved. Elizabeth Fry was warmly engaged on her behalf. Astonished and chagrined at Sidmouth's first rebuff, she pressed the point with all the ardor of her nature, all the conviction that right was on her side, all the urgency of knowing that a life was at stake. She did not know her man. She supposed, in the innocence of her heart, that the Home Secretary was trying to judge the case on its merits. Her letters were in vain, and he refused to see her. Time was passing, and Elizabeth made one last desperate effort. Her old friend the Duke of Gloucester was in London, now safely married to the faithful Princess Mary, daughter of King George III, for whom he had waited so long.[17] Surely the Prince would help her, remembering those old days of heartfelt gayety at Earlham. Indeed he would. He went with her to Newgate, saw Harriet Skelton, and heard their statement. He went with her to the Directors of the Bank of England, and begged their favorable intervention, and he went with her and Lady Harcourt to the Home Secretary's Office.

It was useless. Sidmouth had entrenched himself in sulky obstinacy. The consciousness of pressure, and of the fact that he was, in the eyes of all those who were aware of the circumstances, being put in the wrong, made him peevish. Not even at the request of a Prince of the Blood would he see that odious, that dangerous, that too fascinating woman, Mrs. Fry. In fact, he dared not see her. And he rudely and curtly refused. It was a good morning's work for Viscount Sidmouth. Elizabeth Fry was humiliated and Harriet Skelton was doomed.

It did not take this experience to convince Elizabeth Fry of the futility of palliatives. She would never lose her keen pity for the individual case, but she turned her main energy toward the general principle. Her influence with the public was immense, had she chosen to exert it. She had it always behind her, that vague, easily summoned power, in all her dealings with authority. And she had great personal influence with Buxton. Far more than the gentle Hannah, she

[17] The marriage was delayed by her brother, the Regent.

put ammunition into Buxton's political guns and helped to form the liberality and humanity of his opinions.

No one would have rebelled more against petticoat government than that very dominant man. Yet it can be demonstrated that what Buxton said in Parliament was often what Mrs. Fry would have said had she been there. It was what she was saying out of Parliament, in her letters, journals, and conversations. But she went farther than he did.

Buxton considered himself very advanced, and was considered so by others, for proposing to do away with the death penalty for every crime but murder. But Elizabeth Fry early decided, and experience only confirmed her in it, that the death penalty should be done away with altogether.

In 1827, in her Prison book, she wrote that "the terror of the example" — the chief argument for capital punishment — "is rendered abortive by the notion vulgarly prevalent among thieves, that 'if they are to be hanged, they are to be hanged, and nothing can prevent it.'" Capital punishment had a hardening effect. "It lowers their estimate of the life of man." It had "a direct and positive tendency to promote both murder and suicide." And she calmly enunciates this great axiom, "Punishment is not for revenge, but to lessen crime and reform the criminal."

4

That twenty-eighth day of April, 1818, was to be, as E. F. afterward put in her journal, a day of ups and downs in a remarkable degree.

"When under great humiliation in consequence of this [affair with Sidmouth] Lady Harcourt took me with her to the Mansion House, rather against my will, to meet many of the royal family at the examination of some large schools." So the lady who could not be received by the Home Secretary in the morning was in the afternoon presented to the Queen. "It was a subject for Hayter" — the platform ablaze with bishops, ladies, fans, feathers, jewels, and orders; the hall lined with spectators, "and in the centre hundreds of poor children brought there to be examined from their different schools." But young Katherine Fry tells it best, in a letter to Aunt Hannah Buxton, "a description of our day at the Mansion House": —

"With infinite difficulty we got into the ante-room. In a few minutes some men in very grand liveries came in a great hurry to clear the way and lay down a piece of scarlet cloth; the cry was 'The Queen is coming!' We looked through the entrance-door and saw mamma(!) with the Bishop of Gloucester (!) and Lady Harcourt with Alderman Wood. Silence had been previously ordered as a mark of respect, but a buzz of 'Mrs. Fry, Mrs. Fry' ran through the room. It was to our utter astonishment that we saw them come in and walk along those spread carpets, Lady Harcourt in full court-dress on the arm of the Alderman in his scarlet gown, and secondly the Bishop of Gloucester (Ryder) in lawn sleeves leading our darling mother in her plain Friends' cap, one of the light scarf cloaks worn by plain Friends, and a dark silk gown — I see her now! her light flaxen hair, a little flush on her face from the bustle and noise she had passed through, and her sweet, lovely, placid smile. In a few minutes the Queen passed, followed by the Princesses, the Royal Dukes, the Lady Mayoress, and other official personages. . . .

"The Lord Mayor placed us behind the hustings on which the Queen was. We asked him for mamma. He burst out laughing: 'There she is on the bench of Bishops!' There were eight of them there. We heard people pointing her out to one another: 'That is she, with her hair over her forehead.' . . . 'That must be Mrs. Fry, with the Bishops.' . . . 'Look now! you may see Mrs. Fry; she rises to receive the Queen's salute.' Towards the close, after 'God Save the King' had been sung, everybody began to clap violently, and we asked the cause. 'Why, the Queen is speaking to Mrs. Fry.' When Queen Charlotte rose to go, she paused and passed to the side where the Bishops sat, — of course all had risen, — and Lady Harcourt presented our mother. The Queen, who is so short, courtesying, and our mother, who is so tall, not courtesying, was very awkward. Her Majesty asked our mother if she were not afraid of going into prisons, how far she lived from London, and how many children she had. The shouts in the hall were tremendous, and were caught up by the crowds outside. It was told why they shouted, and it was repeated again and again, till it reached our father, sitting in his office at St. Mildred's Court, that 'the Queen is speaking to Mrs. Fry.' " [18]

[18] When Katherine Fry wrote many years later her account of this scene in the *Memoir*, she had not this letter to refer to. It was preserved among the papers of Hannah, Lady Buxton. To compare the two accounts — the immediate warm impressions of the girl of seventeen, and the faded memories of the woman of forty-five — is an interesting study in the tricks of memory and the effects of time. See *Memoir*, I, 340.

XIII

PUBLIC LIFE

1

MRS. FRY was now the fashion. One of the entertainments of the *haute noblesse* was to go down to Newgate and see her in action. The American Ambassador wrote home to say that he had now seen the two greatest sights of London — St. Paul's Cathedral, and Mrs. Fry reading to the prisoners in Newgate. Jaded aristocrats and discouraged bishops found the scene in the prison strange and very moving; quite a new sensation. And it was all the more valued because only a few could be admitted at a time, and those not without a permit.

"I accompanied Mrs. Fry on two occasions. . . . Tier above tier rose the seats at the end of the room, a gallery of wooden steps many feet high extending from wall to wall; and on that gallery the women prisoners . . . were seated. . . . It was a shocking and most distressing spectacle, that range of about a hundred women's faces with . . . vice and crime written on the lines of almost every one. On some the bleared flatness of face from whence all trace of womanly feeling had disappeared; on others the vulgar snivel, seeming from time to time to twist the lips and nose together. . . . But there they sat in respectful silence, every eye fixed upon the grave sweet countenance"[1] of Mrs. Fry. She read that day the fifty-third chapter of Isaiah, in itself one of the greatest pieces of prose in the English language. ("All we like sheep have gone astray; we have turned every one to his own way; and the Lord hath laid on him the iniquity of us all.")[2] "Never till then, and never since then, have I heard anyone read as Elizabeth Fry read that chapter — the solemn reverence of her manner, the articulation, so exquisitely modulated, so distinct, that not a word of that sweet and touching voice could fail to be heard. While she read, her mind seemed to be intensely absorbed in the passage of Scripture and in nothing else. She seemed to take it to her own soul the words which she read and to apply them to herself; and then she raised her head and after another pause of silence, she spoke to the wretched women before her.

"Her address was short and so simple that it must have been intelligible to the capacities of her hearers. . . . Tears flowed freely from eyes which perhaps had never shed such tears till then. . . . What struck me as most remarkable in her speaking, and no doubt that which won its way so powerfully to the hearts of those abandoned women, was that she always seemed to class herself with them; she never said 'you,' but 'us.' "[3]

The crowds of visitors were at first most disconcerting to Mrs. Fry. She writes about it with distress in her journal as "making a show of a good thing." The reading to the prisoners had been one of her greatest pleasures. Whenever they heard she was going to read, they would flock upstairs after her joyfully, "as if it were a great pleasure I had to afford them." So unlike the attitude of her own household!

[1] Rev. C. B. Tayler, *Personal Recollections*. Hare, I, 283.
[2] The King James or Authorized Version. By the substitution of the word "Jehovah" for the words "the Lord" or "God," the revisers have spoiled the rhythm of most of the finest passages.
[3] Tayler, quoted by Hare, I, 284.

But to most of the prisoners, the Bible was entirely new. They listened to it with unfeigned rapture. Mrs. Fry's readings were to them a theatre and a concert, a church and a superior family circle, all rolled into one. Drama and poetry, exciting stories and sublime thoughts, came new and fresh to their ears. The unused powers of imagination stirred within them. They glimpsed the moving pillar of fire and cloud, they thrilled to the blast of trumpets and the shout that brought down the walls of Jericho, they saw the angel's ladder bright and near, and they touched the hem of a seamless robe whose wearer had shown mercy to the prostitute. In their raw and crude fashion, they worshiped. And some of them were profoundly changed. How, then, could the fashionable world be absorbed into such a scene as this?

To come down to Newgate filled with the intimate problems of prisoners and to find a Duke or two, some ladies of fashion in velvets and furs, a famous authoress like Maria Edgeworth, a sprinkling of clergy, and an ambassador from foreign parts, entirely altered the character of the assembly. But what it lost in intimacy, it gained in publicity. Elizabeth Fry saw that it was ultimately good for the prisoners that the world of rank and power should come inside the prison and see and hear for itself. It built up a public opinion which could presently crystallize into laws. So she accepted the situation, rose to it, and dominated it.

A responsive audience calls forth the best powers of a fine reader; and on the rare occasions when Joe Fry snatched time to look in at the prison and see what his wife was doing, and beheld her so at home, so queenly and composed, the centre of a hundred eyes, yet unembarrassed and concentrated on her task, did he recall those early days of her married life when even to read to himself and brother William and one visitor had covered her with confusion so that she had had to hand the Bible to him "to finish"?

ELIZABETH FRY READING TO THE PRISONERS AT NEWGATE, 1823
Painted by Jerry Barrett

2

In the autumn of 1821, Elizabeth Fry and daughters Katherine and Rachel accompanied Joseph Fry on one of his business journeys. Elizabeth took the opportunity to visit the prisons in every place at which they stayed, including Nottingham, Lincoln, Wakefield, Sheffield, Leeds, York, Durham, Newcastle, Carlisle, Lancaster, and Liverpool. In each place she interested local ladies in forming Ladies' Prison Committees, and in each prison she was requested to read to the prisoners. She later made a similar journey through the North of England with her brother, Joseph John Gurney, visiting Friends' Meetings and prisons, and at other times made journeys in Ireland and Scotland, as well as innumerable other trips in England with her husband. And between 1839 and 1843, she made five journeys on the Continent of Europe. Popular attention fastened on what it could see, the dramatic and the picturesque. The Quaker lady with Madonna face [4] reading the Scriptures in the prisons and having everyone — hardened criminals, fashionable observers, rough turnkeys — alike in tears touched the sentimental fancy of the nineteenth century. So, as Florence Nightingale became the Lady with the Lamp, Elizabeth Fry became the Angel of the Prisons, forever seated with a Bible.

She published in 1827 a book in which much might have been learned of a different character, but it was not the kind of book to have a popular appeal. It was little more than a pamphlet, of ten short chapters, and was aimed directly at ladies who wished to organize committees for prison reform. The edition was small and soon exhausted. Its title is *Observations on the Visiting, Superintendence and Government of Female Prisoners.*

[4] Maria Edgeworth said E. F. had "a Guido Madonna countenance."

The book begins with a note of her old diffidence, "well knowing my incompetency for writing for the public." But it proceeds in a straightforward manner, certain and well-informed and with an excellent simplicity. Much of it is of a definite, technical character for the immediate purpose in hand, and some of it has been already quoted or implied in these pages. But there are passages which shed an unconscious light upon the author's mind and heart.

"The visitor must go in the spirit, not of judgment, but of mercy. She must not say in her heart 'I am more holy than thou,' but must rather keep in remembrance that '*all* have sinned etc.'

"The good principle in the hearts of many abandoned persons may be compared to the few remaining sparks of a nearly extinguished fire. By means of the utmost care and attention united with the most gentle treatment, these may yet be fanned into a flame, but under the operation of a rough or violent hand, they will presently disappear and be lost for ever."

The work of reformation is a slow one but, "sensible of the natural corruption of our own hearts, let us learn patiently to bear with the hardened and the profligate." All female officers in prisons should be "gentle, yet firm, in their demeanour," and "should themselves be daily examples to the prisoners of right womanly conduct. To such a person also the women under her care can freely communicate a knowledge of their circumstances and pour forth their sorrows as to a wise and sympathising friend."

But she advises visitors not to talk to prisoners about their own crimes. Above all, show confidence in them, and encourage them by frequent rewards. She reiterates her objection to solitary confinement. To miss rewards is usually sufficient punishment. The sick should be properly nursed, in a suitable ward, by fellow prisoners qualified for such work. Medical attendance should be regularly provided.

Suitable, clean bedding for every prisoner, sick or well, must be a part of prison equipment.

Prisoners should be provided with books "not only of a religious but of a generally instructive nature, as it is most desirable to turn the channel of their thoughts, to improve not only their habits but their *tastes*, and by every possible means to raise their *intellectual* and *moral* as well as their religious standard."

But is not this rather strong-minded? Did the reader see a woman here exercising — and tacitly recommending to her fellow women — the faculty of reason, instead of the God-given faculties of instinct and emotion which were her rightful prerogative? It was well known, in 1827, that women could not reason. And this theory, carried to extremes, resulted, among other things, in the auction of wives among the lower orders. Hardy's Mayor of Casterbridge had a hundred counterparts in the daily press. While among the upper classes a more genial masculine tyranny was rife. Jane Austen's humor offers it complete in Sir Thomas Bertram's reproaches to his gentle niece Fanny, for refusing to marry the gentleman of his choice: "I had thought you peculiarly free from wilfulness of temper, self-conceit, and every tendency to that independence of spirit which prevails so much in modern days, even in young women, and which in young women is offensive and disgusting beyond all common offence. But you have now shown me that you can be wilful and perverse; that you can and will decide for yourself."[5] To this terrible indictment the guilty Fanny could only answer by tears.

Quakers were different. Their women held a privileged position. But even Quakers were apt to say at times, to a very public-spirited lady, that woman's place was the home.

Elizabeth Fry does not approach this dangerous ground unconsciously. She has given the matter much anxious

[5] *Mansfield Park*, published 1814. Chapter 32.

attention, and she has arrived at a point of view. Well might Sir Thomas Bertram shudder at offensive independence of spirit. Mary Wollstonecraft's *Vindication of the Right of Woman* had burst like a bombshell upon mankind in 1792, when Elizabeth was twelve years old. It is impossible that she should not have heard it discussed, by the Opies and the Enfields, and their friends; and in later years by the Lloyds, after Charles Lloyd became intimate in the Godwin circle. It is unlikely that she ever read it. It was banned in many circles as the work of an atheist and an immoral person, as the books of Shelley were. But the ideas it had let loose were in the air, and could not be caught again. Some of them, without her knowing it, were in the upright mind of Elizabeth Fry, and were fostered there by religion itself. So, in the introduction to her book on Prison Work, Elizabeth Fry makes her apologia for womanhood, its rights and duties: —

"I wish to make a few general remarks which have long impressed me respecting my own sex and the place which I believe it to be their duty and privilege to fill in the scale of society.

"Far be it from me to attempt to persuade women to forsake their right province. My only desire is that they should *fill that province well;* and although their calling in many respects materially differs from that of the other sex, and may not perhaps be so exalted a one — yet a minute observation will prove that, if adequately fulfilled, it has nearly, if not quite, an equal influence on society at large.

"No person will deny the importance attached to the character and conduct of a woman in all her domestic and social relations, when she is filling the station of a daughter, a sister, a wife, a mother, or mistress of a family. But it is a dangerous error to suppose that the duties of females end here. . . .

"No persons appear to me to possess so strong a claim

on their compassion and on their exertions as the helpless, the ignorant, the afflicted or the depraved of *their own sex.*

"During the last ten years much attention has been successfully bestowed by women on the female inmates of our *prisons* . . . but a similar care is evidently required for our hospitals, our lunatic asylums, and our workhouses."

She does not mean that ladies should neglect the poor near their home, or the education of their own children, but "the economical arrangement of time, and more especially a subtle division of labor, will enable them to accomplish without difficulty all their charitable objects.

"All reflecting persons will surely unite in the sentiment that the female, placed in the prison for her crimes, in the hospital for her sickness, in the asylum for her insanity, or in the workhouse for her poverty, possesses no light or common claim on the pity and attention of those of her own sex who through the bounty of a kind Providence are able 'to do good and to communicate.'

"Were ladies to make a practice of regularly visiting them, a most important check would be obtained on a variety of abuses."

Mrs. Fry's influence succeeded, before her death, in establishing Ladies' Committees for visiting prisons, not only all over England, but all over Europe. And had they been composed of people of her own calibre, there would be nothing left for future generations to accomplish in the way of prison reform. Indeed, if Mrs. Fry's theory of the reforming power of kindness, education, and religion was corrected, crime itself might have been eradicated. But difficult as it is to put one's finger on the exact secret of her genius, there has so far been only one Elizabeth Fry.

The best of the prison visitors were more like Amelia Opie. That popular novelist — now widowed and Quakerized — recorded in her journal for April 14, 1827: "Rose low and self-abased. At the jail [Norwich] read tracts to the women and the Prodigal Son; was satisfied with the manner of two of them, but have no faith in their amendment, in one way, while the turnkeys are men, and men on business are admitted where women could do as well; but this is, I fear, a thing which will never be remedied."

Yet, when she wrote those words, the remedy of that particular evil had, by Elizabeth Fry's pressure and Buxton's influence, become incorporated in Sir James Mackintosh's Bill for Criminal Reform, and had become law by Act of Parliament.

3

Meanwhile, in 1818, when her readings in Newgate were the latest theme of fashionable dinner tables, Mrs. Fry was concerning herself with a question that she had been asking ever since the night of her first transport. What happened to the women convicts when they got to the other side?

Strange. Nobody seemed to know. Members of Parliament, people in the Colonial Office, captains of ships, were all equally vague and noncommittal. It was a very obvious question. Surely it must have been asked before. But all Mrs. Fry could learn was that there was some arrangement, the women were taken care of in some way, there was some system of hiring them out to work for the settlers, and so on. Convicts themselves seldom communicated with friends at home. When they were transported they dropped over the edge of the world. They were lost, almost as if they had died.

But Mrs. Fry did not cease courteously to ask her question. And she made her felon friends promise to let her know, if they could, how they got on over there, under the Southern Cross. Her suspicions were dark, but they were less than the truth.

In the spring of 1819 she received a letter from the Antipodes. It was dated February 23 (again February), covered many pages of close handwriting, and was a regular *cri du cœur*. The writer was the Reverend Samuel Marsden, an Anglican clergyman, chaplain at Paramatta, New South Wales: —

HONORED MADAM,

Having learned from the public papers, as well as from my friends in England, the lively interest you have taken in promoting the temporal and eternal welfare of those unhappy females who fall under the sentence of the law, I am induced to address a few lines to you respecting such as visit our distant shores. It may be gratifying to you, madam, to hear that I meet with those wretched exiles who have shared your attentions, and who mention your maternal care with gratitude and affection.

For twenty years, the gentleman went on to say, he had been struggling to get government action on behalf of the women transports, if only to the extent of the building of a barracks for them. But

to this day there never has been a place to put the female convicts in when they land from the ships. For the last five-and-twenty years many of the convict women have been driven to vice to obtain a loaf of bread or a bed to lie upon. Many of these have told me with tears, their distress of mind on this account: some would have been glad to have returned to the paths of virtue if they could have found a hut to live in without forming improper connections. . . . Many do not live out half their days from their habits of vice. . . . When they have been brought before me as a magistrate . . . I was often at a loss what to answer. . . . When I am called to visit them upon their dying beds, my mind is greatly pained, my mouth is shut, I know not what to say to them. . . . To tell them of their crimes is to upbraid them with misfortunes. They will say, "Sir, you know how I was situated, I did not wish to lead the life I have done. . . . I could not help myself, I must have starved if I had not done as I have." . . . I rejoice, madam, that you reside near the seat of Government, and may have it in your power to call the attention of his Majesty's Ministers to this important subject — a subject on which the entire welfare of these settlements are involved. If proper care is taken of the women, the Colony will prosper, and the expenses to the mother country will be reduced. On the contrary, if the morals of the female convicts are wholly neglected, as they have been hitherto, the Colony will be only a nursery for crime. . . .

It was the custom for some years, when a ship of female convicts arrived, for soldiers, convicts and settlers to go on board and make their choice. This custom is no longer pursued openly, but the total lack of provision for the women convicts makes the real situation just as bad as ever. And so it will remain, till they can be provided with a barrack.[6]

Mr. Marsden also poured forth the tale of his personal efforts, intelligent and energetic, all indeed that could be done by a man without influence. In the year 1807, when back in Europe for a three-year furlough, he had memorialized the Archbishop of Canterbury, the Colonial Office, and several members of Parliament, and had obtained promises of immediate attention. Returning to Botany Bay in 1810, he had been surprised to find no change in the conditions, but had waited patiently for five years. He had then approached the Governor, who denied having received any instructions to build a barracks. After a further wait, Marsden sent in a written memorial of conditions to the Governor with a petition that he build a barracks on his own responsibility. And at the risk of losing his own post and livelihood, he forwarded to England both a copy of this memorial and the Governor's negative reply. "However, nothing has been done yet to remedy the evils of which I complain"; and Mr. Marsden does not know how to get the ear of England. Perhaps Mrs. Fry can do it. He eagerly points out that her "good intentions and benevolent labors will be all abortive" if something cannot be done at the Australian end.

In the meanwhile, some of her trained women are respectably self-supporting, in spite of everything: —

[6] *Memoir*, I, 394.

Mrs. B—— who came from Newgate in the *Friendship* often mentions your kindness. She lives near me, with her husband. They are well and doing well, and conduct themselves with much propriety, will be useful members of society, and are getting forward very fast in worldly comforts.

Mrs. Fry lost no time in presenting Marsden's information in the proper quarters. She urged the matter upon the authorities, with a ready plan of action. Cannot the men convicts at once set to work to build a barracks for the women? Surely delay is impossible!

Authority was flurried. Marsden was a mere voice crying in the wilderness, but Mrs. Fry had the ear of England, if and when she chose. She could be dangerous, though no one knew it less than Mrs. Fry. Over a scandal of this kind, properly aired, the governor of a colony might lose his post. A government at home might fall.

Peremptory instructions were instantly sent to the Governor of New South Wales. And Mrs. Fry was suavely assured that her interesting correspondent was out of date. A barrack was in building for the women at Paramatta. These things, she must understand, were slow work in the colonies.

In March 1820, Mrs. Fry answers a letter from Sir Byam Martin, Comptroller of the Navy, and after thanking him for promising to attend to some arrangements regarding soap and towels in the convict ships she adds, with innocent irony, that "she is glad to find the building for the women in New South Wales is begun; she wonders that Samuel Marsden as Chaplain should not have been better informed about it."

It was indeed a singular circumstance that a gentleman resident at Paramatta should have been so ignorant of what must have been going on (if the home authority spoke correctly) under his very eyes.

However, the barracks were built, and were in due course

available. Thereafter the women, although disembarked as usual at Sydney, were taken by boat sixteen miles up the river to Paramatta, and housed in the new prison, called the Factory, until suitable work was found for them outside. Women who bore a certificate of good conduct from the ship's officers were certain of immediate employment. Refractory prisoners were detained indefinitely, and all could be returned to the prison for punishment at the complaint of their employers.

In 1836, a member of Mrs. Fry's Newgate Committee visited Australia and was, as she says, commissioned by Mrs. Fry to investigate the state of the women convicts. Armed with a courteous *carte blanche* permit from the Governor of New South Wales, the lady took the steamboat from Sydney to Paramatta, and passed through that flowery and lovely landscape in the glory of a late afternoon — sunset tints on the river, and wild peace. Mr. Marsden's house stood on a hill, overlooking the large, straggling village of Paramatta, and his family gave the visitor a most cordial reception. The Factory, visited the next day, proved to be a large, airy building, well situated, and remarkably clean. It contained at that time seven hundred prisoners, divided into three classes. In the third class, the worst and largest, the lady spoke of Mrs. Fry and gave a general message from her. It opened the confidence of the prisoners, who gathered round her and entreated her to listen while they told of wrongs which no one heeded: of bad masters and cruel mistresses; that in service they were treated "like dogs" and seldom spoken to without an oath, or "as devils" more than human beings. Two of the prisoners had committed murder on the person of their master, a Captain Waldrom, to whose service they had been assigned. "They were both young and extremely pretty; one especially lovely." They were anxious to clear themselves with the lady and one repeated, "I am *not* a murderer, for I never meant to kill the man. We were in liquor when we did it, but we could n't help that he died, and we were sorry for it; although he deserved it."

The lady left the place much saddened, and did her best to organize a Ladies' Committee for a check on these abuses and a general enlightenment of the prison. And she published a little book[7] on her return to England, in order to rouse a public opinion at home.

The convicts who were doing well were those who were working under good employers, outside the Factory. There was a Matron, and there were women warders in the prison; but there was little kindness, a spirit of revenge rather than reform, and a row of dark punishment cells such as Mrs. Fry would have eliminated from every prison. So the last state was not such a great improvement on the first.

The better colonists themselves were opposed to the whole system of transportation, and after years of protest, aided by such outside observers as the anonymous friend of Mrs. Fry, obtained the Parliamentary Investigation and Report of 1837. Thereafter the system died a lingering but natural death.

Mrs. Fry's recommendation to Sir Byam Martin in relation to convicts was no sentimentalist theory: "I believe kindness does more in turning them from the error of their ways than harsh treatment." She could have summoned as evidence the record of the Newgate women even in the colonies, established in habits of self-support and self-respect. And she could have cited the reduction in Newgate of reconvictions by over 40 per cent.

4

While Mr. Marsden's letter was making the tedious journey from Paramatta to London, Mrs. Fry had become

[7] Timpson, 157. "The Prisoners of Australia" by Miss A——.

and Buxton brought a bill into Parliament to forbid the practice of suttee within the British Empire. It became law in 1829.

Meanwhile, the century took shape. George III died in January, 1820, and his son George IV, the Regent, succeeded to the throne. The royal divorce proceedings and Queen Caroline's abortive effort to attend the coronation scandalized the country. Fortunately for the peace of society, the queen did not long survive the public disgrace.

In May of this year a Mrs. Nightingale, wife of an obscure English country gentleman spending the spring in Florence, presented her husband with a daughter. They had already a baby girl named after her mother; so they called the unimportant little second one after the city of her birth, and the name of Florence Nightingale was written for the first time.

One year before, also in May, a baby girl had been born to the Duke and Duchess of Kent, sojourning in Kensington Palace, London. She was christened Alexandrina Victoria, and no one could then foresee that in eighteen years' time she would grow up to become, in her own sole right, the Queen of England, and give her name to an era.

But amid all public events, known and unknown, and amid all the increasing demand from Europe, including now the Russian court, for advice regarding prisons and lunatic asylums, and amid all her own visits to various prisons, the year 1820 meant to Elizabeth one thing above all — the increasing illness of Priscilla.

For over a year she lingered and faded, at Earlham and at different health resorts. The winter of 1820 she was at the Isle of Wight, and from there she wrote to her sister Betsy a tribute worth remembering: "There is a certain understanding which I feel with thee that I can hardly feel in the same way with any other mortal. . . . What a support and stay and refreshment, in short what a *mother* hast thou been to us both!" The summer was passed at Earlham, but as autumn advanced she was removed to Cromer Hall, recently purchased by Fowell Buxton. The doctors hoped that bracing sea air might revive her. Since her fancy turned particularly to Sam and Betsy, those two, the busiest of the Gurney family, were summoned to Cromer in February. Sam left a banking crisis, and Betsy — what did not Betsy leave? Sam wrote to his wife: "As far as the circumstances of the case admitted, Betsy and I had a very pleasant journey . . . although leaving London at a critical moment has given me some pain. Not that I doubt the propriety of my coming, under the information I then had; and I must therefore leave matters to take care of themselves. Indeed," adds the great financier, "it sometimes happens they do best by themselves, and work their own way better than we can for them."

As the swallows returned with news of spring, Amelia Opie wrote, "I hope that warm weather and great care will make this faint bird of paradise tarry amongst us some time longer."

But Priscilla did not wait to see another April. On March 25, 1821, the seven sisters were together for the last time. There is a chariot that they cannot stop, stand linked as they may.

XIV

TROUBLED WATERS

1

ELIZABETH FRY was now forty years old. Twenty years of girlhood and twenty years of married life lay behind her. She stood on that uncomfortable peak which is often the summit of a slow decline, and the retrospect from which is not seldom scattered with lost ambition and broken hope. But never had life beat in her more strongly. She looked back through the years at William Savery and Deborah Darby and it seemed that they had been the messengers of God, setting her feet on a foreordained road. She saw her vague girlish dreams of usefulness and power coming into a fulfillment beyond her imagination. Through every fibre of her being she felt the supremely satisfying knowledge that she had found her right place. Again her life fell into pattern, and this time with a polarity as steady as that of the stars. Comets might flash into that inward universe, meteors might fall, clouds might obscure, but the pattern itself would never change again. Order at last was hers. Not the order of well-planned routine that she had once dreamed of, — temperament and circumstance alike forbade, — but above and behind all temporal confusion and trouble was the starry pattern. Let her daily timetable fall to pieces as it might, her life was now knit together by a great public purpose.

Any sudden and stupendous success in reform such as that of Elizabeth Fry means not only that a natural genius with a simple cut-the-knot technique has come into a situation, but that he has come at a peculiarly psychological moment. England was going through all the acute discomforts of the change from one form of civilization to another. Reform was in the air. The old stand-patters, bred in the eighteenth century, and looking back with longing to its charm, its widespread happiness, did not see why, now that the war was over, things could not return to pre-war conditions; and, by way of helping that, resisted strenuously all innovation. But prison reform — that, now, was something everybody could agree about. It was comparatively compact, concrete, nonrevolutionary. Conservative-minded and liberal-minded alike could unite to support Mrs. Fry. Prison reform, as they saw it, was to tinker fairly comfortably with an effect without inconveniently probing into a cause. So long, of course, as new legislation was not in question.

But new legislation was. The death of Napoleon coming very aptly just before the coronation of George IV neatly marked the end of an era. He had frightened England, but he had united it. Now he was dead, and the integrated nation fell apart into struggling factions. All that war had destroyed became gradually apparent. Plenty and security and content and the mutual dependence of class on class had gone. Even the old authority and soothing consolation of the Church had gone. There were Dissenters everywhere. One social order was broken to bits, another must be made. Eighteenth-century government had been that of an aristocracy. The nineteenth century demanded the government of a democracy. And the early years of George IV's reign seethed not only with panaceas for distress but with the attempt to tackle evils at the root by schemes for Parliamentary reform, for national education, for the removal of the disabilities of Dissenters and Catholics, and for drastic amendment of the criminal laws. Buxton and his friends were beginning to form a solid little bloc in the House, a bloc whose collective vote was worth obtaining.

Mrs. Fry is the most outstanding example in history of a woman other than royal who accepted marriage and many-times motherhood, and still maintained an active public life. But she is also an example of the difficulty of the double feat. The wide opportunities that were opening out before her required time, attention, and vigor. But her life had to swing, like a pendulum, constantly and daily, from the large to the small. A Parliamentary committee and the menu for to-morrow's dinner; discussion of public measures with Buxton and Wilberforce and the reprimanding of a housemaid; receiving deputations from foreign parts on the methods of prison reform, and the settlement, on return home, of a nursery riot.

All her immediate circle regarded the small domestic matters as her real life, the larger public matters as extraneous to it — at best, worthy and admirable leisure-time pursuits. And her emotions themselves committed her to the same point of view.

Elizabeth confides to her diary: "The prison cause affords a wonderful opening. I believe if I had time I should have enough to do without attending to almost anything else; and what is more the attention paid to this subject brings so much fruit with it." There were other matters which took up heaps of time and seemed to bear simply no fruit. "My household cares at times a weighty burden, which peculiarly cast me down, and appear as if they must swallow up much of my powers. It is what I have no natural taste or power for, and therefore it is so difficult to me. . . . Then one almost constant source of anxiety, and may I not say sorrow, are our expenses, as in our reduced circumstances I feel it an absolute duty to spend moderately, and a *real want* of knowledge of economy renders it almost impossible to do it, but money appears to *leek* on every side and it seems almost impossible to prevent it. How I can feel for those fallen in life."

2

The *Times* of June 4, 1821, carried an important column on a mass meeting in the Freemasons' Hall, London, for Prison Reform, presided over by the Duke of Gloucester, the platform packed with noble lords, — of Buxton's committee and others, — including also Ryder, the Bishop of Gloucester. Mrs. Fry was present (not as a speaker) and received a tremendous ovation, while speech after speech referred to her ideas and her work. But where was her heart? Throbbing with pain for Priscilla's recent death, and with excitement for daughter Rachel's approaching marriage; with anxiety over money matters, and over disagreement with her dear, her obstinate husband.

Her life ran in a very full tide. "A very busy morning. Went early to town, visited Newgate, Milbank Penitentiary and Tothill Fields prison." Another day: "Visited Newgate, Giltspur Street Compter,[1] and Clerkenwell Prison." She calls on the Duchess of Gloucester and is presented to the Crown Prince and Princess of Denmark. Receives Lord and Lady Torrington to tea, and brother Buxton. Is suddenly informed that the Princess of Denmark proposes to breakfast with her at Plashet next morning. "She came and remained some hours."

But Mrs. Fry's head is not turned by the "high people"

[1] Equivalent of the modern police station; a temporary lock-up, whence people arrested by the watch were distributed to the jails, before the days of police.

with whom she is forced to mix and the attention she now excites everywhere. Of what use to her the admiration of dukes and princesses if Joe is a little offish and her children tart and rebellious? "As far as I know my own heart, never less disposed to exaltation. . . . Several things cast a cloud over me, the first seeing my beloved partner in life so devoted to some things that I am confident are most injurious to his best welfare. . . . Then my elder children, sweet as they are and much comfort as I at times have in them and strong marks of principle as I occasionally see, yet there is a want, a great want. . . . And two of them . . . are induced to treat me and to speak to me at times in a manner that cuts me to the very quick."

But she turns her clear eyes upon her own conduct with uncommon impartiality. "I feel full of love to others, particularly those near me, but I have not towards them that patience and forbearance that I ought to have, and I think I am too-easily provoked — not sufficiently long-suffering with their faults. I do not sufficiently remember that the wrath of man worketh not the righteousness of God."

The fact was that the growing children were increasingly rebellious against Quaker dress and Quaker speech and all the repressions which belonged at that period to the plain Quakers. Elizabeth Fry forgot that she had had ample outlet for frivolity and high spirits in her youth, and had adopted the ways of the plain Quakers with all the ardor of a voluntary discipline. Not so with her own children. To them the Quaker life was a discipline imposed from above, against the grain of their natures, and against their maturing wills. They had never been to a dance, to a concert, or to a theatre. But as their mother mingled more with the world, they met plenty of young people who had. And adolescent discontent was waspish.

Joe Fry, "my beloved companion in life, to whom I believe I may say I am increasingly attached," is also not in complete unity, and though he encourages his wife's activities, he does not share them. There is a deep cause of disagreement, if not dissension, between him and his wife. "We in measure draw two ways, which not only hurts us but the children, that have come to an age of understanding." It is music that is the rub. Joe Fry was addicted to music as another man is addicted to drink.

Unable to obtain music in his own home, he had fallen into the habit of going out to obtain it elsewhere. There were "music meetings" at the houses of worldly friends; and Fry would even slip off to the opera disguised in the costume of the world, leaving his Quaker coat to bear mute witness against him in the cupboard.

Had he been a reflecting man, he might have looked back with regret at the lost opportunities of that first disturbed year of their married life. Had they had quiet and leisure then, he might have been able to win her over to his own love of music, might have been able to establish it as a *good* thing. She had been so soft and open to him, so eager to please. And she had at that time herself only just relinquished music, with pain. But they had not had time or peace. And Fry did not know how to defend music on principle. He was never ready with words. He had been brought up in the strictest, narrowest circle of Quakerism, where music was banned, and how he ever acquired the art of it and the taste for it is a mystery.

He was never quite sure that it was "right"; and his wife's opposition to it (hounded on by the elders) made him gradually grow to feel that it was "wrong." But it was a venial sin, and he had to have it. He also did not hesitate to take his sons with him, as he took them off on shooting and fishing trips.

The blame for everything which, from the strict Quaker view, they did amiss fell on Elizabeth. All resentment for her eminence, all human spite and jealousy, found entry here, under cover of church discipline, along with sincere remonstrance from pure but narrow souls. What, a "recognised minister" of the Society, and her family doing thus and so? Ah, if she only stayed at home and gave proper attention to her husband and children, they would not go astray in this fashion! Elizabeth was very sensitive to blame. She recognized it as a weakness, and struggled with it, but she always felt it.

The resentful children did not realize this pressure from without. They only knew that it was their mother, and not their father, who insisted upon this and that. They knew it was their mother who drew up recommendations and advice for the tutor who took a sixteen-year-old son and three other youths abroad for an educational tour, and was warned: "Never allow the boys to be out alone in the evening; nor to attend any public place of amusement with any person, however pressing they may be. I advise thy seeing that they never talk when going to bed, but retire quietly after reading a portion of the holy scriptures. In the morning that they be as quiet as possible and learn their scripture texts while dressing. . . ."[2] (Visiting in good families, nature, and geology were approved.)

They did not know that under the evangelical puritan revival that was permeating England there were many other parents, not Quakers, who were just as misled. They did not know that the poet Cowper himself believed music to be a debauch, yes, even the oratorios of Handel played in church of a Sunday afternoon. They could not foresee that in years to come a Prince Consort and a Queen of England would, without any pressure from any sect, draw up a not dissimilar set of recommendations for the tutors of the

[2] The young Francis Hare, at eleven years old, could write to his parents, without any sense of singularity, "I read every day for one hour in the morning one of those prayers that you left me, and thirteen chapters in the Bible, and two Psalms, and some of the *Grandeur de Dieu.*" (*Memorials of a Quiet Life*, I, 103)

Prince of Wales. Nor could they look back into their mother's past and see how her natural easiness over trifles had been pressed by church discipline into a stiffer frame.

The elders and overseers of the Society of Friends were rather apt to find fault. Their minute interference with the daily life and habits of members in the early nineteenth century was only comparable to the tyrannical directorship sometimes practised by priests of the Roman Church. Young Mrs. Fry had often found it hard, in the first days of her marriage, to take all their doings in a sweet spirit. She could not help feeling even in those days (when *all* her time was given to her home and her children) that she and her husband were under a rather special surveillance. And she was not wrong, though she never could quite understand the reason. In fact, Joseph Fry was suspected of a touch of unorthodoxy, of being secretly touched with worldliness; and Elizabeth — extraordinary as it would have seemed to her sisters — fell under a similar suspicion. Why? Because she was one of the Gurneys of Earlham and because her early breeding had stamped her deeply and indelibly with an air and manner that was too polished, too elegant, for current Quaker standards. When, in 1806, a committee had been appointed to visit Friends suspected of being "delinquent" in the training up of their children, Elizabeth was astonished and mortified at being one of those visited. And at the next Monthly Meeting a good deal was said with respect to "dress and parents dressing their children"; and some of the "details entered into" were so patently allusions to the little Frys and their mother that they were "not very agreeable," though Elizabeth Fry tried to be grateful to Friends for their watchful care over her youth and inexperience.

In her maturity she grew used to being "eldered" for every variation from a very narrow line — used to it, quite touchingly expectant of it, but never hardened to it. Subjects of censure varied from raising her bell-like voice with unwomanly clearness in meeting, to "allowing" her husband to take two daughters and two nieces for a month's far-too-gay holiday on the Continent, ostensibly searching for some lost Friends who were traveling there in the ministry. Joseph Fry and his four girls had the time of their lives, wearing non-Quaker fripperies, hearing music, attending places of public amusement. It was terrible.

From this period onward Mrs. Fry was from time to time attacked even in public press for neglect of family, and as regularly defended by some friend or other who took up the cudgels on her behalf. Just as Joseph John Gurney later, in a similar manner, defended Florence Nightingale from detractors who called her public activities unwomanly.

Florence Nightingale, before she had attained her freedom, was tantalized by being told by her family that they would have no objection to her undertaking a mission, "like Mrs. Fry," provided there should first be a Mr. Fry to protect her. But Miss Nightingale knew better. In one of her passionate outbursts she writes: "Where do we see the woman with *half* her powers employed? . . . What is she to do? Her best plan would be to have a pursuit of her own; *with* her family, if any of them like it; *without* them if they don't or can't do it, like Mrs. Fry or Mrs. Chisholm. But then what a cry the world makes!"

But Mr. Fry did stand by his wife. That autumn, after a long prison trip with her husband in the north, she writes: "My husband and myself have had a very uniting journey together. I deeply feel the separations that attach to this place [that is, work] and desire to make pleasing him one of my first objects.

"My little children are a great comfort, and glad and thankful as I feel to avoid lyings-in yet I think my pleasures are certainly diminished by not always having babies."

So tenderly maternal in her natural reactions, it was a pity that with her older children she could not take the advice of Madame de Maintenon: *"Êtes-vous mécontente du peu de progrès que font vos filles? Eh! n'êtes-vous pas assez heureuse? Traitez les toujours avec douceur, donnez leur un bon exemple. Priez pour elles — et attendez le reste de Dieu!"*

3

Rachel Fry's marriage let a flood of fresh air into the domestic situation. For Rachel married "out," — that is, married a man who was not a Friend, — and she was therefore automatically "disowned." [3] That solved the problem of Rachel's Quakerism. Yet Elizabeth liked her son-in-law, Francis Cresswell, very much, knew it to be a good match, and joined with her husband in full consent. The young couple were married at Runcton by Uncle Francis Cunningham, vicar of the parish. Though the strict rules of the Society of Friends at that time prevented Elizabeth Fry from attending the wedding, she presided at the reception afterwards. A fog began to clear from her mind. Rachel, as a married woman, was no longer a troublesome and wounding little daughter. Met on equal terms, she proved to be a delightful friend. And when, a year later, on November 1, 1822, Elizabeth Fry's last child and Rachel Cresswell's first were born on the same day, what a close link was forged between them. "How striking to me it was. . . . R. and myself had each a darling boy born. Both of us very graciously and wonderfully helped."

This eleventh and last child was named Daniel Henry, and went by the name of Henry. And as for little Cresswell, he might well be a cocky child. It is not many babies who can boast a twin uncle.

---

[3] Dropped out of membership in the Society of Friends. This destructive practice has of course long ceased.

This completed the tale of Elizabeth's children, six daughters and five sons. All but one grew to maturity, and most to a ripe age, in contrast to Gibbon's dictum that "the general probability is about three to one that a new-born infant will not live to complete his fiftieth year."[4] And still more in contradiction to Buffon, whose data is depressing indeed: "Of a given number of new-born infants, one half, by the fault of nature or man, is extinguished before the age of puberty and reason — a melancholy consideration!"[5]

Yet this generally high child mortality was no exaggeration. The Buxtons had had sad proof of it. Even a mother who stayed at home all the time with her children might not be able to protect them any better than one who freely and boldly took onerous outside duties. In April 1820, Fowell and Hannah had lost four children in five weeks. The first, a boy of ten, came home from boarding school with inflammation of the lungs; and the three others, four years old and under, died of simultaneous whooping cough and measles. The four were buried at Hampstead in one grave, with the simple inscription, "Eheu. Eheu." It was after this overwhelming experience that Fowell Buxton sold the house in Hampstead and moved to Cromer Hall, with his wife and two remaining children.

On December 14, 1822, Elizabeth records in her journal: "I yesterday for the first time since my lying-in went to London and visited Newgate. My greeting there was warm from the prisoners, friends of the committee, etc. My dearest babe who I took with me suffered apparently much by the drive to and from town, so that its little crys almost overcame me." In April: "Newgate, and overdone with company there, so as greatly to prevent my usefulness to the prisoners. (There was a sale of the work of our poor

[4] Gibbon's *Autobiography*, 20.
[5] *Supplément à l'Histoire Naturelle*, VII, 158–64.

prisoners in Newgate, many of the great of this world present.)"

But, born nurse and doctor as she is, she cannot resist calls upon her medical skill, nor can her desperate relatives resist the temptation to call her away from her unique and exacting work to serve their individual dear ones. In May, a young cousin's wife was due for a first confinement. "I have passed through a scene of deep affliction in attending dear Mary Hanbury. I was called to her on the 6th. She was delivered the next morning early of a nice boy, did well at first, and after great reduction and illness she died on the 16th, leaving her beloved father, husband and helpless infant behind her. I," says Elizabeth, simply, "suckling the babe at times, helped to support it."

As one of her biographers remarked soon after her death, "She set an unusual value upon infant life; she was almost displeased at the death of little children being lightly considered: 'You none know how good or how great they may live to be.' "[6]

It was necessary after such a statement to explain that there was nothing really impious in Elizabeth Fry's attitude. She did believe — oh, indeed — in submission to the will of God.

The year 1823 was a prosperous one. "We have lately been much pressed by company, which leads to handsome dinners," and that, of course, tends to make the children more worldly. And "my husband taking a small place where he may go and fish and take the children etc.," did not seem right to Elizabeth at first, not only because it encouraged frivolous friendships, but because — well, was it not only last year that money seemed to "leek"? However, she grew to enjoy Dagenham very much, its informality and simplicity, two jolly little houses on a piece of land that jutted out into the Thames estuary, all among water and

[6] *Memoir*, II, 68.

boats and willows and the greenest of grass; and it grew to be an economy and a rest to close for a while the comparative grandeurs of Plashet and go away to picnic for quiet weeks down at Dagenham.

Another piece of extravagance that year leaves us much indebted to Mr. Fry. In March, "My J. F. appointed Leslie the painter to come and take him and myself, which from peculiar circumstances I have appeared obliged to yield to, as so many likenesses of me have already appear'd and it would be a trial to my family to have only these disagreeable ones to remain instead of a good one. . . .

"Sat to the artist, but got forward with letters for Newgate sale."

In December she is thankful "that we have not exceeded what we think it right to spend — providential provision — abundant kindness of some near to us." And in April 1824: "Money has lately very unexpectedly dropped in a good deal to myself, many hundreds if not perhaps £2000, and this of course must excite much thankfulness and pleasure — really wanted." And the year 1824 was on the whole "a year of much increase of property, so as to remove many of those distressing fears that I have often had on the subject of money, which has come when wanted."

A spirit of opposition to the prison cause and to the interference of ladies had now had a chance to gather head, and had given her much trouble. She is in no sense a debater, and shrinks from controversy: "The burden and perplexity of the opposition in the prison cause is almost too much, it is so much against my nature to take my own defence, or even that of the cause in which I am interested, into my hands." . . . And indeed "my *mind* feels really *worn* and as if I were driven by the almost innumerable calls upon me almost out of measure . . . great opposition and difficulty in getting committees into prisons."

In April she was very ill, with attacks of faintness and

JOSEPH FRY IN 1823

Reproduced from the painting by Leslie with the kind permission of the owner, Miss A. Isabel Fry, Loughton, England

prostration, and was taken to Brighton for a cure. Her famous name caused her to be applied to by large numbers of poor people, and as soon as she was well enough she organized, with the aid of local clergy and gentry, a District Charity Society for the visiting and care of the poor. It was the first of the kind, and arose out of a combination in Mrs. Fry's mind of personal efforts for the poor, such as her own at Earlham, London, and Plashet, and the organized Provident Societies for encouraging the poor to save, which she had heard of from Dr. Chalmers. The success of the Brighton District Society caused many others to be formed in other places. But of course in this, as in other of her organizations, she expected each individual to have her own ardent, personal touch, and flawless good manners; whereas often both were wanting, and the name of charity fell into disrepute. There was also another side line of her visit to Brighton.

Attacks of faintness at night made it necessary to carry her to the open window for air. At such times she constantly saw on the sky line the solitary figure of a man, pacing the cliffs. She was told he was the coast guard; and she became interested in his lonely and dangerous life and that of his fellows. The next time she was out for a drive, she stopped to speak to the coast guard on duty, but the man told her, very civilly, that it was against the rules for him to speak to strangers. The next day she was called upon by the officer in command of the station. He professed himself at her service to answer all inquiries, and a conversation took place in which Mrs. Fry finally suggested that the chief need of these lonely men — whose very duties in preventing smuggling and remaining clear from bribery and collusion prevented them from ordinary human intercourse — was clearly books.

The officer heartily agreed. Mrs. Fry enlisted her husband's help in this project, and began to collect information on which to base plans. Nothing could be done in a hurry. A Navy Department was involved, any amount of red tape, and a considerable sum of money. But before ten years had passed every coast-guard station on the coasts of England had a library.

There were five hundred coast-guard stations, and Mrs. Fry estimated the minimum cost at three pounds apiece. Bibles were given out at once free by the Bible Society. But a grant was finally made from Sir Robert Peel of five hundred pounds and a strong committee was formed to raise the extra thousand and to buy and distribute the books. This committee included an admiral and twelve naval captains, as well as Joseph Fry and two or three of the wealthy Barclay cousins. The Reverend Thomas Timpson was its secretary.

The complete list of books furnished to each library may be found in Timpson's *Memoirs of Elizabeth Fry*. They numbered fifty-two, of which twenty were books of adventure and travel, four or five were biography, one was Bunyan's *Pilgrim's Progress*, one was a Book of Nature, and ten were of an exclusively religious character, as Baxter's *Saint's Rest*.

While they were about it, observed Mrs. Fry, why not libraries for the cruisers? And why not schoolbooks and other reading books for the children of the crews of stations? Mr. Spring-Rice, the Chancellor of the Exchequer, was applied to, made further grants of £460, and the additions were made accordingly.

Mrs. Fry performed a similar service later on a small scale for the lonely shepherds of Dartmoor, whom she happened to notice on a journey.

4

But in 1825 the coast-guard libraries were still only in their first inception, just one more of the "great press of company and engagements" which multiplied "so that I am at times almost afraid for my mind and understanding lasting long, the press upon me is so great."

Her eldest son, John Gurney Fry, married a cousin of the Barclay clan, Rachel Reynolds, in August, and took up his residence at Mildred's Court. By November he had, to his mother's dismay, installed a piano there. Shades of Father Fry! However, reasoned Elizabeth to her diary, what could she do? It was her son's house now. One could not tell people not to put things in their own room. Her mind, after the first shock, was further cleared by this event. When one's children became adult, they deserved the same tolerance and courtesy that one would extend to other adults. And she was careful not to treat John and his wife as if she had authority in their house. Were there some useful memories of William?

More serious affairs presently made even a piano at Mildred's Court seem almost trivial. In December, there was a panic in the money market. "Several large banking-houses in London and many in the country have stopped payment. A great many are in danger, strong as well as weak ones." The Fry house is one.

On the fifteenth, Gurneys' intimated that "they wd do no more, and without some help our house must then stop in *that hour*. My brothers Joseph and Sam came to tell me of it and to consult me whether they shd run the risk of some thousands to do it for that day only. This was taking a great weight on myself. Deeply try'd as I was I *did not* give up hope and was still for *every effort* being made. The next morning they came to this conclusion that if our house had strength to stand through 1st and 2nd day *alone* (without their aid) they would then try to carry us through, if not *we must fall*."

The crisis was met for that time. But the shock was one that had staggered the whole country. In December 1825, the shortage of gold was such that England was "within twenty-four hours of barter."[7] And brother Sam, if Elizabeth had but known it, was very near the core of the trouble.

The flare-up of artificial prosperity after the long wars offered an opportunity for speculation that was irresistible. The idea of forming joint-stock companies crystallized in the minds of a few financiers as a way of making money quickly. Of these, Samuel Gurney, now about forty years old, was one of the leaders. "The launching of the Alliance Assurance Company of 1824 under the combined patronage of Nathan Rothschild and Samuel Gurney was an initial event in a speculative mania as exciting as the South Sea Bubble."[8]

One of the most popular schemes of this company was that of rehabilitating the South American gold and silver mines and equipping them with steam engines to strike for deeper ores. Another company in which Samuel Gurney had an influential voice secured grants of land in South America for mining and for emigrant colonies. South America gleamed like El Dorado in the imagination of the British public. The mania was on.

Early in the spring of 1824, gold and silver were exported to the distant continent by millions, yet nobody appeared to notice that there was too much money abroad. The private banks had gone on issuing as many notes as they could, till the country was deluged with paper money. In 1825 there was 40 per cent more paper out than in 1822. Bankers were willing to discount bills at very long dates. The fever of speculation reached epidemic proportions. On July 6, 1825, the King's speech dismissing Parliament for the session stated confidently that "the general and increasing prosperity on which His Majesty had the happiness of congratulating his parliament at the opening of the session continued to pervade every part of the kingdom."

But the tide had already turned. No returns were com-

[7] Leland Hamilton Jenks, *Migration of British Capital*, 57.
[8] *Ibid.*, 52.

ing from the huge speculations in South America. An anxiety to collect debts became apparent. Here and there a commercial house became unable to meet its pressing liabilities and was declared bankrupt. In vain the leaders of finance tried to suppress the demand for ready money. So many firms failed, one after the other, each spreading disorder in its own sphere of influence, that any kind of property became questionable as security. Then the banks began to totter, the securities they held for their rash advances having become for the time little better than waste paper. The run upon the weaker country banks was immediate. In December, an important London bank (Poles' in Lombard Street) failed, dragging with it forty-four provincial banks. Another Lombard Street banker failed the next day. And a few weeks saw the downfall through the country of more than a hundred banks.

Rothschild and Gurney and other men of stability and genius were called in to advise the Cabinet. Restoration of credit was imperative, and for that gold was the magic secret. The Mint was set to work to coin gold, and gold poured forth at the rate of one hundred and fifty thousand sovereigns per day.[9] Privately hoarded gold was demanded. The Bank of England agreed to make advances of gold to traders upon deposit of goods. But merchants did not need the gold in their hands as long as they knew that they could get it. Trust was restored, mutual confidence, that intangible necessity called "credit"; and cautious trading began to revive. The immediate crisis was over. The regulation of banking had begun.

But the King's speech at the opening of Parliament in 1826 — always colored on principle by the maximum of optimism — was compelled to confess that "the depression had abated more slowly than His Majesty had thought himself warranted in anticipating."[10]

[9] *Annual Register*, 1825, 124.   [10] Hansard, XVI, 11.

"Was abating" would have been a more correct term; and even that would have been on the extreme edge of the truth. By 1830 the distress in England was so fearful that the royal speech was obliged to take unvarnished notice of it. Yet money was abundant throughout this period. The depression was accompanied by riots, rick burnings, machine breaking, trades-unions and strikes, cholera epidemics, cut-throat competition which exploited child labor and threw grown men into idleness, and the usual schemes of artificial employment such as setting thousands of unemployed men to work upon the roads.

Samuel Gurney had ridden the tide of speculation; he had been instrumental in the brilliant and more difficult operation of restoring his own and the national credit; and he had incidentally saved, for the moment, the banking house of Fry. Only just saved it. In February 1826, Elizabeth confides to her journal: "Sam has given me leave to use 200 pounds of my little remaining property for John and Rachel's bills.[11] Ours are not heavier than we can expect, rather better perhaps. I was near sending out of the house some of our valuable pieces of furniture to get money to pay everyone that which is due."

But there are charming comforts incidental to this time of stress. "Last evening my J. F. brought me a present from dearest sister Louisa of 100 pounds sterling. My dearest husband brought me 50 pounds which unexpectedly came in to him and my sweet dear son Wm. out of his *own* money *saved me five* as a little present."

There are also galling feelings of self-consciousness and humiliation. "The very neat things the children and I had on (though partly presents) were rather a burden to me lest those who knew our circumstances should think me extravagant." And that leads her to this quite striking conclusion, "I fully unite in the Christian duty of true simplicity in

[11] Her son and his wife.

dress but I think it is rather too much dwelt upon by us as a Society. . . . I also can hardly bear to hear Friends make us out as of a chosen people above others."

A holiday at Dagenham in July is a great respite. To come "to this quiet abode — refreshing influence — But the perplex'd state of our business . . ." It is hard to be really at peace.

Yet it is under this very pressure of adversity that all the little troubles with her children are finally laid. After all, her cleared vision perceives that "experience has proved in my beloved brothers and sisters that much of the unity of the spirit and the bond of peace may be experienced where we may not see eye to eye."

To emphasize this, brother Daniel comes in August to Plashet for a visit, with his aristocratic wife, the Lady Harriet Hay, a daughter of the Earl of Erroll.

Elizabeth likes her, is "glad that her brother has got such a dear companion. . . . He is a dear, kind brother to me, considering his circumstances, difference of age etc. to myself, he might naturally have turned his back upon me in the day of trouble instead of warmly and steadily doing all he can to help us.

"My other dear brothers are also now actively endeavouring to serve us and set our affairs in order."

Again she takes a moment from her various business to record her gratitude: "I am well provided for and have been all this year, a good deal through the abundant kindness of my brothers and sisters. I am able to give freely to the poor through the abundant kindness of my dear Uncle Barclay and cousin Hudson Gurney. They nearly kept us one half-year whilst the business was in so trying a state."

It was a refreshment, although of a fatiguing kind, to cut loose from oppressive responsibilities, and travel with Joseph John Gurney to Ireland, visiting Friends' meetings and prisons. They were away three months, from February to

May, 1827. Elizabeth was overdone, and her health precarious, but they accomplished a vast amount, as their Report of the Prisons of Ireland bears witness. Joseph John's peremptory methods of taking care of his sister (and himself), of ensuring horses to travel with, and regular food and rest, have been ill-naturedly but graphically described by a discontented Irish Quaker who was disowned later for misconduct.[12] Even this, Elizabeth Fry's only ill-natured critic, can give her no worse nickname than "Friend Stately."

Lord Lansdowne, the Secretary of State, and Spring-Rice, then Undersecretary, needed her advice and information on prison matters on her return. But Joseph Fry was touchingly glad to have her back. Strolling with her in the garden in company with an Irish Friend visitor, and caressing her hand upon his arm, he became for once — though in all bluff simplicity — courtier-like. "What pretty hands you have, m'dear!" And to the Irishman, "Did Friends in Ireland remark what pretty hands my wife has?"

In August she was summoned to Earlham. Rachel Gurney was dying. Sitting beside her dead sister in the Blue Room, shaded against the scented August heat, Betsy takes her journal and pours out the warmth of her heart in loving reminiscence — over this sister in particular, her early beauty, her sad love; and then over every brother and sister in turn, their virtues and their worth. Nor does she praise the Quaker ones any more tenderly than the others. They are all, now even more than in the days of childhood, formed after her own heart.

5

Early in 1828, "public business" had once more to be laid aside on account of a "call to Birmingham to attend the

[12] Mrs. Greer, author of *Quakerism*.

funeral of Charles Lloyd.[13] Numbers of children and grandchildren of various descriptions from Dr. Wordsworth [14] to plain friends . . . others interesting to me whom in early life were dear to me, particularly James Lloyd to whom I was once engaged to be married in my young and gay days. . . . My dear brother Sam! accompanied me." Elizabeth Fry spoke at this funeral.

But her reverie afterwards turned quickly to her children, as in the midst of all her concerns it did constantly and naturally. "My little Harry has been very poorly but is now better. . . . I have also had to settle my Gurney in at school again with some anxiety because he has not appeared so happy there. Tried to make my visit pleasant to all the boys by taking them a walk and giving them oranges." Harry was now six years old, and Gurney twelve.

In spite of her music complex, Elizabeth Fry was moving now very rapidly into broader paths. Was it contact with the cultivated and scholarly Lloyd circle, coming close on her appreciation of the qualities of the "fine company" into which her public fame more and more took her, that caused the next remarkable entry in her journal?

"I long, I crave, I desire for more of the spiritual life amongst us, and I should much like more intellectual cultivation and taste amongst us. I think, as a family, it would tend to our profit and our pleasure."

But as the year advances, the attention of the Fry family is forced to concentrate on mere physical necessities. Real poverty, though it cloaks itself still in outward comfort, has entered Plashet. "When I see my own family generally in full prosperity and see myself and my family laid low before them as dependants almost for daily bread, and really in temporal things under their control, I feel almost ready to complain. . . . Fowell and Joseph have been kinder than

---

[13] Father of Lamb's friend, Charles Lloyd.
[14] Master of Trinity, brother of the poet, and husband of Priscilla Lloyd.

I know how to express to me, and Sam, I am sure, means the same, but from his fearful mind and extreem caution in business he has not in this time of deep distress shown himself so strong and firm a helper as they have, nor did he in 1825, partly I believe, because his judgment is against helping us through, and he is weary of the folly and great imprudence of our house. However, no brother can be dearer than he is to me and one of the deep sorrows of times like these is being wounded in the house of our friends. Frank [15] has behaved delightfully and been a son indeed to me in every way during the time he has been with us."

In April, Joseph Fry had to go on one of his business journeys, and took her with him, an arrangement which always gave a spirit of holiday to them both. Their daughter Chenda and her fiancé, Foster Reynolds, accompanied them. Lynn, Leicester, Nottingham, and Derby gave J. F. business contacts, and E. F. Friends' meetings, lunatic asylums, and prisons; and then a real rest at Matlock in a "quiet, comfortable inn . . . on the side of a high hill, the river Dove at the bottom, full with the late rains, flowing over rocks." [16] The ineffable country peace of an English April soothed the spirit, even though the weather was wet. And the presence of mind of Foster and J. F. saved the inn from burning down when Elizabeth's cloak, left to dry on a chair, caught fire.

In June, there was another pleasant interlude in the marriage of Richenda to her cousin, Foster Reynolds, a Quaker wedding, though Chenda, as a married woman, promptly discarded Quaker dress.[17]

But Joseph Fry's ability and industry cannot alone save the sinking ship. The rumblings of coming storm are

---

[15] Cresswell, her son-in-law.   [16] *Memoir*, II, 75.

[17] My husband's aunt, Anna Braithwaite Thomas, as a little girl, remembers seeing Mrs. Reynolds, as an old lady, sitting regularly in Westminster Meeting, London.

nearer. Firms are going down on every side, and every one that founders drags others down with it.

On August 26, Elizabeth Fry makes her last record — though she does not know it — of what might be called a normal Plashet day. "I expect this morning — 1st, sister El.[18] on important business — next Josiah Forster perhaps to elderise me — next our clergyman [19] to see after our poor — next Foster and Chenda and most of our family together. I have felt, as I often do, the various influences to which I am so peculiarly liable — particularly to-day, just expecting to be closeted hours with dear Josiah Forster who I may call one of our most authordox [20] friends, and then to be hours in near contact with our very authordox high Church Clergyman; both young men of strong minds, views and influence. I have real love for dear Josiah and much unity though I feel from our very different circumstances and education we do not in all things, I believe, see eye to eye, and my degree of fear of him arises in my mind from the high value I have for the good esteem and unity of those in religious profession with myself, and apprehension that he does not fully understand us."

But with what a deep sigh of relief she catches up her journal after their visits to add, "I had a satisfactory time with both the young men. Dear J. Forster only came from friendship."

6

Brother William had made complaint to Elizabeth as far back as 1825 that neither she nor her husband nor brothers "had acted right respecting them [21] in our time of deep trouble." And Elizabeth had murmured to her journal

[18] The unmarried Elizabeth Fry, resident now at Plashet Cottage, though often living with William and Eliza.
[19] Angelzaark's successor.
[20] E. F.'s spelling.   [21] William and Eliza Fry.

that if she had not "to look to a very expensive husband and children, but *only myself* I may say I believe I could make almost any sacrifice of private advantage to please him and his family, so dear are they to me." After weeks of consideration and observation, however, she had been convinced by events. "I have since, from what has passed, seen that that which was done by my beloved brother [22] in business was a *right* and *prudent* measure, and he had good reason to act as he did, both for our sakes and others, and we should have been saved trouble indeed had our hopes attended to him."

But "imprudence in business," combined with the misfortunes of firms with which their money was entangled, brought at last its inevitable result.

On November 15, 1828, Elizabeth notes hurriedly: "The storm has now entered our own borders. The expenses of the year have been so very heavy that it will be very difficult to make ends meet, my own money not coming in as usual." On the twentieth, "Some glimmering of light has arisen on our dark picture as to outward things. I have still money for all private debts, and *for the present* to live comfortably."

But she was to touch the very bottom before long. She records it succinctly. Of what use comment?

"*December 3, 1828.* Here I am in my own room expecting an officer in, who is going round the house to take an inventory of all that we possess for our creditors. Another about the grounds taking an account of all that we have there — another in another part of the house watching over the rest of our property."

The Banking House of Fry, as reputable and as long-established, if not as far-reaching, as the House of Gurney, had closed its doors on a run. Joseph Fry was bankrupt.

The Gurney clan rallied quickly to the help of its fallen member. "Since writing the above, my dearest sister

[22] Reference is to Samuel Gurney.

Hoare [23] has given us in the most free and generous manner 286 pounds, brother Buxton 100, Priss [24] 25, and Anna Gurney [25] and Sarah Buxton [24] 50; therefore we are now well provided for. . . ."

(In the midst of this, she was called away to Newgate to visit "poor J. Hunton," who said he was a Quaker, and was about to be hanged for forgery. He was not a Quaker, but she did for him what she could.)

"Oh, if any read this Journal may it lead them to a most tender compassion for those in perplexed and reduced circumstances."

Letters of sympathy and loyal friendship poured in from every side. Wilberforce wrote, and Francis Cunningham, the Marquis of Cholmondley, the Committee of the Ladies' Prison Society, many members of the Society of Friends who loved and admired her, and her old friend Amelia Opie. And sister Kitty, the ever-faithful, hurried down from Earlham to console her in person.

Bankruptcy had seemed the bottom; but there was one step further. "Today the case of my beloved husband will be brought before our Monthly Meeting."

Friends, then and now, exercised a strict oversight on the business integrity of their members. But in those days they were much more ready to "disown" on slight provocation. Perhaps the state of business panic was an excuse. So many Quakers were concerned in banking that fear for Quaker credit may have urged disciplinary severity upon business failure. Whatever the reason or excuse, Joseph Fry was "disowned" — cast out of membership in the Society of Friends — and undoubtedly unjustly. Not only he but Elizabeth bitterly felt the blow to pride and even to self-respect.

In March 1829, Elizabeth wrote: "Now it comes near to the point I feel the prospect of my husband's disownment

[23] Louisa.   [24] Sister of Fowell Buxton.   [25] A cousin.

very much. It is so striking a *cut down* to our family in so many ways. Yesterday at our Monthly Meeting, whether from my naughty nature or not I cannot say, but I could not but observe the wonderful contrast of my circumstances with some present. Looking at the dear Upton [26] family, Sam! and Eliz. and their children in the midst of prosperity, spiritually and materially."

Friends did not exercise tact in the choice of a disciplinary committee. "A Friend and his wife greatly raised in life, and he visiting my husband as *a delinquent*. I might in truth say, a wonderful change!"

Now indeed her children have a reason to be "grieved with Friends," and most heartily do they express it. The fact that in the long run only one of the Fry children remained in the Society of Friends (Richenda Reynolds) is to be traced, not to their mother's public work, but to their father's disownment. The bitterness which its harshness and injustice aroused in their young and proud minds crystallized their youthful rebellion against the restraints of the Society of Friends.

There is record of how Joseph Fry himself felt about it. Four years afterward, in the year 1833, Fry went through a spiritual experience, not specified, which was to his different temperament something of what the Norwich Sunday of 1798 had been to his wife. The only clue to its nature is that it occurred in the month of May and "was a powerful visitation of Judgment mingled with mercy." It may have had to do with the cholera that was raging in England at that time. Or with one of Fry's numerous escapes from accidental death — overturned whiskies and so on. In fact, it may have been a parallel to Joseph John Gurney's impressive anecdote of the skeptical doctor who was terrified of death in a runaway coach. "The Lord applied that alarm to the highest purposes."

[26] Ham House, Upton, near Plashet.

But however it occurred, it was of lasting influence, and thereafter Joseph Fry kept a desultory sort of journal, to keep himself up to the mark and to "renew his covenant": Sometimes he would only put down one entry in a year. And some years, none. His entry for May 14, 1837, reads as follows, "Our Monthly Meeting, which had disowned me (not I think on sound or at all just grounds) at the time of our failure in 1828, my honor or uprightness never having been even called in question or ground given, has, during the past year, re-instated me in membership. I apprehended it my duty to apply for it, although I have never yet believed myself (since) required to conform in outward appearance or speech to the customs of the Society or its peculiarities. My dress is simple and plain. . . ."

The humiliation, however, cut him deep. All the deeper, perhaps, — who knows? — because of his wife's celebrity. Something that belonged to his essential self was killed, and never raised its head again. His tone suggests that even he dimly perceived that a tragedy was here.

"But in all these changing things the most remarkable change I have experienced has been relative to my great love joined to some taste for music, with a correct ear and some cultivation in singing, which love seems to have passed away like a summer cloud, or died off like the leaves in autumn."

In September 1829, Elizabeth recorded, "My husband is likely to have all his private debts paid to the full about the end of this month."

The hold of the customs of Friends is very strong upon her, tolerate others as well as she may, and she cannot help clinging to her husband's Quakerism for him, even in its outward aspects, disowned as he may be. She met him first, and loved him finally, in a Quaker coat. But Joseph, when he can afford another, is glad to be rid of it; especially in the sore state of his feelings. In September 1830, Elizabeth writes, "My dearest husband has been at home, and his company I have enjoyed, and if it were not that I deeply lament his intention of entirely casting off the appearance of a Friend, which he means to do, and I fear, a good deal of his esteem for the Society and its principles, I should think in other respects I have cause to trust that he is in a happyer and even more peaceful state than sometimes."

It was so. There was a relief from years of strain in knowing the worst. There was almost a serenity in Joe Fry's sturdy acceptance of the worst, and in his immediate reconstruction of his life and business on other and more moderate lines. The promptitude with which, at any sacrifice (of Plashet, of Dagenham, if necessary of all that went with them), he cleared off his private debts is sufficient evidence of his character.

Elizabeth had less to do with the reconstruction. She could only feel the public disgrace and the pinch of the retrenchment. Her spirits at the end of 1829 were low. "I have now had so many real disappointments in life that my hopes, that have so long lived strong that I should see much brighter days in it, begin a little to subside."

7

Baron Bunsen, sometime Prussian Ambassador to England, wrote to a friend, "If the merchants of England, like those of Tyre, may be called princes, Samuel Gurney was indeed a prince." However cautious Sam may have been in supporting the fortunes of a sinking house, — probably feeling that to do so was simply throwing good money after bad, — he had a reputation for genuine generosity of character uncommon in a man whose adventurous genius could not resist juggling with the world's finance. It is on record that when a City friend in whose integrity he had perfect confidence was put on trial for forgery, Sam Gurney, having no actual evidence to offer, went down and stood beside his friend in the dock. That silent weight of confidence secured the man's acquittal.

The lustre of the name of Gurney in the City is reflected in Gilbert and Sullivan's *Trial by Jury*, not written until 1875.

> I soon became as rich as the Gurneys!
> An incubus then I thought her
> And I threw over that rich attorney's
> Elderly, ugly daughter!

Samuel Gurney was not quite easy under his great riches. When from time to time an unworldly Friend would deal with him faithfully about giving too much time and attention to the pursuit of business, Samuel would listen gently and apologetically. "But what am I to do? I am not bookish, like my brother Joseph!" His charities amounted to twenty thousand pounds a year (a hundred thousand dollars) and a hundred allotments on his estate were given rent-free to the poor or unemployed of East Ham who would display energy enough to cultivate them. Being careful not to let his right hand know what his left hand did, he slept well o' nights and, stimulated by the queer drug of success, probably secretly agreed with Anna Buxton's estimate of him — "a well-poised vessel, by some peculiar fortune fitted for pleasant traffic *here* and certain also of a good market above! At least," she murmured, in a lower tone, with the faintest tinge of doubt, "if Sam is not a good fellow, who *is* good?"

His sister Betsy was probably the person in the world whom he most admired. And now that the Fry business had come to its foreseen and unpreventable ruin, Samuel Gurney came forward with practical help. Joe Fry was giving up Plashet. He needed a house. Sam Gurney had a house to offer.

By June 1829, Joseph and Elizabeth and their family were comfortably established at Upton Lane. Their garden joined the grounds of Ham House, into which they could freely overflow. They were still in the neighborhood to which both their hearts were so closely attached. And a dignified economy was at their command.

Thank goodness, daughter Katherine was old enough to undertake the housekeeping. Joseph Fry and his sons were giving all their energies to the tea business, which was still solvent.

"We are now nicely settled in this our new abode, and I may say although the house is small and garden, yet it is pleasant and convenient, and I am *fully* satisfied and I hope thankful for such a home under such afflicting circumstances as ours are. A delightful view of Greenwich Hospital park and the shiping on the river and other parts of Kent, as well as the cattle feeding upon the marshes.

"I have felt much comfort in my Newgate visits, and having but little company I have been able more than common to attend to the prisoners."

It was not too uncomfortable (never worth a murmur) to drive into London by the stage, instead of in one's own carriage. And it was interesting in 1829 to see the new, uniformed policemen patrolling the streets, called "peelers" or "bobbies" after Sir Robert Peel. The world moved. Interesting things turned up all the time. There were steamers on the Thames now, and Sam was always joking about some day having a steam carriage of his own, to go without horses, in which he would go tearing into London at ten miles an hour. But the seesaw of existence was painful, too. "I still hear from different quarters *evil* reports of me. . . . I have been raised up in no common degree and cast down in no common degree."

XV

ROYAL PROGRESS

1

To many a woman, it would have been easier to go right away from the neighborhood in which for twenty years she had been a principal figure, dispenser of charity, and beneficent mistress; not to live within an easy walk of the manor house, or to see it closed up in the charge of caretakers, and to watch its loved and lovely grounds become gradually choked with weeds. But Elizabeth Fry had now for more than ten years been experiencing the deep inner satisfaction of successful work. In the world's eye she was not Mrs. Fry of Plashet House but Elizabeth Fry of Newgate. And after the first shock of bankruptcy and removal, she found a sense of release in being cut off from a mass of domestic detail and village responsibility.

She so graciously and simply adjusted herself to the new conditions that Upton Lane became, from the first, a place of contentment and simple elegance. Not the old life impoverished, but a new kind of life, simpler and perhaps freer.

Dagenham was retained, as an inexpensive family resort, not only for Joseph Fry's family, but also for married sons and daughters, and the two roomy cottages there were occupied the summer through, year after year, by happy family parties, freely passing from one house to the other; rowing and fishing in the larger boat *Elizabeth Fry,* or the smaller, or both, and coming home in the early evening over the water, singing to the beat of oars. Grandmother secretly loved to hear the children sing. Her grandchildren could do what her children could not.

Her first journals at Upton Lane are full, not of struggle to make ends meet or vain regrets or weak submissions, but of her relations with her children and the problems of education. She is advancing in sympathy and understanding.

"I feel more hopeful on account of my family. . . . I see in many of them, if not all, much that is good. Naturally," she confesses to herself, "I consider them a very favoured family, particularly in talent and power of mind, and open, generous dispositions."

William, her favorite son, decided to discard his Quaker coat, and she does not want to be unreasonable, she wonders why she minds so much. "The longer I live, the more difficult do I see education to be; more particularly as it respects the religious restraints that we put upon our children. To do enough and not too much is a most delicate and important point. I begin seriously to doubt whether as it respects the peculiar scruples of Friends, it is not better quite to leave sober-minded young persons to judge for themselves. . . . I have such a fear that in so much mixing religion with those things that are not delectable, we may turn them from the thing itself. I see, feel, and know that where these scruples are adopted from principle, they bring a blessing with them, but where they are only adopted out of conformity to the views of others, I have very serious doubts whether they are not a stumbling block."

Perhaps being called to the bedside of John Pitchford's[1] dying boy that year took her back to the days of her own

---

[1] Pitchford had married at last and settled in the neighborhood of Ham House.

JOSEPH WILLIAM STORRS GURNEY
HANNAH HENRY KATHERINE LOUISA

THE CHILDREN OF JOSEPH AND ELIZABETH FRY LIVING
AT HOME, FEBRUARY 1830

*Reproduced from the painting by Leslie with the kind permission of
the owner, Miss A. Isabel Fry, Loughton, England*

rebellious girlhood, and gave her the point of contact with her children that she had sometimes lacked. Maturity and experience were to her mellowing influences.

Then their love affairs stirred her lively interest. It was no use wanting them all to marry Quakers. William, who was so kind a son, and had so sweet and affectionate a disposition, — and such talents! — was at present in love with a daughter of Lord H——d, though he actually married (in 1832) the daughter of Sir John Henry Pelly, Baronet.[2] Both were fashionable young ladies, but as "sweet, amiable and well-disposed" as any Quakers. "It is my solid judgment," considered Elizabeth Fry, "that real love is not a thing to be lightly esteemed, and when young persons of a sober mind come to an age like Wm., more than 24 years old, it requires very great care how any undue restraint is laid upon them in these most important matrimonial engagements, and that we are all so short-sighted about them that the parties themselves should after all be principally their own judges in it."

Elizabeth Fry's own loyalty to the Society of Friends had itself been severely tested. If she, and other liberal-minded Friends, had left the Society, it would have died of the stranglehold of its own restrictions in the nineteenth century. But she remained and, by the gentle force of her growing stature, lifted the church.

At the Yearly Meeting of 1830, freed for the first time from the burden of hospitality, — never more would Mildred's Court keep open house, — Elizabeth Fry gave her whole mind to the state of the Society, and the tenor of the part she played in the meetings — which are the heart of the church's policy — may be judged from the entry in her journal. "The state of our Society as it appeared in the Yearly Meeting, was very satisfactory, and really very comforting to me: so much less stress laid upon little things, more

[2] Governor of the Hudson Bay Company.

upon matters of greater importance, so much unity, good-will, and what I felt, Christian liberty amongst us. . . . I am certainly a thorough Friend, and have inexpressible unity with the principle, but I also see room for real improvement amongst us; may it take place! I want less love of money, less judging others, less tattling, less dependence upon external appearance. I want to see more fruit of the Spirit in all things, more devotion of heart, more spirit of prayer, more real cultivation of mind, more enlargement of heart towards all; more tenderness towards delinquents, and above all more of the rest, peace and liberty of the children of God."[3]

2

From time to time Mrs. Fry was summoned to appear before a Committee of the House of Commons — or, once, of the House of Lords — and would go escorted perhaps by Buxton and brother Sam and Lady Pirie, and would patiently repeat her recommendations for permanent legislative reform: women warders for women prisoners,[4] solitude in the night, association by day, paid employment, education, rewards, reformation.

Never did she fall into the error of Howard regarding the supposed benefits of solitary confinement. Nor did she adopt the opinion of J. J. Gurney that trouble should be taken to render prison "irksome and unpopular." In their joint report on the prisons of Ireland, chiefly written by Joseph John Gurney, she cannot prevent his urging the use of the treadmill for men prisoners. But she immediately inserts a statement that it must not be used for women prisoners.

Strangely enough, her eye was always on the return of the prisoners to society. What will best fit them for that? She

[3] *Memoir*, II, 121.
[4] The first prison in the British Isles on this basis was opened in Dublin in 1837.

is sure — as the necessity for building new prisons became manifest with the decline of transportation, and the idea of solitary confinement began to loom large among the followers of Howard — that "solitude does not prepare women for returning to social and domestic life, or tend so much to real improvement as carefully arranged intercourse during part of the day with one another, under close superintendence."[5]

Then again, — even more important than model prisons, — what can be done to prevent crime? Very early she had come to the conclusion that the chief causes of crime were ignorance, irreligion, and poverty. In her eager, amateur way she attacked these evils wherever they came within her sphere of influence, but she wanted Acts of Parliament to deal with them in a large and drastic way. She kept a very close watch on all bills of a social slant that came before the House. Yes, and an effective watch. They were, she knew, a woman's business. And so also thought Harriet Martineau.

The same wave of bankruptcy that had engulfed the Frys engulfed also the Martineaus of Norwich. And young Harriet Martineau rejoiced in being freed at a stroke from the burden of gentility and forced to earn her own living. Fancywork, her mother suggested — indeed, she tried to enforce the suggestion. But the bent of Miss Martineau's mind was otherwise. The bent of Miss Martineau's mind was in the direction of political economy, a subject then not taught in any university; and since she believed that theory could best be learned by concrete example, she started a series of tales on various aspects of economics. Her Poor Law tales were the first of these, and were avidly read, not only by the public but by members of Parliament, who found them filled with mental stimulus, the clarification of issues, and accurate information which could be used in debate. Elizabeth Fry read them with admiration (they were clearly not

[5] E. F.'s statement before Parliament in 1832.

novels) and so did Fowell Buxton and Joseph John Gurney. And in 1833 an interview took place between Miss Martineau and Mrs. Fry.

We are indebted to Miss Martineau for a full account of it.[6] Mrs. Fry apparently never mentioned it. The curious omissions in Elizabeth Fry's journal are partly due to the fact that even after she began to realize that her journal might be used by later biographers, and gave specific permission for it, — "even if my weaknesses are acknowledged," — she wrote it, after all, for herself. Whereas Harriet Martineau left a complete autobiography for publication.

A conversation between two such women has an intrinsic interest of its own, but it is still more interesting in the direct evidence it affords of Elizabeth Fry's conscious influence in Parliamentary affairs.

It was she who requested the interview. They met at Newgate in the Matron's room. Miss Martineau, knowing the conversation was to have to do with politics, astutely brought a witness. The careless, easy Mrs. Fry never thought of such a thing. But the clergyman friend was a quiet fellow; and the mutual admiration of the two ladies made the conversation easy. Mrs. Fry had heard that Miss Martineau was informed on some of the measures, especially in Poor Law Reform, that were shortly to come before the House of Commons. And she wondered if it would be honorably possible for Miss Martineau to pass on some of that information in order, said Mrs. Fry candidly, that "our section of members might come prepared." Miss Martineau was able to give useful information on the principles of the proposed measures without betrayal of confidence, and willingly did so. Mrs. Fry took notes, gave her cheerful thanks, complimented Miss Martineau on her books, and the ladies parted, with expressions of mutual esteem. The results were excellent. "Our section" of members came well prepared,

[6] Harriet Martineau's *Autobiography*, I, 173.

and one and all "unflinchingly supported" the reform measures.

At the time of this naïvely wire-pulling conference, Miss Martineau was thirty-one and Mrs. Fry fifty-three. No doubt Mrs. Fry, always conscious of intellect when she met it, regarded Miss Martineau half-enviously as "realy clever." But Miss Martineau regarded Mrs. Fry as nothing less than "sublime."

3

In 1834, the Duke of Gloucester died — the Prince who had made such holiday at Earlham Hall, so very long ago. Elizabeth Fry was a frequent visitor at Gloucester House, and most earnestly and candidly did the royal Duchess pour out to her the story of the Prince's last hours and easy, Christian death. It was to Elizabeth the losing of a friend, and the breaking of yet another link with the past.

But her heart is now more warmly engaged with the future. Her life is flowing on down the generations. What a family can now collect at Upton Lane for special celebrations: "There is very great blessing to look round upon our lovely family — children and children's children — without natural defect, bodily and mentally." And she can now feel, in spite of all, "the pleasure of having with my children the double tie not only of mother and children but a friendship formed upon its own grounds. I certainly think that in no common degree my children feel me their familiar friend."

The accession of the elderly William IV to the throne in 1830 had marked out Princess Victoria as the Heir Presumptive to the English throne. Mrs. Fry called upon the young Princess and her mother to interest them, on Buxton's behalf, in the question of slavery, and had been much taken with the Princess Victoria's childish charm. She had also been presented to Queen Adelaide, and was in some demand among the ladies of the nobility as an unofficial spiritual adviser. They would send for her when in trouble, and depend upon her common sense, her dispassionate sympathy, and that extra something from Beyond that belonged to her religion. Perhaps no one of the period, outside some of the dignitaries of the Roman Church, was the repository of more curious secrets.

This side of her life, though well known to her family and intimates, and mentioned, time after time, — sometimes with a sigh, — in her journal, had no publicity. And Byron, in his "Don Juan," attempts to take Mrs. Fry to task for neglecting the upper classes: —

> Oh, Mrs. Fry! Why go to Newgate? Why
>   Preach to poor rogues? And wherefore not begin
> With Carlton or with other houses? Try
>   Your hand at harden'd and imperial sin.
> To mend the people's an absurdity
>   A jargon, a mere philanthropic din,
> Unless you make their betters better; — Fy!
>   I thought you had more religion, Mrs. Fry.
>
> Tell them, though it may be perhaps too late,
>   On life's worn confine, jaded, bloated, sated,
> To set up vain pretense of being great
>   'T is not so to be good; and be it stated
> The worthiest kings have ever loved least state;
>   And tell them — But you won't, and I have prated
> Just now enough.

However, that was just what she would, and did, with her perfect simplicity and her beautiful manners. She would even remonstrate gently in the highest quarters about the extravagance displayed at royal coronations, weddings, and christenings, in such a time of widespread poverty. Her "courtly politeness knew no change in the palace of a prince or in the cell of a convict. She respected human nature."[7]

[7] Lord Ashley, 1846.

But there was one place where she carried no weight; one house where she was nobody. And that was Runcton Hall, where brother Daniel was master. A sister and a welcome guest, certainly; but nothing more. Daniel had very definite ideas about the place of woman. Elizabeth's reaction is rather unexpected. "From Earlham I went to a *totally* different atmosphere. . . . Dan would not even allow me to read the Scriptures with himself and children. To myself I feel it a previlige and an advantage to be for a while where I am not looked up to or depended upon for religious help in the degree I am at home. I feel it an advantage to myself to be *thought little of*. I think it leads to a more watchful and humble deportment and a more *just* view of myself. I delight in the quiet and liberty of my own room, and I spent, I think, some of the sweetest hours here I spent anywhere, not being driven by so many interests as at home."

In the latter years of Daniel's life, the bank at Lynn failed, and he was allowed two thousand pounds a year by his wealthy widowed sister, Lady Hannah Buxton. A suitable womanly act.

The year of Queen Victoria's accession saw Mrs. Fry's fifty-seventh birthday and Mr. Fry's sixtieth. As the years passed, Mrs. Fry had put on flesh, and now had the Roman-matron look of the well-known Richmond portrait. Joseph Fry, pressed by business cares, was having considerable trouble with his younger sons, particularly Gurney. In Gurney's case, it was more than a taste for music that was in question. The harassed father came to the conclusion that for his own sake — for the sake of the peace and rest and comfort of having her about, and at the helm and centre of the little domestic ship — Elizabeth must stay at home more. He made himself extremely clear, and Elizabeth was humbled, astonished, and distressed.

"*June 18th*. This morning my dearest husband really *feelingly* expressed his deep feeling of my constant engagements — calls of duty from home. I deeply felt it, for much as I make a point of always dining at home and spending evening and morning with him and my family yet my mornings are much occupied by public and relative duties — ministerial, Public, children, brothers and sisters, their children and others in illness, sorrow, etc. etc. I felt greatly cast down at his remark, desiring to be a faithful loving wife."

As a matter of fact, it was Joseph Fry who next left home. Gurney's "sense of sin" and smouldering unhappiness and reticence therein brought on a condition so serious, "so very low and morbid," that both parents realized that his was a case for a medical man. By the doctor's advice, Joseph Fry shortly left for the Continent with Gurney, taking Harry along for company. Travel, change, and recreation were the prescription, with a parting hint relative to the benefits of a suitable marriage. They came back from the Continent with news of Gurney having "an affair" with Sophia Pinkerton, daughter of Dr. Pinkerton. It ended in an engagement. "My Gurney going on improving."

While they were away, Elizabeth had been to Earlham to bid farewell to Joseph John Gurney, who was about to set off "to travel in the ministry" in America. She and Sam and Elizabeth (Sam's wife) went with him to Liverpool, where Elizabeth Fry "put sweet flowers in his cabin," and wept to see him go. "We made things comfortable for him. I attended to the books, and that a proper library should go out for the crew, passengers and steerage passengers." [8]

Returning to Lynn and Earlham for a further visit, Elizabeth had her first journey by railway (from Liverpool to Birmingham), "meeting with an accident by the way which might have been serious, but we were preserved from harm." [9]

Nothing could be less enjoyable than this new mode of travel. It was too fast to see the scenery properly, "the noise is deafening, the motion jarring, particles of cinders or

[8] *Memoir*, II, 268, 269.   [9] *Ibid.*, II, 268, 269.

iron dust get into your eyes and blind you for the time and make your eyes weak for a day or two afterward." And the crowd, and the packages! Indeed, it made the comfort of one's own carriage rise up vividly in wistful retrospect. But so many people had no carriages of their own nowadays. And one could not deny that the railway was one of the greatest marvels of the age.

4

Joseph Fry was fond of travel on the Continent and had been there several times. Elizabeth had been no further than the Channel Islands. His accounts of his journey with his sons, the messages he brought from some of her correspondents, and his encouragement of her concern made her apply for a certificate to travel in January 1838, and in that unpromising season she braved the rough Channel crossing and the rigors of winter to set foot in France for the first time. Her husband was her escort, and two Quaker friends accompanied them, with a concern for Quaker meetings and the Bible Society.[10]

It seems extraordinary lack of judgment to plan such a journey for such a time of year. It can only be explained by assuming either that Joseph Fry was called to Paris on business, and Elizabeth took the opportunity to accompany him, or that both of them found they had that rare chance, a month or two when each could cut loose from his various affairs at the same time, and so seized it, regardless of prudence. Needless to say, Elizabeth reached Paris feverish and ill, and was confined to the hotel for some days. She received there many distinguished visitors, was later on able to visit various prisons, was presented (with her husband) to the King and Queen of France[11] and the Duchess of

[10] Josiah Forster was one, and a woman Friend the other.
[11] Louis Philippe.

Orléans; and finally wrote a memorial to the King on the state of the prisons. She found it all extraordinarily fascinating. At a dinner given for her at the British Ambassador's (Lord Grenville) the conversation became so moving that many of the exalted people present were in tears.

Hidden springs of hope and faith were touched on many fashionable occasions, and the worldly people went away temporarily aware that life was short, that there might be God; that they could do something, if they tried, for the betterment of suffering mankind, and so assuage their own secret pain. It was extraordinary how she brought with her another air.

When she left for England in April, she was pressed to return. And so intended.

Homecoming was a sad fall. Gurney was no longer "very far astray," but he was trying, low-spirited, and irritable. His birthday celebrations did not go off very well. "Gurney's birthday, 22-. I gave him a beautiful Bible and his father a present; but I am sorry to say instead of appearing pleas'd or much so, he appear'd rather disposed to complain that the Bible was not something else and the present of money might be spent some way different to what his father wished. How discouraging! but at times for all this I see kindness, love and gratitude in him, but he is in a low state this morning."

Dr. Pinkerton crossed over unexpectedly from Europe early in May, and came to visit the parents of his intended son-in-law. They were exceedingly open with him as to Gurney's condition, as far as they understood it. And Dr. Pinkerton, forming his own opinion, decided that the marriage could go forward.

Gurney "seemed low" and produced a final distressing symptom. He announced that in future he intended to go to church instead of meeting. "I thought part arose from bodily infirmity," writes the anxious mother. "I therefore gave him quinine, and it is curious to observe his improvement." It would, however, take more than quinine to keep Gurney Fry a Quaker.

The wedding took place at Frankfort-on-Main on July 12, 1838, and Gurney brought his bride back to England in August. He had departed in rather a sullen frame of mind, saying that "he felt as if there had been too much said upon *turning*, meaning, I think, that he had already endeavour'd to take a turn and wanted a little encouragement on that head. I felt there was some truth in it," confessed his candid mother, "which made me sorry that I had not seen it before."

His return was therefore waited apprehensively. "Our dearest Gurney brought his dear wife home to us the 2nd of this month. With no small anxiety. . . . We were much pleased at Sophia's appearance, pleasing though not handsome — gentle, very unaffected, sensible, sweet in her manners to Gurney. Gurney at first appeared an altered man, so very sober, happy and agreeable." The "at first" was able to be extended. Sophia's sweet manners continued to work their magic. Perhaps what Gurney Fry needed was someone to look up to him. After a visit to Scotland that autumn, making a report on the horrors of solitary confinement in the Scotch prisons, Elizabeth Fry records on her return that "my dearest husband and Katherine appear'd happy and Gurney and Sophia remarkably so."

The Scotch had loved Mrs. Fry because she had loved their mountains and their flowers. But carrying her domestic trouble in her heart, she had been unaware of the impression she had made on certain keen-eyed men and women of the world who had met her more intimately. One of them, the Duke of Argyle, wrote of her: "She was the only really very great human being I have ever met with whom it was impossible to be disappointed. She was, in the fullest sense of the word, a majestic woman. She was already advanced in years, and had a very tall and stately figure. But it was her countenance that was so striking. Her features were handsome in the sense of being well-proportioned, but they were not in the usual sense beautiful. Her eyes were not large or brilliant or transparent. They were only calm and wise and steady. But over the whole countenance there was an ineffable expression of sweetness, dignity, and power. It was impossible not to feel some awe before her, as before some superior being. I understood in a moment the story of the prison. . . . It is a rare thing indeed in this poor world of ours to see any man or woman whose personality responds perfectly to the ideal conception of an heroic character and an heroic life." [12]

Baron Bunsen, then Prussian Ambassador, was presented to Mrs. Fry in London in March 1839, and has left his description of her: "A tall, large figure, about 60 years of age, with eyes small but sweet and commanding expression — a striking appearance, not plain, but rather grand than handsome. This was Mrs. Fry, my favorite saint." [13]

5

From this time onward, Elizabeth Fry became increasingly restless. There was so much to do, so many opportunities were open to her, such prompt results occurred in reform wherever she appeared (outside the obstinate family circle), that she felt driven hither and thither in the effort (as she said) to work while it was yet day.

She did not want to disregard her husband's protest; and she did not want to leave him. So on many occasions she persuaded him to accompany her; and on many more, she used the opportunities afforded by accompanying him on his necessary business journeys.

[12] George Douglas, 8th Duke of Argyle, *Autobiography and Memoirs*, I, 414.
[13] *Memoirs of Baron Bunsen*, I, 316.

In March 1839, Elizabeth Fry again visited France, accompanied by her husband, her daughter Katherine, and Josiah Forster. The youngest son, Harry, joined them in Paris.

So great was her reputation by this time that at Boulogne she was recognized at once, and almost mobbed in her hotel by people eager to see her; nor was she allowed to leave Boulogne until she had visited the prison. When she reached Paris, the servants of the hotel, who remembered her interest in them on her former visit, beguiled her into the kitchen, and listened eagerly to her broken French (alas! poor M. Lesage!) as she tried to tell them a little about faith and practice. Then they must all shake hands with her, from the chef downward.

The next day "the great" claimed her, and social events, meetings, and prisons took up her days. On this occasion, Mrs. Fry was given a letter from the Minister of the Interior granting her and her husband and Mr. Forster permission to visit all the prisons in France. They remained six months and made a very extended tour. Mr. Fry probably felt that these long absences from England were incompatible with business, and it was his last. But ever since that mysterious day of the new covenant in May 1833, he had thrown himself much more heartily into his wife's concerns. During this French visit he not only gave her the physical support and care which protected her constantly from unnecessary fatigue, but also took a definite interest in her prison work. There is a very long letter written by his hand, on his wife's behalf, to some of the French authorities on the subject of solitary confinement. He emphasizes the need that all methods of correction in prison should have as their aim the restoration of the prisoner to society as an efficient being. "Too much silence is contrary to nature, and physically injurious both to the stomach and lungs. And as regards the faculties, we are credibly informed of the fact (in addition to what we have known at home) that amongst the monks of La Trappe, few attained to the age of sixty years without having suffered an absolute decay of their mental powers, and fallen into premature childishness."

The extent to which practical suggestions from Fry influenced Elizabeth throughout her whole career can never be known. But the daily conversation of a long and affectionate married life is far from negligible in its effects, difficult as those effects may be to tabulate or analyze. Some hints there are, however, to guide conclusions. As long as he had abundant money, she had his purse to draw upon. He was the most easy of men in tolerating her absence from home — nay, in respecting her right to be absent as almost equal with his own. And he engaged in a businesslike way in a definite practical job now and then, in support of her schemes, as in the coast-guard libraries, where a businessman could be of the utmost help. He says of himself in his journal, in a remark that is as near to self-analysis as he ever came, "I don't think my nature would lead me into any sort of Public service," but he has been working to get a Provident district society established at Plaistow, "believing that it would have very beneficial results."

And he was, from first to last, an exceedingly devoted father. "I am this day commencing a journey on business for the benefit of my sons" is a not infrequent entry. And his last entry of all, in 1857, is one of distress over his youngest boy.

6

In 1840, Elizabeth Fry made her third journey to the Continent, this time with her brother Samuel Gurney and his daughter Elizabeth (who later married a son of Baron Bunsen) and a fellow Quaker, William Allen, and his niece.

Before going, Mrs. Fry and her brother were called to

have an audience with the young Queen, who was about to be married to the German Prince Albert of Saxe-Coburg. Elizabeth did not much enjoy this interview. "Lord Normanly came to introduce us and informed us that we were only to reply to the Queen's questions and not say what we liked; this was very cramping."

They went in February and returned in May, and included Ostend, Brussels, Antwerp, Amsterdam, and Berlin. If anything could have exceeded the enthusiasm of Mrs. Fry's reception in France, it was her reception in Germany.

With the touching belief of the English that their language only needs to be made into baby talk to become intelligible to the childish foreigner, she moved graciously about among the populace in Holland, Germany, Belgium, France, offering little tracts from a well-arranged store in the floor of the carriage, and murmuring "Booky! Booky!" in her melting voice.

Some of her interpreters hinted that she could say anything in that voice and it would be all the same! A German prince, translating her into the vernacular to a group of prisoners, saw the hardened audience melt into tears before they understood what had been said, and, moved himself, exclaimed, "*C'est le don de Dieu!*"

Niece Elizabeth proved the tenderest and most thoughtful of companions, and brother Sam's lavish expenditure certainly added éclat to their progress. Sam thought nothing of hiring a room in a hotel large enough for two hundred people in order that sister Elizabeth Fry might be able to hold suitable receptions.

But the high point of the 1840 itinerary was the visit to Kaiserswerth, although its importance was not apparent to Elizabeth Fry, and it obtains the scantiest notice in her journal. Indeed, some of the reasons which made it worthy of remark were still in the future. Perhaps Mrs. Fry would not have thought of going there at all, had it not been for

Bunsen. But he had particularly reminded her to be sure not to miss it.

Kaiserswerth was an ancient town on the Rhine, six miles below Düsseldorf. In the year 1823, the failure of the silk mill which employed almost all the inhabitants had plunged the whole area into literal destitution. But it was possessed of a pastor, Theodore Fliedner, who was young, energetic, and sensitive. Unable to watch his people starve or to find for them alternative employment, he set off on a journey to Holland and England to raise funds for their relief. In England, the little Princess Victoria headed his list of subscribers. And various wealthy Quakers, such as Gurney, Buxton,[14] Fry, Hoare, and Barclay, also figured on it. Fliedner met Mrs. Fry, was one of the numerous visitors, "interesting and occupied by subjects of importance," at Mildred's Court. He heard everywhere of Mrs. Fry's fame, went down to Newgate to see for himself, and had several conversations with her on the treatment of criminals in prison, and the need for helping them to reinstate themselves in honest ways after their discharge. These conversations included also her other two great interests, the establishment of schools and the care of the sick.

The contact with Elizabeth Fry and her ideas and work was a turning point in Fliedner's life. He was passionately impressed. When he returned to Kaiserswerth, with his immediate object accomplished, he saw a life work opening out before him. He lost no time in establishing, on Mrs. Fry's lines, the Rhenish-Westphalian Prison Association. His position as a minister made it easy for him to enter the local prisons, and gave weight to his steady pressure for reforms. He married a wife in unity with his work, and in 1833 — in a tiny summerhouse in their garden — they opened a refuge for the reception of a single discharged prisoner.

[14] Buxton, of course, was not a Quaker; but he was imbedded in that group.

In '34, Fliedner paid a second visit to England, partly to raise funds, and partly to talk over his plans with Mrs. Fry. She gave him of her best, and he passed a whole day at her house — a day marked to him for life with a white stone, and to Mrs. Fry distinguished by nothing whatever. She was doing that sort of thing all the time, for the entire civilized world east of the Atlantic. She made no special note of Fliedner's visit, and forgot all about it. Three years later Fliedner and his wife added, on an equally modest scale at first, an Infant School, and a hospital in which to train volunteer nurses, and a small training department for teachers.

How intense, then, was Fliedner's feeling when on May 8, 1840, Mrs. Fry, with her party, came to visit this little tree of her planting. Did she know that she had planted it? Impossible to say; it is the kind of thing she never mentions, or very slightly. Yet Fliedner must, in his honest enthusiasm, his spirit of humble discipleship, have tried to make it clear to her, as he made it clear after her death in a letter to her daughters.[15] "Of all my contemporaries, none has exercised a like influence on my heart and life. . . . Thus may my happiness be estimated when Mrs. Fry . . . came in person to see and rejoice over the growing establishment at Kaiserswerth." She, at any rate, behaved beautifully. She went into every room, gave motherly advice to the twenty Deaconesses and the young probationers, and to the twelve young ladies in training for teachers. She inspected the wards of forty or fifty sick; and went over minutely, with Fliedner, the rules and regulations of the establishment, eagerly submitted for her inspection. "Truly," said Fliedner, glowing at the recollection, "God was in the midst of us."

From these humble beginnings had grown (before the World War of 1914) a great congeries of famous institutions — thirty in Germany; and others at Jerusalem, Alexandria, Cairo, Beirut, Smyrna, and Bucharest.

[15] Cresswell, 459.

But perhaps it is equally important that sometime before the autumn of 1846, Florence Nightingale had heard of Kaiserswerth and that it had become "the home of her heart." Tradition, based on every probability, says that she obtained that information first from Elizabeth Fry herself, in a personal interview, sometime between 1844 and 1845. There is no proof of this, though there is evidence of the ardent girl's hero worship for the famous older woman, who alone of her sex was living the full life. What chiefly matters is that, after prolonged struggle with her family, Miss Nightingale came to Kaiserswerth in 1851, and there found what she needed for the start of her own great career.

The visit to Kaiserswerth in 1840 reminded Elizabeth Fry of something that she had left undone. Back in 1829 the poet Southey had written to his friend Mrs. Amelia Opie "to engage her sympathies and those of Mrs. Fry in establishment of Societies for reforming the internal management of Hospitals and Infirmaries; so as to do for the hospitals what Mrs. Fry had already done for the prisons."[16] Amelia had passed on the word to Betsy, and Mrs. Fry replied, "I have seen the thing wanted to be done, ever since the days of my youth." She had indeed mentioned it in her Prison book in 1827. But Amelia Opie was inert in the matter, and Elizabeth Fry had never seen an opportunity to begin this new and large field of work.

However, she was now sixty years old. All of her work must before long be passed on to others. It seemed legitimate to initiate yet another piece of work for others to carry on, using, what she could not be entirely unaware of, the vast power of her name. On her return from Germany, therefore, in 1840, she made the initial plans for a nurses' training home in London. At first they were called Protestant Sisters of Charity, but the name was changed to Nursing Sisters, and they were usually briefly spoken of as the

[16] Celia Lucy Brightwell, *Life of Amelia Opie*, 337.

Fry Nurses. Sam Gurney's wife, Elizabeth, undertook the work of organization, once the project was launched. The Queen Dowager consented to be Patroness, Lady Inglis was President, an effective committee was promptly in existence; funds of course were forthcoming; and the Bishop of London, approached by Mrs. Fry, gave his support. The whole project was to be, by Mrs. Fry's direction, entirely unsectarian.

Twenty young women were selected as a start, trained for a probation period in one of the larger and better hospitals, and finally admitted as Sisters. They lived in the Home, wore a simple uniform, and received an annual salary. They went out to cases, "living in" or going by the day as convenient. To the poor, they went free of all charge. To the well-to-do they made a charge of a guinea a week, which went into the joint exchequer of the Home. Every nurse who served a stated number of years was to receive a pension on retirement, and a fund was started for that purpose. Mrs. Fry herself had one of the Fry nurses in her last illness, and Florence Nightingale took some of the Fry nurses with her in the first band that went out to the Crimea.

This was the first attempt in England to train and standardize nurses, and put nursing on a professional basis. But Mrs. Fry was as far as Mrs. Nightingale from considering nursing as a possible profession for her own daughters. The Fry nurses were respectable women of what was in those days called the lower class, the sort of women described by Jane Austen as "Nurse Rooke" in *Persuasion*. That kind of nurse was already obtainable, if you knew where to find them, trained merely by experience and practice, and heard of by personal recommendation, but able to nurse "most admirably." Sairey Gamp, by the robust genius of Dickens, has set her mark upon the period; but Nurse Rooke was probably almost as common. A grateful patient said of her, "She has a fund of good sense and observation which, as a companion, make her infinitely superior to thousands of those who, having only received 'the best education in the world' know nothing worth attending to." [17]

To train more of that sort of women, and to make them more readily available, especially to the poor, was Mrs. Fry's aim.

7

Elizabeth Fry was sixty years old, and was tired. She had returned from her travels feeling that it would be sweet to pass her declining years quietly at Upton with her husband, visiting and being visited by her children and grandchildren, and pressing all of her prison reforms into the permanent laws of the land by her contacts with authority.

But there was the May Yearly Meeting. And there was the Annual Meeting of the British Ladies' Prison Society; and there was the French Ambassador to dine — "with a large party" — at her home; and there was her new nurses' scheme on her hands. The days were too full, too full. "The morning began with a meeting of Friends in London; afterwards she waited upon the Duchess of Gloucester — had a short interview with the Duke of Sussex — drove from London to Upton with the Duchess of Sutherland and Lord Marpeth to meet, at Ham House, the American Delegates who had come to England on the subject of slavery." [18] And Newgate and the other London prisons were badly needing her renewed attentions. She was caught upon a treadmill from which it was almost impossible to escape.

Meanwhile, her brother Buxton has been made a baronet; and her son William has reopened the manor house of Plashet, and is living there with his wife and family. Prosperity begins to smile. John and Rachel have built themselves a fine new house, and no longer need her to pay their

---

[17] Jane Austen, *Persuasion*, Ch. 17.   [18] Cresswell, 463.

debts, as of old. And she counts up eighteen [19] children and twenty-six grandchildren. After all, between days of press of business, she can snatch days of domestic peace, as long as she remains at Upton.

Had she been able to remain there, busy as her years must in any case have been, she would doubtless have prolonged her life, and also have been able to give a permanent character to some measures that at present depended upon her own life and interest for their maintenance. Bunsen had urged this upon her, and she was not indifferent to its importance. But time, and the mere staying in one place long enough to apply steady and constant pressure, were needed.

Why then, should Joseph John, wishing to travel on the Continent in 1841, urge his famous sister to accompany him? But he did. And letters from Europe, constant, innumerable letters, from the Queen of Prussia downwards, were pouring in to Elizabeth Fry daily to enforce his request.

Her hesitation was considerable. But she finally thought it right to go. The journey this time was to include Holland, Germany, Prussia, and Denmark. The Prince Consort offered letters of introduction to the King of Prussia.

Elizabeth's health was far from good, but "my brother Joseph, his daughter Anna, my dear niece Elizabeth Gurney and my own maid go with me, with the prospect of every comfort this life can afford." Even so, she found the "roughs of the journey" very hard to bear. The best hired carriage is uncomfortable when it strikes a bad road, with "sand up to the axles." They were away from the end of July to the beginning of October. Royalties and prisons liberally besprinkled their passage, but the great event this time was acquaintance with the King of Prussia. Between this kindly monarch and Elizabeth Fry there sprang up, even in their first interview, an extraordinary friendship. Warmth met warmth and simplicity met simplicity. "The King began easy and

[19] Including in-laws.

pleasant conversation with me about my visiting prisons. I told him in a short, lively manner, the history of it. He said, he heard I had so many children, how could I do it? This I explained. . . . Our very serious conversation was mixed with much cheerfulness. . . . I concluded by expressing my earnest desire that the King's reign might be marked by the prisons being so reformed that punishment might become the means of reformation of criminals; by the lower classes being religiously educated; and by the slaves in their Colonies being liberated. The King then took me by the hand and said he hoped God would bless me."

But Joseph Fry, who met his wife at Dover, was shocked at her appearance, and took little account of anything but her shattered health. He would not risk the journey home, but bore her to the neighboring seaside resort of Ramsgate to recuperate. Indeed, during the return journey down to Ostend, Elizabeth had suffered severely. A business emergency (perhaps relative to his approaching third marriage) had put Joseph John into a flurry, and he had traveled with six horses to make the greater speed. Elizabeth was in no condition to stand it. She had been seized with a stiffness in the limbs. It had taken two men to get her in and out of the carriage and up and down stairs. "I might have had the same attack at home," she said, patiently. And she had written to her husband, "I have a board in the carriage, so that when Joseph and Anna are outside, I can quite rest and make a real sofa of it, when I need it, which I do for one or two stages in the day. Mary and François [20] are very active and kind. I am indeed yours most faithfully and lovingly, E. F."

She would never hear Joseph John blamed.

All that autumn Elizabeth reposed, at one place and another, in the tender care of her husband and children. Her body suffered, but her spirits were serene. It was almost worth being ill, she said, to be so petted and nursed. Joseph

[20] Servants.

John remorsefully gave her a little carriage, and her sons provided her with horses for it. William called at Upton Lane for a few minutes every morning on his way in from Plashet to the city, and cheered her, as always, by his pleasant talk and promising manhood. And what a comfort it was to have "a dear, valuable, single daughter at home."

Distinguished visitors began to come out to see her, including the Duchess of Sutherland and Baron Bunsen and his wife. And Katherine [21] was kept hard at it, writing and answering letters on matters that were of moment to the welfare of thousands of the oppressed and the miserable all over the British Isles and Europe. Treat prisoners as if they were redeemable, treat lunatics as far as possible as if they were sane; teach children, but do not overwork them or treat them harshly; these, in various contexts and applications, were the tenets of Elizabeth Fry's gospel. And it had weight. It produced effects. In Russia, in Germany, in Denmark, in Holland, in France, in Scotland and Ireland and England, chains were removed, old cruelties were stopped, men jailers were taken away from control of women prisoners, lunatics were allowed books and occupations and sunshine, and to sit at table for their meals, instead of being fed like beasts, at the word of Elizabeth Fry.

By January 1842, she was so far recovered as to accept a very important invitation from her friends, Sir John and Lady Pirie. Sir John was this year Lord Mayor of London, and he and his lady gave a luncheon at the Mansion House on January 17, at which Mrs. Fry was the guest of honor. "I hardly ever had such kindness and respect shown me," she wrote in her journal with unaffected satisfaction. But there had been vicissitudes. "I was at first greatly try'd by the carriage not driving up to the door — my having to get out and walk through the mob, driven about on every hand, exceedingly dirty'd even up to the knees that we were doubtful

---

[21] The "dear, valuable, single daughter."

whether my gown were not ruined. I knew I was after the time and had the most hurried and confused dressing, the Lord Mayor waiting at the bed-room door for me, sending for me again and again. I much feared this flurry would overwhelm body and mind but as I walked into the drawing-room with the Lord Mayor, on his arm, I felt much quieted and supported and very soon in great degree recovered. And as Prince Albert, Sir Robert Peel, Sir James Graham, Lord Aberdeen, the Bishop of London etc. came and spoke to me, I was quite self-collected and enabled I trust to put in the word in season.

"An important conversation with Sir James Graham, our present Secretary of State, on a female Prison being built; upon Patronage, Society, etc. . . .

"With Lord Aberdeen, Foreign Secretary; I requested his help for anything I want for the continent of Europe.

"With Lord Stanly, our Colonial Secretary, upon the state of our Penal Colonies as it respected the women in them and opened the door for further communications with him on these subjects. . . .

"I walked into dinner with Sir Robert Peel, our Prime Minister, and sat between him and Prince Albert. . . .

"His ear (Sir R. P.) appear'd perfectly open to me and the Prince entirely at home — indeed we both felt I believe as if we had long been friends. I felt perfectly easy to rise upon any religious occasions. . . . But I could not rise for toasts, a mode of showing rejoicing and good will that I did not approve."

She therefore refused to rise for any of the toasts, explaining to her distinguished neighbors, and gracefully wishing them health and best wisdom when their healths were drunk. She did rise for "a solemn grace" and also for "God Save the Queen," "feeling it as a hymn . . . but I told the Prince I did not unite in praying for victory, for I wish'd only for peace and no war, therefore no victory. . . .

"Sir Robert Peel proposed a toast for the Lady Mayoress and at the same time spoke of me in terms of regard and high esteem and said there was not a table in Europe that would not have been honor'd by my presence."

E. F. felt she ought to rise to express her unworthiness, but "I felt silence easyest and I trust it was safest."

8

That same January, 1842, Frederick William IV, King of Prussia, came to England for the christening of the infant Prince of Wales. "The King of Prussia is come," wrote Lady Lyttleton, Lady in Waiting to Queen Victoria, "most brilliantly and affectionately received by the people, and magnificently indeed by the Queen. . . . The King is fat and tall, and looks at first sight only plain, like a good-natured farmer; but his eyes, though small, are observant, and he talks like a sensible man." [22]

The King soon found out how to approach his friend, Mrs. Fry. Another Mansion House party was in order. He appointed Sunday, January 30, as the day on which Mrs. Fry and her husband and daughter were to meet him at lunch with the Lord Mayor. It threw Mrs. Fry into rather a flutter. Some of the stricter elders had already cast her "under a cloud" for her participation in the other banquet. Were there not toasts and music? Her presence as the guest of honor had seemed to give her sanction to these unquakerly habits.

Mrs. Fry foresaw toasts and music at the second party. And worse, it was to be on a Sunday. But she desired eagerly to see her friend again. And a royal invitation was not to be refused. Escorted by Joseph Fry, who had learned to keep appointments by the clock, they were in excellent time, and

[22] *Correspondence of Sarah Spencer, Lady Lyttleton*, p. 324. She was later made governess to the royal children.

it was Mrs. Fry who waited in the drawing-room, and the King of Prussia who was late. He had been attending service in St. Paul's Cathedral, cynosure of hundreds of onlookers. But he came in, attended by the Duke of Cambridge, and greeted Mrs. Fry with the simple warmth of a plain gentleman — "My dear friend!"

As they took their seats at table, Mrs. Fry softly asked the Lord Mayor if toasts might be omitted — as a favor to her? — since it was Sunday? The Mayor whispered a plea just to drink the Queen's health — and that of the King guest? But the King, whose mastery of English was perfect, had overheard, and said that he was sure Sir John would do exactly as Mrs. Fry wished. So Elizabeth hoped to pacify the elders, and gave herself up peacefully to enjoyment of the occasion. That it was enjoyable also to the King of Prussia is shown by the fact that before they parted he had made two engagements with Mrs. Fry: one to meet her the next morning in Newgate, and hear her read, and see the prisoners at work; and the other to take lunch at her house at Upton Lane.

Mrs. Fry received both with her own royal simplicity. And both were kept. Sam Gurney and his wife and Lady Pirie supported her at Newgate. The King listened humbly to her reading and speaking, as to *his* "favorite saint." Mrs. Fry, having reminded the prisoners and the large brilliant company alike that they were all in the presence of the King of Kings, read the passage from Saint Paul's Letters that expresses the complete and vital democracy of the Christian faith: "For as we have many members in one body, and all members have not the same office: so we, being many, are one body in Christ, and every one members one of another." [28] As long as she was there, they truly felt it. She made the vital, connecting link between the King and the prisoner, and life flowed through her from the one

[28] Romans, XII.

to the other. After her death, there was no one to take her place.

Meanwhile, those in charge of the King's visit were scandalized that one of the first monarchs of Europe, closely related to the English reigning house, should go to eat lunch in a simple middle-class home. Even Mrs. Fry became aware of some objections being made. But her account is unselfconscious.

"There were difficulties raised about the King's going to Upton, but he chose to persevere. I went with the Lady Mayoress and the Sheriffs, the King with his own people. We arrived first. I had to hasten to take off my cloak, and then went down to meet the King at the carriage-door, with my husband and seven of our sons and sons-in-law. I then walked with him into the drawing-room, where all was in beautiful order — neat, and adorned with flowers. I presented to the King our eight daughters and daughters-in-law (Rachel only away) our seven sons and eldest grandson, my brother and sister Buxton, Sir Henry and Lady Pelly,[24] and my sister Elizabeth Fry — my brother and sister Gurney[25] he had known before — and afterwards presented twenty-five of our grandchildren.[26] Our meal was handsome, not extravagant, but fit for a king. I sat by the King, who appeared to enjoy his dinner, perfectly at his ease, and very happy with us. We went into the drawing-room . . . and found a deputation of Friends with an address to read to him. This was done, and the King appeared to feel it much. . . . We then had to part, and when either he or I said perhaps we may never meet again he wept aloud at parting, and hardly let me leave hold of his arm the whole time he was here, except when at table."

The unavoidable publicity of this affair brought great pressure to bear upon her, as everybody thought if she could

---

[24] Parents of her son's wife.   [25] Mr. and Mrs. Samuel Gurney.
[26] This excluded the Cresswell family, none of whom were present.

do all that, she must be recovered and could do "all most anything," and pressed her "out of the measure of my strength." Besides which, she felt the cloud of disapproval of the strictest Friends, and received "a strong and painful judging letter," accusing her of worldliness in relation to her Mansion House luncheons and the King of Prussia's visit. It hurt her, but it opened her eyes more fully to a fact that she had been more or less discerning for some time — the danger of the narrow interpretation of the outward forms of religion. Quakerism, in its inception, had been a great breaking away of the spirit into freedom from the bondage of outward forms. But in the eighteenth and nineteenth centuries it had made new and straiter forms of its own. Looking back over her life, Elizabeth Fry felt that herself had fallen into an error in making too much of dress and speech and other outward things. As a private discipline, it might have its value; she still felt that, to her, it had. But she could have helped her children more into what she called "the liberty" of the true Quaker faith had she made less of the unessentials.

One of her last messages to her children and grandchildren at a family gathering shows how she has come through. She warned them against "undue love of riches"; against "too much partaking of the indulgences and luxuries of life," and against "extravagance, vanity and immodesty in dress"; but "above all I fear whether there is not a danger of quenching or grieving the Holy Spirit of God by too much attention to outward rather than the inward teaching of the Holy Spirit."

Her health was still very delicate, and she looks forward now at last to a time of comparative peace at the close of life. "I have much valued my dear husband's company, and feel it sweet that in our declining days we can so thoroughly enjoy being together, and that we unite so much in our principles and tastes.

"I think a quiet spirit before the Lord, and not always looking out for concerns, but knowing how to be still, is a very great point in the religious life." But she feels that her temptation has always been to take things too easily! It is on this fear, of not doing enough, of not using life to the full while it is hers, that the restless energy of Joseph John can seize.

Joseph John Gurney, in April 1843, had a concern to visit Paris with his new American bride, — who was a recognized minister among Friends, — and desired his famous sister's company. What an introduction to Europe it would be to Mrs. Joseph John Gurney to travel in the company of Elizabeth Fry! The change would no doubt be beneficial to Elizabeth, and she might clinch some of the good beginnings that she had already made in French prison reforms.

She went. Weary as she was, she came, under the powerful influence of her brother, to feel that perhaps it was her duty. She was welcomed by the King and the Queen of France, and the Duchess of Orléans and other distinguished admirers. Crowds greeted her carriage in the streets. She visited prisons, and tried to speak to the prisoners. But her once-clear voice was faint, the interpreter could hardly distinguish her sentences. Several times she writes, "I was tired and poorly, my flesh and my heart ready to fail, but the Lord strengthened me."

Behind her, in England, the new model prison at Pentonville has gone up on the plan suggested long ago by Howard: solitary confinement, day and night, for every prisoner; silence; dark punishment cells. And even in the regular cells, the glass is of such a nature that the prisoner cannot see the sky. The criminal world of London has christened it the Bastille. And to remedy its grim, inhuman defects was Elizabeth Fry's last struggle. By letters to the Home Office, by personal appeal at the Mansion House banquet to

Sir Robert Peel and to the Prince Consort, she had sought to abolish the unnecessary cruelties. "Let them see the sky! Indeed, I should prefer more than the sky." And again she repeats: "I am *certain* that separate confinement produces an unhealthy state both of mind and body . . . and that a sinful course of life increases the tendency to mental derangement as well as bodily disease." And conversely, "I am as certain that an unhealthy state of mind and body has generally a demoralising influence; and I consider light, air and the power of seeing something beyond the mere monotonous walls of a cell, highly important. . . . When speaking of health of body and mind, I also mean health of *soul* . . . for I do not believe that a despairing or stupefied state is suitable for salvation."

But Mrs. Fry has been taken away from this piece of work, just when the steady influence, reiterated from different quarters, which she could uniquely exercise was needed to move the inertia of accomplished fact. It might have been the suitable occupation, and the final crown, of her last years.

Instead she spent her failing energies in Paris, an object of interest and admiration to the kindly French. And the handsome person of Joseph John Gurney attended her everywhere with assiduous care. They returned to England at the beginning of June.

It became gradually apparent that Mrs. Fry was in the grip of a slow, encroaching illness. Sandgate, Tunbridge Wells, and Bath were tried in turn.

"My complaint is a very distressing one — so difficult to rest or do anything. As to sitting Meeting, it is real suffering!"

In the autumn she writes at Upton: "I have been home nearly a fortnight. My illness has increased. I very much keep my bed. I am entirely nursed and it is a very serious compleat illness, one of a very low description." Her husband would often sit beside her an hour at a time, comforting her by holding her hand. And, clinging to him fast, she would murmur to herself her old ritual of endurance: —

"Come what come may,
Time and the hour run through the roughest day." [27]

[27] Cresswell, 544.

XVI

TIME AND THE HOUR

HER illness had its ups and downs. She knew now that she was near the end. The dark descent was before her that she had dreaded all her life. How often the unction had descended upon her for others, and appropriate and soothing words of Scripture had flowed in a hypnotic chant from her lips. Now others tried to minister to her, but the exhausted mind withdrew uncomforted into the sore discomforts of the body. The more she failed, the less she found they helped her. They tried to read her "a very interesting religious biography," but she drifted into sleep and, waking, begged them to desist. "It is too touching — too affecting."

She looked back, with her old honesty, and saw herself at many a cottage deathbed, and said, after a pause, "How I feel for the poor when very ill; in a state like my own, for instance; when good ladies go to see them. Religious truths so strongly brought forward, often injudiciously."

She thought wistfully of the great Jesus — "the exquisite tenderness of his ministrations — His tone and manner to sinners."

A niece was married, a baby great-niece died, scarlet fever broke out at Plashet and cut down little Juliana and her father, the favorite son William; still her vigorous constitution resisted the onset of mortal disease and overwhelming sorrow. The one perhaps deadened the other.

She roused herself to write again in her journal, that little friend of her heart — prayers and tears. She even had herself borne to meeting, and as one raised up by miracle addressed the assembled Friends from her wheel chair with a touch of her old power. She wrote letters again with her own hand, and Scriptural phrases flowed.

And the turn of the year passed her, and her brother Buxton died, and her daughter Hannah, with her husband Streatfield, was ordered by the doctor to Madeira.

And then her weary heart and body, worn with partings, weak with pain, turned to the happy days of childhood, radiant in retrospect. She longed for Earlham, the broad lawns and the shady trees, the shining river, the peace and leisure of the days of youth when they could recline upon haycocks and listen to poetry. Even death, perhaps, at Earlham would seem less terrible.

But death avoided still. Her youngest son became engaged to Lucy Sheppard, one whom she loved, and above all a Quaker. So a spark of joy revived her, and she returned by slow stages to London, and attended two sittings of the Yearly Meeting and spoke about different temperaments being used like different stones in the building of God.

And June came in, and she once more saw the roses, and met, at her meetinghouse at Plaistow, the Annual Meeting of the Ladies' British Society, and took a lively part, though sitting throughout. Her mind clear and cool as ever, her prisons, she felt, in good order, she yearned now over the most fallen of womankind, and longed to be given strength to establish a refuge for *"repentant"* prostitutes. This she did not live to see, but the "Elizabeth Fry Refuge" was established in her memory.

June waxed, and she saw her darling youngest son married; "a ray of light," she said, "upon a dark picture."

Hope for her health revived, and she was taken to Ramsgate for sea air. Her tiny grandson, Willie Fry,[1] was her constant companion, lisping the Bible to her, drawing pictures for her, sorting shells with her, chatting of this and that, golden head and gray head together, each equally busy and happy.

The heats of August drew on. Willie went home. Her journal was got out and written in for the last time, about the marriage of her son to Lucy, and of her dear niece Elizabeth to young Ernest Bunsen. Another ray of light.

Her family gathered around her with a sense of impending farewell, and with them to support her she attended the small neighborhood meeting on September 19 and spoke upon the imminence of death. "She walked rather better, she looked less distressed, her appetite was improved, and her nights not so disturbed"; but there was a new symptom — occasional severe pains in the head. She also — striking change — refused all decisions. "Just as you like, dear — just as you like."

Her diminishing energy was bent upon the coming dreaded hour. Oh, that she might in mercy be unconscious when the time came — go to sleep on earth and wake in heaven!

She selected some texts "for a young person who desired her autograph," and refused her spectacles, saying that her sight was much better. This was secretly regarded as a new and serious symptom.

And before she knew it, she was in the valley. Her grandchildren had tried to read the Bible to her, and the words did not reach her. She answered the doctor's questions correctly, but she was already far off.

The hours passed, and she lay powerless and beyond all help. Here it is then at last, that which she has dreaded all her life. Where now is her unction? Will her faith still serve?

[1] Son of William, who had died recently.

Her fluent texts were still, her habit of impressive speech all lost. Silent she lay hour after hour, and the shadows closed around her. All her old terrors were there. The night was in her room, and Death was in her room, and outside her window she could hear her old enemy the sea.

Hours. And the slow gray dawn of Sunday morning came, the twelfth of October. The watchful maid saw a slight stir, bent quickly over the bed.

Through the thin crust of the minister's habit there broke Betsy Gurney, never entirely lost, always alive and throbbing there, the Betsy of the early journals, simple, sincere, and clear.

"Oh, Mary, Mary — it is a strift! — but I am safe!"

BIBLIOGRAPHY

ASHTON, JOHN, *The Dawn of the XIXth Century in England.* 1886.
AUSTEN, JANE. Novels. 1775–1817.

Biographical Catalogue. London Friends' Institute.
BRAITHWAITE, JOSEPH BEVAN, *Life of Joseph John Gurney.* 2 vols. 1854.
BRIGHTWELL, CECILIA LUCY, *Life of Amelia Opie.* 1834.
BUXTON, CHARLES, ESQ., B.A., *Memoirs of Sir Thomas Fowell Buxton, Bart.* 1866.
BUXTON, SIR T. FOWELL, *Inquiry Concerning Prisons.* 1818.

COOK, SIR EDWARD, *Life of Florence Nightingale.* 2 vols. 1913.
CORDER, SUSANNA, *Life of Elizabeth Fry.* 1856.
Correspondence of Sarah Spencer, Lady Lyttleton, 1787–1870. Edited by Mrs. Hugh Wyndham. 1912.
CRESSWELL, RACHEL, *Elizabeth Fry.* 1856.

DIXON, HEPWORTH, *John Howard and the Prison World of Europe.* 1849.
DU THON, ADÈLE, *Histoire de la Secte des Amis suivie d'une Notice sur Madame Fry et La Prison de Newgate à Londres.* 1821.

Elizabeth Fry's Journeys, 1840–41. From a diary kept by her niece, Elizabeth Gurney. Edited by R. Brimley Johnson. 1931.
EMERSON, EDWIN, JR., *A History of the XIXth Century Year by Year.* 1902.

FREMANTLE, ALAN FREDERICK, *England in the 19th Century.* 1929–30.
FRY, ELIZABETH, *Observations on the Visiting, Superintending and Government of Female Prisoners.* 1827.

GELDART, MRS. THOMAS, *Memoir of Samuel Gurney.* 1857.
GEORGE, M. DOROTHY, *London Life in the XVIIIth Century.* 1925.
GREENE, J. R., *A Short History of the English People.* 1895.
GREER, MRS., *Quakerism or the Story of My Life.* 1851.
GUMMERE, AMELIA, *The Quaker; a Study in Costume.* 1901.
GURNEY, J. J., Autobiography addressed to his nephew John Gurney, on his voyage to the United States. 1737. Manuscript volume.

HANKIN, CHRISTIAN C., *Life of Mary Anne Schimnelpenninck* [neé Galton]. 1859.
HARE, AUGUSTUS J. C., *The Gurneys of Earlham.* 1895.
—————— *Memorials of a Quiet Life.* 1873.
HAYDON, ROBERT BENJAMIN, *Autobiography and Memoirs, 1786–1846.* Introduction by Aldous Huxley. 1935.
HOWARD, JOHN, F.R.S., *The State of the Prisons in England and Wales, with an account of some foreign prisons and hospitals.* 1742.

JENKS, LELAND HAMILTON, *Migration of British Capital.* 1927.
Journal of the Friends' Historical Society.

LATIMER, ELIZABETH WORMELEY, *England in the XIXth Century.* 1895.
LAWLESS, HON. EMILY, *Maria Edgeworth.* 1904.
Letters of the Wordsworth Family. Edited by William Knight. 3 vols. 1787–1811.
LEWIS, GEORGINA KING, *Elizabeth Fry.* 1910.
LUBBOCK, PERCY, *Earlham.* 1922.
LUCAS, E. V., *Life of Charles Lamb.* 2 vols. 1905.

MCCARTHY, JUSTIN, *England in the XIXth Century.* 1899.
MACGREGOR, MARGARET ELIOT, *Amelia Alderson Opie, Worldling and Friend.* Smith College Studies in Modern Languages, vol. XIV. 1933.
Manuscript journals of Elizabeth Fry, William Savery, Joseph Fry, J. J. Gurney.
MARTINEAU, HARRIET, *Autobiography.* Edited by Maria W. Chapman. 2 vols. 1885.
—————— *The History of England from the Commencement of the Nineteenth Century to the Crimean War.* 4 vols. 1864.

———— *Illustrations of Political Economy.* 9 vols. 1834.
Memoir of the Life of Elizabeth Fry. Edited by two of her daughters. 2 vols. 1847.
Memoirs and Correspondence of Eliza P. Gurney.
Memoirs of Baron Bunsen. 2 vols. 1868.
MITFORD, MARY RUSSELL, *Our Village.* 1893.
MUIR, RAMSAY, *A Short History of the British Commonwealth.* 1922–23.

Newgate Monthly Magazine. 1824–25.
Nineteenth Century Letters, selected and edited by Byron Johnson Rees. 1899.

PERKINS, JANE GREY, *Life of Mrs. Norton.* 1909.
PITMAN, MRS. E. R., "Elizabeth Fry," in *Famous Women Series.* 1888.

QUENNELL, MARJORIE, AND C. H. B., *A History of Everyday Things in England.* 1918.

RENDER, WILLIAM H., *Through Prison Bars. The Lives and Labours of John Howard and Elizabeth Fry.* 1894.
RYDER, EDWARD, *Elizabeth Fry.* 1883.

SEEBOHM, BENJAMIN, *Memoirs of Stephen Grellet.* 1860.
———— *Memoirs of William Forster.* 1865.
Sketch of the Origin and Results of the Ladies' Prison Association. 1818.
Social England. Vol. V, From Accession of George I to Battle of Waterloo. Edited by H. D. Traill. 1896.
SOMERVELL, D. C., *English Thought in the XIXth Century.* 1929.

TAYLOR, FRANCIS R., A.M., LL.B., *Life of William Savery.* 1925.
THACKERAY, ANNE ISABELLA, *The Book of Sibyls* (Mrs. Barbauld, Miss Edgeworth, Mrs. Opie, Miss Austen). 1883.
TIMPSON, REV. THOMAS, *Memoirs of Elizabeth Fry.* 1847.

WALLACE, ALFRED RUSSELL, *The Wonderful Century.* 1898.
WEBB, BEATRICE POTTER, *My Apprenticeship.* 1926.
WOODFORDE, SAMUEL, *The Diary of a Country Parson,* 1758–1803. Edited by Beresford. 5 vols. 1924.

www.ingramcontent.com/pod-product-compliance
Lightning Source LLC
Chambersburg PA
CBHW060551230426
43670CB00011B/1773